DOCTORAL EDUCATION'S REFORM IN SWITZERLAND AND NORWAY

LUKAS BASCHUNG

DOCTORAL EDUCATION'S REFORM IN SWITZERLAND AND NORWAY

A PUBLIC MANAGEMENT ANALYSIS

PETER LANG
Bern · Berlin · Bruxelles · Frankfurt am Main · New York · Oxford · Wien

Bibliographic information published by die Deutsche Nationalbibliothek
Die Deutsche Nationalbibliothek lists this publication in the Deutsche National-bibliografie; detailed bibliographic data is available on the Internet at ‹http://dnb.d-nb.de›.

British Library Cataloguing-in-Publication Data: A catalogue record for this book is available from The British Library, Great Britain

Library of Congress Cataloging-in-Publication Data
Baschung, Lukas, 1980-
Doctoral education's reform in Switzerland and Norway :
a public management analysis / Lukas Baschung.
p. cm.
Author's doctoral thesis, University of Lausanne.
Includes bibliographical references.
ISBN 978-3-03-431262-2
1. Education, Higher–Switzerland. 2. Education, Higher–Norway.
3. Education and state–European Union countries. I. Title.
LA937.5.B37 2013
378.1'55–dc23
2012044782

Published with support of:

- Société Académique Vaudoise (SAV)
- Fondation du 450e anniversaire de l'Université de Lausanne

Société Académique Vaudoise

Cover design: Thomas Grütter, Peter Lang AG

ISBN 978-3-03431-262-2 pb. ISBN 978-3-0352-0171-0 eBook

Hochfeldstrasse 32, CH-3012 Bern, Switzerland
info@peterlang.com, www.peterlang.com

Printed in Switzerland

Acknowledgements

I am indebted to many people who have been involved in different ways in my doctoral thesis. From a scientific view, I am particularly grateful to all members of the "Steering of University-project" (SUN). Under the lead of Catherine Paradeise, senior and junior researchers from six European countries regularly met to discuss and present the overall SUN-project and, in particular, the doctoral students' individual doctoral researches. Such scientific exchange activities went on even after the SUN-project's formal end. I appreciate this engagement a lot and could benefit in a significant way from it. A second scientific platform which contributed a lot to the progress of my thesis consists in the Euredocs conferences. Explicitly conceptualised for doctoral students and young researchers who work in the field of higher education studies, this European forum is extremely precious because it allows to get inputs from European leaders of the field and doctoral students from other countries. Thirdly, I also thank all my colleagues from the Observatoire Science, Politique et Société at University of Lausanne, in particular Gaële Goastellec, Martin Benninghoff and my thesis director, Jean-Philippe Leresche, who were always at disposal when I asked for some advice. The success of qualitative research projects always heavily depends on the good will of the interviewees. Therefore, I thank all 100 interviewees who, in spite of their mostly overloaded agendas, spent some of their precious time to answer my questions. I hope that the results of this project somehow constitutes a service in return.

This project also included a linguistic challenge. I am particularly indebted to Kari Lund Mestre who helped me acquiring patterns and finesses of the Norwegian language and who thereby contributed to my discovery of Norwegian higher education as well as this charming country and society.

A comparative research project may also involve some logistic challenges. I was lucky having always been supported. Concerning "scientific infrastructure", I particularly thank Ivar Bleiklie, Stig Slipersæter and Christine Musselin who made it possible to host me during several months in their respective institutions, that is to say in the Department of Administration and Organization Theory at University of Bergen, the Norwegian Institute for Studies in Innovation, Research and Education (NIFU-STEP) and the Centre de Sociologie des Organisations (CSO) of Sciences Po Paris. Several people helped to find or suggested me great places to live during my sojourns. I thank Gigliola Mathisen, Marte Mangset, Oda Radoor, Julien Barrier, Pauline Ravinet and Franck Paris for their great help. All of the latter as well as many members of the mentioned scientific institutions also contributed to this adventurous project by informal scientific exchanges, moral support but also social activities like invitations to dinner, having a beer together and football games… All that was very important for me in order not to forget that there is a life besides the doctoral thesis.

In the same vein, I would like to thank my family, friends and all other people who accompanied me in a way or another during those four years for their moral support and indulgence towards this personal project.

Last but not least, I was lucky to rely on generous financial help which is indispensable for the good devolution of a doctoral thesis and its publication. The one-year grant from the Swiss National Science Foundation was particularly helpful for finishing my research. Two foundations that are very close to the University of Lausanne, that is to say the *Fondation du 450e anniversaire* and the *Société académique vaudoise*, generously supported this publication. I would like to thank all of them very cordially.

Table of Content

Introduction

During the last decades, higher education has become an increasingly popular field of study among political and social scientists. This statement, which is illustrated for instance by the steadily higher number of specialised journals, might be explained by higher education's growing relevance for economy and society at large, and perhaps also by the theoretical and analytical challenges that the complex field of higher education poses to researchers. However, political and social scientists have been studying higher education through political science's three classical dimensions, that is to say polity, policy and politics. Higher education institutions (HEIs) – i.e. universities, colleges, polytechnics and other institutions at tertiary level – have often been in the centre of such analyses.

Many scholars have been focusing on the question of how and by whom HEIs are governed (see e.g. Neave and van Vught 1991). On the basis of their analyses they developed models that should allow to qualify what is generally called *University Governance.* Among those models, "Clark's Triangle" (Clark 1983) is the most famous and discussed one. Since then, further models have been developed, for instance by Braun and Merrien (1999), Musselin (2001) and de Boer, Enders and Schimank (2008). Those models are often elaborated on the basis of comparative or single case studies of countries which frequently focus on general patterns of *polity and politics* of higher education in order to dress an overall, often national picture of university governance. Some studies also use particular *policies* as a point of departure for observing and discussing potential changes in polity and politics of higher education, or in other words, within university governance (see e.g. Paradeise et al. 2009).

This book, resulting of a PhD project, also focuses on the governance issue. By choosing doctoral education's reform in Switzerland and Norway as its topic, the present study adopts the approach which goes out from particular policies in order to observe potential changes in university governance. Thus, the first, general research question can be formulated in the following manner: can one observe any changes in the Swiss and Norwegian university governance (polity and politics) on the example of doctoral education's reform taking place during the first decade of the 21st century, and, if yes, how can those changes be characterised? Many among the existing university governance studies draw general conclusions for a whole national higher education system. Yet, in reality, higher education systems are often very complex and diversified. By choosing two different countries, this study also integrates the national variable. However, in addition, this study considers three further variables, that is to say, the type – in terms of disciplinary composition – and size of HEIs as well as scientific disciplines. Thus, the second, more specific research question can be formulated in the following terms: to what extent do observed changes in university governance vary according to those four variables?

In order to answer the first two research questions, this study builds on a large range of interviews with academic and administrative actors outside and especially inside HEIs. This provides the opportunity to go beyond a macro analysis, which would be limited to observations of changes in university governance for instance in terms of the relationship between the state, the HEIs and/or the academic profession as a whole. In other words, the actors' framework, considered in this study, is redefined to some extent: further actors are added (intermediary bodies like public research funding agencies and rectors' conferences) and "classical" actors or units are considered under a different label (for instance instead of using the academic profession as unit of observation, professors and doctoral students are observed in a more distinguished and individual manner).

A considerable number of higher education studies dealing with the governance issue underline the rising role of "New Public Management" (e.g. Braun 1999; Schimank 2005). In their "Governance Equalizer" de Boer et al. (2008) used among others a range of central elements of New Public Management as a *normative benchmark* in order to characterise and compare university governance of different countries. Considering that this narrative is useful but not sufficient to analyse the governance issue in higher education, two other public management narratives, namely the ones of "Network Governance" and "Neo-Weberian-state" are added to complement the analytical framework. Thus, using the example of de Boer et al. (2008), this study will choose a number of central elements of the three narratives in order to characterise and, as far as possible measure changes in university governance.

However, why should one analyse potential changes in university governance on the basis of doctoral education's reform? In the field of higher education policies, doctoral education occupies – since about one to two decades – an increasingly important place on the reform agendas at European, national and institutional levels. Among others, it has become a hot topic in the framework of the Lisbon agenda and the declaration of Bologna (Kehm 2006). Various national Ministries of higher education, research funding agencies, rectors' conferences as well as individual higher education institutions (HEIs) began to plan and implement varying types of reforms. Being considered a non-issue until recently, doctoral education has been recognised among others as a key resource for the creation of scientific research. Improvement with respect to doctoral education is also expected to guarantee the attainment of higher summits in terms of quality and quantity of research production. From an economic point of view, doctoral education and doctoral graduates are also seen as an important tool in the "Knowledge based Economy". Hence, the increasing interest of a larger number of actors for doctoral education raises the governance issue. A second reason to raise the governance issue consists in the arrival of new forms of doctoral education: one central component of doctoral education's reform in Europe consists of the establishment and running of "structured doctoral programmes" or "doctoral schools".[1] Inspired by American "Graduate Schools", various forms of doctoral schools have been increasingly emerging in many European HEIs. Until recently, European doctoral education has been mainly shaped by the so called "apprentice-ship model", that is to say the idea according to which a professor recruits and trains his[2] doctoral students within a binary

1 Varying denominations figure in higher education studies and political documents. Besides the mentioned terms, "research school" – especially in Nordic countries – or "graduate school" are also in use. The term "graduate school" may be particularly misleading because in the country of its origin, the USA, it includes both the master and doctoral levels, whereas in many European HEIs, it is limited to the doctoral level. In the present study, three terms, that is to say "structured doctoral programmes", "doctoral schools" and "research schools" are used interchangeably.

2 In order to facilitate the lecture, only the male form is used.

relationship without any interference through other actors. Thus, with respect to the governance issue, existing literature generally underlines the prevalent role and power of the academic profession. Since forms and contents of doctoral training have mainly been determined in the framework of the "apprentice-ship model", professors have largely controlled them. Due to those new forms of doctoral education, some authors (e.g. Gingras and Gemme 2006) interrogate the power of the academic profession on doctoral education. Thus, some changes in the governance of doctoral education may have been occurring, in particular through doctoral schools.

Finally, doctoral education has a central place among HEIs' missions because it is more or less directly related to all of them. Doctoral students participate in research and often also in teaching and activities related to universities' third mission. As a consequence, changes in doctoral education's governance may give insight on broader tendencies in university governance.

The governance issue cannot be examined without studying, at least to a certain extent, the actual reform of doctoral education. Hence, this study also seeks to identify the principal changes in doctoral education's practices. Thus, the third research question is formulated in the following manner: what does doctoral *education's* reform in terms of practices consist of? Making the hypothesis that changing practices may vary according to the studied case, a fourth research question is again related to the four determined variables: to what extent do reform elements vary according to the national higher education system, the type and size of HEIs as well as according to scientific disciplines? Arguing that changes in doctoral education's practices are related to changes in doctoral education's governance, the present PhD project also seeks to establish the link between the governance issue and the actual reform.

From an empirical point of view, those four research questions are examined on the basis of a case study design covering four contrasting scientific disciplines within two countries. Considering the importance of "doctoral schools" within the reform movement of European doctoral education, four Norwegian and four Swiss "doctoral schools" in the fields of biology, materials science, humanities and finance have been chosen as empirical centre. Each case study is scrutinised within its respective institutional and national environment. Empirical data principally rely on semi-structured interviews with 100 institutional and national actors involved in the selected "doctoral schools" and the reform of doctoral education. It is complemented with the underlying legal frameworks and available quantitative data.

The structure of the present book is divided into three major parts. The first part – "Setting the Field" – includes chapters one to three which have a preparatory character. Chapter one develops more in detail the arrival of the issue "doctoral education" on the reform agenda at the various mentioned levels and doctoral education's analysis in scientific literature. Chapter two deepens the research design and the underlying methodological thoughts. Furthermore, it describes collected empirical data and data treatment. The first part is concluded by the third chapter which develops reasons for the analytical framework's choice, exposes the three public management narratives, and discusses the relationship between them and their use in the analysis. In addition, the slightly redefined actors' framework used in this study is exposed.

The second part – "Empirical Results" – constitutes the empirical core of this study. In order to embed the individual case studies, it begins by exposing the national frameworks of doctoral education and recent reforms carried out in Switzerland and Norway. This fourth chapter presents recent qualitative, legal and quantitative developments. It then concludes by exposing some reflections about possible wider implications regarding the respective national higher education systems. Chapters five to eight are dedicated to the eight case studies. Chapter five deals with the case studies in biology, chapter six with those in material sciences, chapter seven develops those in humanities and the last ones concerning finance are exposed in chapter eight. Each time, changes in governance and practices of doctoral education are described and measured on the basis of the three public management narratives' main elements, developed in chapter three. After having established the link between observed changes in governance and actual reform elements, wider observations related to those changes are pointed to and discussed.

The third part – "Transversal Analysis" – is composed of two chapters. Chapter nine summarises and compares the case studies in terms of triggers of and obstacles to reform, observed governance patterns and resulting reforms. Thereby, all four research questions are answered. A further section of this chapter summarises the link between changing governance patterns and resulting reforms, whereas a last section resumes the discussion about wider implications of observed changes in governance and practices of doctoral education on academic work. Chapter ten is dedicated to reflections with respect to recruitments of doctoral students on the international market. This recruitment issue is an additional outcome of this broadly induction based research. On the basis of collected empirical data, identified recruitment mechanisms are analysed more in depth. Finally, this book ends with a general conclusion.

The present book is one product of a European research project called SUN – Steering of Universities. SUN was one out of a series of projects constituting the European Network of Excellence PRIME ("Policies for Research and Innovation in the Move towards the European Research Area"), funded through the 6th European Framework programme. SUN has had the objective to analyse the steering issue of universities in particular on the basis of two tracers, namely doctoral schools and research funding. A number of doctoral students have studied those issues in a deepened way in a series of European countries. Besides the present doctoral study focussing on doctoral schools in Switzerland and Norway, another doctoral study is dedicated to doctoral schools in France (Aubépine Dahan). The second tracer, that is to say research funding, is studied in France (by Julien Barrier), Great-Britain (by Felipe Camerati), Italy (by Marco Seeber) and Norway (by Gigliola Mathisen).

Part 1:
Setting the Field

I. The Reform's Initiation and First Analysis

This first chapter is divided into two main sections. The first section deals with the arrival of the issue "doctoral education" on the European reform agenda at several levels, whereas the second section develops doctoral education's analysis in scientific literature.

I.1. The Arrival on the Reform Agenda

Within a few years doctoral education in Europe developed from a non-issue to an object of policy making. "The doctoral level of training, learning and work has been a stepchild for many countries as well as for European policies until recently. In recent years, a sense of urgency emerged as far as expansion, institutionalization and financial support for doctoral study are concerned" (Teichler 2006: 36). Thus, it is not anymore considered an affair between the doctoral student and his professor or department. But it became a hot topic at the institutional, national and even supra-national level (Kehm 2006).

I.1.1. European Movements

At the European level, doctoral education is put on the agenda in the framework of two different but complementary policies. The European Union is the creator of the first policy, the "Lisbon Agenda". This policy aims at achieving an extremely ambitious goal for Europe, namely "to become the most competitive and dynamic knowledge-based economy in the world, capable of sustainable economic growth with more and better jobs and a greater social cohesion" (European Council 2000: 5). Several strategies shall help to achieve this goal. One of them is the creation of the "European Research and Innovation Area (ERA)". ERA pursues better integration and coordination of research activities at national and

Union level in order to make them as efficient and innovative as possible. In further related documents, the European Commission (2003; 2003a) underlined the important role of universities and the training of a highly qualified workforce within the process towards the most competitive and knowledge based economy.

The Commission mentions concrete suggestions in order to improve the preparation of future researchers. It points at two issues, namely supervision and type of training: the Commission sees a potential in joint supervision models for doctoral students and suggest to train doctoral students in an interdisciplinary work perspective (European Commission 2003). Furthermore, the Commission underlines the importance to improve career structures and perspectives for researchers in order to make the profession of researchers more attractive. It notes structural weaknesses and differences concerning issues like differences in recruitment methods, contractual and budgetary dimensions as well as evaluation mechanisms. The lack of openness for researchers careers in Europe are also evaluated as hindering the development of proper career perspectives at European level (European Commission 2003a).

The second policy, the "Bologna Declaration" (Ministers responsible for Higher Education 1999), seeks to create the "European Higher Education Area (EHEA)". This aim shall be mainly achieved by the creation of a common degree structure. The implementation of the declaration began with the two-tier structure Bachelor-Master. Since the follow-up conference in Berlin, which took place in 2003, the then 33 participating countries integrated also the third level into this reform, that is to say the doctoral level. According to the communiqué, this measure – which has previously been supported by the European Commission (2003) – shall promote closer links between the European Higher Education Area and the European Research Area. In addition, research and research training as well as the promotion of interdisciplinarity are emphasised as being crucial in maintaining and improving the quality and competitiveness of European higher education more generally. Besides formally integrating the doctoral level into the Bologna reform, the Berlin communiqué did not yet make any clear indications about what type of actions can be expected or should be implemented as a consequence of this decision. Ministers just make the vague statement according to which "networks at doctoral level should be given support to stimulate the development of excellence and to become the hallmarks of the European Higher Education Area" (Ministers responsible for Higher Education 2003: 7).

Although running under the "Bologna label", more concrete steps have not been exclusively prepared by the Ministers but by a wider circle of actors, which notably included a high number of academic community members. In February 2005, the Austrian Federal Ministry of Education, Science and Culture, the German Federal Ministry of Education and Research as well as the European University Association (EUA)[3] organised a "Bologna Seminar" in Salzburg. More than 300 representatives of universities and governments from all over Europe and the USA participated.[4] They elaborated a set of ten basic principles with respect to doctoral education in Europe and recommended to the Bologna follow-up group to base the Bergen Communiqué on those principles. In addition, they suggested that the Ministers should "call on EUA through its members to prepare a report under the responsibility of the BFUG [Bologna Follow-Up Group] on the further development of these principles to be presented to Ministers in 2007" (EUA et al. 2005: 3). Indeed, both recommendations have been accepted to a large extent by the Ministers in Bergen. Among the suggested set of basic principles, the Bergen Communiqué in particular integrated the following points (Ministers responsible for Higher Education 2005: 4):

- "The core component of doctoral training is the advancement of knowledge through original research."
- There is a need for transparent supervision and assessment.
- "The normal workload of the third cycle in most countries would correspond to 3-4 years full-time."
- Interdisciplinary training and the development of transferable skills should be promoted in order to meet the needs of the wider employment market.

---

3 "The European University Association (EUA) represents and supports higher education institutions in 46 countries, providing them with a unique forum to cooperate and keep abreast of the latest trends in higher education and research policies. Members of the Association are European universities involved in teaching and research, national associations of rectors and other organisations active in higher education and research." Source: <www.eua.be/about-eua/>; accessed on November 2009.

4 Source: <www.eua.be/research/doctoral-programmess/doctoral-programmes-in-the-bologna-process/salzburg-seminar/>; accessed on November 2009.

In addition to (part of) the principles suggested by the "Bologna Seminar-Group", Ministers also integrated in the Bergen communiqué the following points:

- An overall increase in the numbers of doctoral candidates taking up research careers in the EHEA needs to be achieved.
- There is a need for structured doctoral programmes.
- Participants in third cycle programmes are considered both as students and as early stage researchers.

As mentioned, the second recommendation of the "Bologna Seminar-Group" has also been accepted: the Ministers "charged the Bologna Follow-up Group with inviting the European University Association, together with other interested partners, to prepare a report under the responsibility of the Follow-up Group on the further development of the basic principles for doctoral programmes, to be presented to Ministers in 2007" (Ministers responsible for Higher Education 2005: 4). However, they also underlined that overregulation of doctoral programmes must be avoided. The Ministers do not add any new relevant decisions regarding doctoral education in the Bologna follow-up conferences taking place in London (2007) and in Leuven and Louvain-la-Neuve (2009). They essentially confine themselves to re-underline decisions which have already been previously addressed (Ministers responsible for Higher Education 2007; 2009).

The European University Association already started working on the issue of doctoral education before it got the formal invitation of the Ministers.[5] Referring to the "Lisbon objectives" and the "Bologna process", it set itself the objectives, first, to identify essential conditions for successful doctoral programmes and second, to promote and encourage cooperation in the development of doctoral programmes at the European level. On the basis of a collaborative project with 48 European HEIs from across 22 countries, it published the following findings: first, compared to the reform of the first two cycles, the transformation of

5 Since 2008, EUA even disposes of a "Council for Doctoral Education", which "creates a strong voice for European universities on doctoral education both inside Europe and internationally and contributes to enhancing the visibility of doctoral/graduate/research schools and programmes." Source: <www.eua.be/events /eua-council-for-doctoral-education/about-eua-cde/>; accessed on November 2009.

doctoral education "presents a different order of challenge" (EUA 2005: 7). Second, the reform is carried out with different paces. Certain countries are only at the beginning of the reform. Third, the re-organisation towards structured programmes which include training courses in a wide range of transferable skills requires adequate funding. Fourth, data collection on completion rates and career outcomes should be carried out in a more systematic way in order to measure the success of structured doctoral programmes with respect to the defined policy objectives. Besides those general findings, this EUA report (2005) also points at a number of "good practices":

- The *definition of common institutional guidelines*, codes and regulations on recruitment, supervision, exam, evaluation and defence of thesis at the highest institutional level.
- The "apprenticeship model" is questioned and structured programmes like *research/graduate/doctoral schools* are put forward as increasing tendency.
- To examine and think about *innovative practices* regarding qualification requirements, responsibilities and duties, training and workloads of supervisors, but also concerning doctoral students' progress assessment, requirements for the doctoral thesis and its defence as well as the follow-up "tracking" of doctoral candidates' career outcomes.
- *Mobility* may lead to wider research experience and career development opportunities.

Another EUA report (EUA 2007) – that is to say the one which has been mandated by the Ministers – presents a series of recommendations with regard to doctoral/graduate/research schools and general issues of doctoral education. The question of the appropriated choice in terms of institutional structure is seen as a key issue. The retained principle concludes that according to the HEI, its specific aims, absence/presence of critical mass and disciplinary differences, the appropriate solution may vary. Furthermore, the report points at a series of elements related to doctoral schools which may provide an added value to doctoral programmes:

- "Define a mission or vision shared by all partners that facilitates the process of training doctoral candidates into excellent researchers;

- Provide a stimulating research environment and promote cooperation across disciplines;
- Provide a clear administrative structure for doctoral programmes, candidates and supervisors, and offering a clear profile and status for doctoral candidates;
- Ensure critical mass and help to overcome the isolation of young researchers;
- Bring junior and senior researchers together;
- Support and facilitate the task of supervising candidates and the role of supervisors;
- Organise admission with transparent rules and regulations;
- Provide teaching and transferable skills training;
- Provide enhanced career development opportunities, including advice on funding opportunities (scholarships, projects);
- Guarantee quality assurance and monitoring;
- Provide a framework allowing the development of codes of practice, procedures and mechanisms within the university structure and act as a [sic] an arbitrator or ombudsman where necessary;
- Enhance opportunities for mobility, international collaboration and inter-institutional cooperation (EUA 2007: 19)."

Concerning more general issues, the recommendations, partly repeat the ten principles formulated during the "Bologna seminar" in Salzburg and elements mentioned in the previous report but also add some more precise elements. Those recommendations concern six issues: first, concerning access and admission, it is recommended that flexibility should be maintained. For instance, the Bologna commitment that the second cycle, i.e. the Master degree, gives the possibility to be considered for admission to the third cycle should be maintained but not be the only route. Simultaneously, greater attention should be paid to the issue of equality of access to the third cycle. Second, regarding supervision and assessment, arrangements based upon transparent contractual framework of shared responsibilities between doctoral candidates, supervisors and the institution should be developed. In addition, multiple supervision arrangements, continuous professional skills development of academic staff as well as performance reviews of supervisors are recommended. Furthermore, the importance of properly recognising supervision activities as a task of academic staff through its inclusion in their workload and task description is underlined. Third, with respect to transferable skills development, the following point is underlined as being important: "to raise awareness among doctoral candidates of the importance of both recognising and enhancing the skills that they develop and acquire through research, as a means of improving their employment prospects both in academia and on the wider labour market" (EUA 2007: 12). Interdisciplinary dialogue among doctoral students from varying scientific fields as well as various forms of courses taught by academics and external consultants from industry and companies are suggested as means to develop transferable skills. Fourth, the report confirms the principle suggested in the Bergen Communiqué according to which a three to four years period is the overall full time duration of doctoral education. However, they underline that part time studies take longer. Considering that in reality, overall duration is often longer, the need to carefully monitor the development of time to degree for doctoral candidates is emphasised. Fifth, universities and authorities are declared being responsible for promoting attractive research careers and career perspectives inside and outside of academia. This should also be done in collaboration with partners outside academia. Finally, the report encourages HEIs to include doctoral programmes in their strategies for internationalisation and to implement them for instance by offering funding instruments which facilitate the mobility of doctoral candidates from all 45 Bologna countries, by recruiting international doctoral candidates and other staff and by internationally suggesting "local" training activities (EUA 2007).

Two other issues, which have been tackled and further developed in EUA reports of 2007 and 2009, concern the "professional doctorate" as well as "collaborative doctoral education" with industrial partners. "Professional doctorates" or practice related doctorates are defined as "doctorates that focus on embedding research in a reflective manner into another professional practice." It is underlined that professional doctorates "must meet the same core standards as 'traditional' doctorates in order to ensure the same high level of quality. It may be appropriate to consider using different titles to distinguish between this type of professional doctorate and PhDs" (EUA 2007: 14). Considering the increased importance of innovation through R&D in the context of the "Knowledge-based Economy" as well as the reality that a majority of doctorate graduates make careers outside academia, "collaborative doctoral education" is given an important focus in EUA's report of 2009. In the framework of the underlying project called "DOC-CAREERS", a number of "collaborative doctoral education" programmes – which are distinguished through the formal or informal participation in the supervisory committee of "industry experts" – have been examined. Among others, learned lessons concern diversity, skills and funding. Regarding diversity, it is noted that there is no "one-size-fits-all" solution for successful approaches. Differences between – for instance American and European – cultures but also size of companies make differentiated approaches necessary. In the same vein, SMEs placed a higher value in doctorate holders with "soft skills" than large R&D companies. However, if all companies generally were satisfied with the acquired knowledge and research skills of doctorate holders, they emphasised the need to develop greater communication skills, knowledge about intellectual property issues and the manner business operates. Last but not least, the necessity for data tracking and public support of collaborative doctoral education, especially for SMEs, is again underlined (Borrell-Damian 2009).

I.1.2. National and Institutional Agenda Setting

Doctoral education's reform has also been put on national and institutional agendas during these last years. According to the country, the national agenda setting took place before or after the one at European level. Several governmental initiatives ended in the – often non-comprehensive – establishment of graduate/doctoral/research schools.

A first example concerns Germany, where the federal government introduced in an unusual top-down manner so-called Graduiertenkollegs in 1989 (Bartelse et al. 2000). As recent governmental reports witness, the reform of doctoral education and graduate schools are still an issue for the German government (Bundesministerium für Bildung und Forschung 2008). Governmental decrees also led to the introduction of so-called écoles doctorales in France. Initially not mandatory, doctoral schools have been gradually introduced since 1992 (Dahan 2007). As we will see more in detail, also the national governments of Switzerland and Norway put the issue of doctoral education and, in particular, the issue of doctoral or research schools on their reform agendas during the last few years.

Finally, three kinds of agenda setting witness of the rising importance of doctoral education and its reform for higher education institutions themselves: first, national rectors' conferences of varying countries, among which Germany, Austria and Switzerland, make various types of statements with respect to doctoral education.[6] Second, individual HEIs sign different kinds of agreements containing guidelines for doctoral education in the framework of inter-institutional networks. The "League of European Research Universities" is one of those networks.[7] And, as we will see in the case studies, certain HEIs have been increasingly developing own policies with respect to doctoral education and its reform.

6 See for instance CRUS et al. (2004).

7 See LERU (2007).

I.2. Doctoral Education in Higher Education Studies

Doctoral education and its reform did not only get an important place of the agenda at various political levels. During the last ten to fifteen years, it has also become an increasingly considered issue in higher education studies. This second section of the present chapter aims at illustrating the rise of this issue by presenting a literature review. By perusing existing higher education studies, it quickly becomes clear that doctoral education and its reform are no issue which is limited to Europe. In opposite, quite a body of literature bears on developments in Anglo-Saxon countries, in particular in Australia and the United States of America. Treated issues are often very similar to those dealt with in scientific literature or political debates referring to European countries (see e.g. comparative study of Kehm 2006a). Therefore, this strand of literature is also integrated in the following literature review. The latter is divided in two parts: the first part develops the main issues (regarding doctoral education) studied in literature. The second part identifies and develops existing knowledge about the steering issue of doctoral education.

I.2.1. Issues in Scientific Literature

A first issue, which however is only sparsely studied, concerns the *recruitment* of doctoral students. Concerning Europe, Enders and de Weert (2004) notice that doctoral students are not anymore exclusively recruited at local level, but increasingly at national and international levels. Reasons are varying: for countries and HEIs, where doctoral students pay tuition fees, the attraction of international students is a mean to increase income. Furthermore, international students are also recruited in order to compensate the lack of "own" candidates. This phenomenon concerns especially natural sciences and engineering (Enders and de Weert 2004). A look to American literature reveals the competitive aspect related to doctoral students' recruitment. Gumport (1993) underlines that the attraction of the "best" doctoral students provides HEIs an important advantage in the competition with other

HEIs. She emphasises that PhD programmes with particularly good reputation may be a mean to attract high quality students.

A second issue, which is more often the subject of higher education studies, consists of *supervision and socialisation* of doctoral students. Several authors point to the problematic nature of the relationship between doctoral student and his supervisor. For instance, Mainhard et al. (2009) emphasise the supervisor's double role as guide and (often) assessor which may be source of tensions. They also reveal that doctoral students' needs in terms of supervision may clash with supervisors' styles of supervision. Needs and styles may vary between "hands on" and "hands off" modes. Pearson (1996) goes even more in detail by adding that, according to the moment, doctoral students need supervision to varying degrees. Furthermore, as indicated by Smeby (2000), gender may also matter in the binary relationship between doctoral student and supervisor. By studying this relationship on the basis of the gender variable in Norwegian graduate education (including master and doctoral levels), he found out that female doctoral students prefer female supervisors, especially in natural sciences. He sees a possible explanation for this finding in the need for role models for female doctoral students who are a minority in their scientific environment. However, Mainhard et al. (2009) emphasise that, in spite of the importance of the supervision issue, the evaluation or even discussion of supervisory experiences among academic staff is uncommon in many HEIs. Besides the binary supervision relationship between doctoral student and supervisor, studies are also dedicated to alternative forms of supervision. In this perspective, Pearson (1996) reveals that doctoral students' overall satisfaction with supervision is higher in the case of multiple supervision. In addition, he argues that other activities like participation in conferences outside of the department are also very important in the process of becoming an independent researcher.

Supervision and socialisation to disciplinary cultures and more generally academia are tightly related, since socialisation may partly happen through supervision activities. In their study, Delamont et al. (1997) were interested in the importance of the transmission of knowledge, techniques and disciplinary cultures through supervisors to their doctoral students for the success of doctoral research and training. Findings indicate that, especially in social sciences, the relation is strong and that, what they call "succession" – that is to say continuing transmission of disciplinary knowledge and culture through academics – may be more important than a "critical mass" of researchers within the doctoral students' research environment. More generally, Weidman and Stein (2003) underline the importance of the role played by faculty for doctoral students' socialisation as academic scholars. They point in particular at four points which promote socialisation: first, faculty who are accessible to students, second, who are themselves actively involved in different kinds of scholarly activities, third, who convey expectations and encourage doctoral students to engage in such activities and fourth, faculty who treat doctoral students as their colleagues.

Unsurprisingly, several studies underline the link between doctoral experience – partly determined by supervision and socialisation – and research careers. Harman (2002) reports that doctoral students' overall satisfaction about their experience, in particular regarding supervision, influences their intention to do an (academic or non-academic) research career. Furthermore, Enders (2002) noticed in his study about Germany that the degree of doctoral students' integration in the scientific community has an impact on careers in higher education.

An important element of the structuring process of doctoral education can be seen in the introduction of a *curricular component*. Currently, little literature is dedicated to this issue. This may be explained by its recent character. If, in certain European countries, coursework was already a more or less stable component of doctoral education of some disciplines, the breakthrough of this idea on a broader disciplinary scale happened only recently. Considering certain political requirements which claim broader and especially interdisciplinary doctoral training in order to prepare doctoral students for the wider, non-academic labour market, the question of a disciplinary or inter-disciplinary orientation of research training is apparently a central one. For the moment, three lessons can be drawn on the basis of existing studies regarding this dichotomy. First, disciplinary professions may give preference to the transmission of disciplinary training. Heen (2002) notices in her study about two doctoral programmes in economics in France and Norway that mono-disciplinary training has been preferred to institutional and/or national requirements of interdisciplinary training. Second, a case study of Holley (2009) about an interdisciplinary training programme showed that there may be difficulties in terms of implementation. For instance, she found out that the interdisciplinary programme has been culturally dominated by one single discipline, that doctoral students were unsecure about the courses to choose and that a (too) large number of courses may get in conflict with work in laboratory. Third, besides interdisciplinary training, so-called "soft skills" are often required in order to prepare doctoral students for the non-academic labour. Harman (2002a) inquired into a doctoral programme, situated between industry and a university, which put particular emphasis on training in skills which might be considered "soft": courses in how to apply for grants, to manage research projects and to write business plans, about leadership and financial skills as well as about how to present research to client groups. Harman was particularly interested in the doctoral students' view. He concludes by noticing that the latter's feedback was rather positive.

A fourth issue identified in higher education studies concerns the *funding* of doctoral education. Here, it can be distinguished between the funding of doctoral education as a whole and the funding of doctoral students' grants and salaries. With respect to the former, Clark (1995) emphasises – for the case of American Graduate Schools – the importance of cross-subsidisation for the solidity of American graduate education. He indicates that graduate education costs many times more than undergraduate education. However, since departments control the distribution of funds, which are largely based on undergraduates' number, they can allocate a more important amount to the graduate level. Thus, the undergraduate level cross-subsidises the graduate level. Concerning the funding of doctoral students, several points are developed in existing literature. A study of Hellström (2004) points among others at the tension between research funding and the learning process of doctoral students. On the one side, doctoral students should be given leeway for making mistakes in order to progress in their learning process. On the other hand, (quick) progress in the laboratory is needed in order to obtain research funding. In other words, financial and time pressure let little room for the learning process. Together with other authors like Gumport or Mendoza, Hellström (2004) also underlines the potentially negative impact of industry-sponsored doctoral research and training. Besides the academic learning process, Hellström (2004) expresses fears regarding the socialisation process, whereas Gumport assumes that such doctoral students are less encouraged to think about problems that benefit the public or problems that are unlikely to result in profits (Gumport 2005). In the same vein, Mendoza notices that academic core values like academic freedom may be at play. However, he also states that the risk of such consequences is highly context dependent. For instance, HEIs which have a mix of varying funding resources – including funding from the federal government – are less exposed to such a risk than HEIs which principally rely on industrial funding (Mendoza 2007).

A fifth issue which is largely debated in higher education studies concerns the *labour markets* for doctorate holders and the related question of *new forms of doctoral education*. Here it can be distinguished between the academic and the wider, non-academic labour markets. Need for reform in doctoral education is identified with regard to both types of labour markets. Concerning the academic labour market, Austin (2002) refers to new economic and societal demands which are addressed to HEIs and their faculty, like solving societal problems and aid local and regional economic development. She argues that the new generation of academics must demonstrate a wider array of talents than their predecessors in order to successfully respond to those new requirements. Therefore, Austin suggests changes in the way doctoral students are prepared for those future tasks. Besides, the provision of regular, ongoing advising and thorough, periodic feedback and assessment as well as deliberate use of informal peer relationships to foster socialization, she suggests organised opportunities for students to learn about the many aspects of faculty work. Besides such measures for an improved preparation for academic careers, Austin nevertheless emphasises that doctoral education also should provide opportunities for students to learn about alternative careers and choices (Austin 2002).

This last point – that is to say the question of non-academic careers for doctorate holders – is treated and developed by a series of authors in the framework of three different types of contexts. First, several studies indicate that the desirability of faculty positions is declining. In their study about the UK, the Netherlands, Germany and Sweden, Huisman et al. (2002) identified as underlying reasons bad career perspectives shaped by many uncertainties and low salaries compared to the private sector. Harman explains the declining attraction of academic careers by the academics' heavy working loads, which, in addition, often consist of actual non-core activities like fund raising instead of research. Observing this situation, doctoral students do not feel attracted by academic careers

(Harman 2002). Second, the issue of non-academic careers is also related to demographic developments. The overall number of doctoral students in Europe is constantly increasing, whereas the number of tenured academic positions is not or at least not as strongly. Thus, an increasing number of doctorate holders have to find employment outside of academia because there are not sufficient academic jobs available (Gingras and Gemme 2006). The third context, consisting of the "Knowledge based Economy" is somehow the opposite perspective of the previous one. Instead of doctorate holders who need to find a job outside academia, it is the "Knowledge based Economy" which needs a higher number of qualified researchers. Authors like Allen et al. (2002), Usher (2002) and Evans (2002) referred to this perspective as a point of departure for their studies. Within these contexts shaped by the wish or necessity to find jobs on the non-academic labour market or the knowledge based economy's need for qualified researchers, claims for new forms of doctoral education are formulated. Campbell et al. (2005: 153) argue that doctoral programmes cannot remain static if trained doctors should be "marketable graduates". This claim seems to be supported by Mangematin et al.'s finding according to which requirements towards doctoral graduates in social sciences vary according to the type of labour market (Mangematin et al. 2000).

Indeed, new forms of doctoral education have been emerging and have become the object of higher education studies. Whether within or outside of Europe, several authors observe the development of an increasing *diversity* in the forms of doctoral education (Boud and Tennant 2006; Enders 2005). Two phenomena are often mentioned in relation with diversity in doctoral education. The first phenomenon is called *"professional doctorate"*. In their case study of a professional doctoral programme in business and administration in New Zealand, Lockhart and Stablein distinguish the analysed professional doctorate from the PhD degree by its increased focus on the application of the knowledge, which has been created through the doctoral research and whose point of departure consists of a practical problem (Lockhart and Stablein 2002). However, several authors emphasise that a clear-cut distinction between PhD and professional doctorate is not simple. Notably Tennant (2004) argues that this distinction is difficult to maintain because academic PhDs move in the direction of professional doctorates, in particular by accentuating the development of generic skills. Evans (2002) agrees on this argument and adds that PhD students – in particular so-called part-time doctoral students – also partly undertake their research in relation with professionally related fields.

The second phenomenon which appears in higher education studies in relation with different forms of doctoral education can be called *industry based doctoral education.* Like in the case of professional doctorates, the term is not clearly delimitated and may contain varying practices. However, the basic idea may be summarised to a situation where a doctoral student is simultaneously in contact with academia and industry. Unlike studies on doctoral education's funding (see Hellström 2004; Gumport 2005; Mendoza 2008), those particularly interested in such forms of doctoral education also emphasise positive aspects. Thune (2009) underlines the importance of the triple role of doctoral students working in between academia and industry: they are crucial, first, in the production of knowledge, second, for the transfer of knowledge to industry, and third, for the maintenance of network ties between universities and firms. With their conception of doctoral students working on the academic-industrial interface as boundary subjects instead of an exploited boundary object, Salminen-Karlsson and Wallgren (2008) express the idea according to which doctoral students are seen as humans who develop "phronesis", which means the capacity to deal with dynamics of practical situations in an appropriated way: do the right thing at the right time and on the basis of the right arguments.

To summarise the issue of new forms of doctoral education, one can refer to Allen et al. (2002) who state that demands on university systems to create innovative and flexible doctoral programmes have been formulated and that countries have responded to this challenge by developing professional doctorates and/or by reinventing the traditional PhD. However, as Usher notes, such new forms of doctoral education are not sufficiently familiar to the academic community and there are fears about the dilution of the PhD's standing. Therefore, he expects that conventional forms of PhD may remain the only form of doctoral education in certain knowledge areas, like for instance in physics and chemistry (Usher 2002). By mentioning possible resistance to changes in doctoral education, for instance coming from the academic community, Usher launches the question which will be developed in the next and last part of this chapter, that is to say, the question of the steering of changes in doctoral education.

I.2.2. The Steering of Doctoral Education and Doctoral Schools

As convincingly illustrated by Herman (2009) for the case of a South-African HEI, doctoral education is strongly determined by actors who control it. In this case study, Herman pointed out to what extent an (authoritative) political regime may shape supervisors regarding the question of the type of research topics and methods which are to be considered "valuable" for doctoral research. In the case of the USA, Gumport indicates that the role of the federal state regarding doctoral education is rather weak and deplores that fundamental questions about purposes and means of doctoral education are not addressed from a system-wide point of view. Instead local solutions have been formulated (Gumport 1993). Yet, from the point of view of Clark (1993), it is precisely this leeway for individual HEIs and the resulting spontaneous adjustment of HEIs and their departments which led to the successful strength of existing American Graduate Schools.

In the cases where HEIs are largely responsible of doctoral education, one can ask which actors within HEIs are steering doctoral education. Still for the American case, Damrosch (2006) states that even though faculty power may have diminished in other spheres, it still remains decisive when it comes to the training and advising of graduate students. Stark et al. (1997) add that the primary influences on course planning are the background, discipline and educational beliefs of the faculty. Yet, with respect to completion, Enders (2005a) notes for the case of Germany that the responsibility is more on the shoulders of the doctoral students than on those of the supervisors. He notices that, to a great extent, a candidate's failure in completing doctoral education has no consequences for supervisors. Damrosch also notes that tenured faculty at doctorate-awarding HEIs are not only the ones who decide but also the ones for whom the existing system worked well (to the extent that they are on tenured positions). However, it is precisely therefore, that they may not see disadvantages of the current system (Damrosch 2006). In other words, they may have little reason to introduce changes in doctoral education. For instance, Usher (2002) argues that disciplinary communities may inhibit the institutionalisation of diversity in doctoral education. With respect to the development of industry-based doctoral education, Enders notes (2005) that senior researchers may protect clear boundaries between the academic and entrepreneurial world and thereby hinder the development of new modes of doctoral education. In the same vein, Mangematin (2000) points at potential conflicts if doctoral students who carry out their doctoral research within industry do not share the same priorities like their supervisors, that is to say for instance rather economic than academic ones. Holley (2009) demonstrated that diverging opinions among supervisors about course components and other issues may also lead to difficulties in the development of for instance interdisciplinary doctoral programmes. Gingras and Gemme (2006) argue that professors have been used for a long time to decide about the content of doctoral training, to the point that this monopole has been taken for granted. Simultaneously, they launch the question of whether this power and traditional forms of doctoral education are currently threatened in the framework of the knowledge based economy.

As mentioned, a central component of doctoral education's reform in Europe consists of the establishment of "structured doctoral programmes" or "doctoral schools". Inspired by the US experience, a "fruitful misunderstanding has contributed to the creation of new forms that actually inspire, in turn, to some extent reform initiatives in the US" (Enders and de Weert 2004: 148). According to Enders and de Weert (2004), the graduate school movement spreads in Europe since the 1980s, though with differences in time according to the country. It can be added that, in countries like Germany, doctoral schools have often been introduced on a pilot basis and do still only concern part of doctoral students (Bartelse et al. 2000). Probably due to the phenomenon's young age, little research has been carried out about structured doctoral programmes and underlying governance mechanisms. An exception consist in Sadowski et al.'s (2008) study about 14 mostly structured doctoral programmes (and programmes which were in the process of being structured during the study) in economics within Germany, Switzerland, Italy, the UK, France and the Netherlands. These authors noticed that the introduction of structured doctoral programmes often resulted of the initiative of one central personality within the respective economics department who identified and convinced a group of like-minded people to cooperate. Furthermore, to some extent, their involvement appears to be idealistic since they do not get any reduction of their working load in compensation, like in terms of teaching load. Therefore, "free riding", through members of the same department, may occur (Sadowski et al. 2008). Thus, although in an unequally distributed manner, the power of those structured doctoral programmes seems to be largely maintained by the academic profession.

What about the power of other institutional actors? The study of Sadowski et al. also examined whether corresponding deans and presidents of structured doctoral programmes got more power. This was not the case (Sadowski et al. 2008). In another study about graduate schools in Canada, the US and the UK, Elgar et al. (2004) examined to what extent graduate school deans were informed about the completion rates of the doctoral students within their graduate schools. Interestingly, most graduate school deans rated completion rates within their schools as good although they were unable to report about completion percentages… (Elgar et al. 2004).

In summary, a number of scholars noticed that doctoral education and doctoral schools have been largely steered and determined by the academic profession. It is argued that the latter has no interest and does not necessarily see the need either to reform doctoral education. However, other scholars launch the question of whether the academic profession's monopole on doctoral training and traditional forms of doctoral education are challenged in the framework of the knowledge based economy. Considering the lack of higher education studies dealing with this question, in particular with respect to European doctoral education and even more regarding European doctoral schools, the present study aims at creating additional knowledge about this issue.

II. Research Design, Methodology, Collected Data and Data Treatment

As mentioned, the present study seeks to deal with organised doctoral education in two main ways: on the one hand, it tries to identify its nature such as it exists today in Switzerland and Norway. On the other hand, it scrutinises the steering of structured doctoral education. This chapter addresses, in a first section, the question about how the phenomenon of structured doctoral education in Europe can be studied. A second section describes the effectively collected empirical data.

II.1. How is a European Trend Focussing on Governance to be Studied?

This first section is structured in the following way: arguing on the foundations of the phenomenon as a "multilevel issue", the research questions, existing research methods, theoretical and practical considerations as well as concrete realisation, the choices in terms of research design are exposed and discussed. Furthermore, reasons are provided why the proposed research design is not only a means to understand existing structured doctoral education better, but also an opportunity to learn about university governance. In this part, some tools in the discussion about governance are suggested. Then, a discussion of choices estimates the strengths, weaknesses, opportunities and threats of the presented research design and exposes some more general observations about the study of higher education.

II.1.1. Structured Doctoral Education in Europe: A Multilevel Issue

It has been demonstrated in chapter I that structured doctoral education has been put on the reform agenda at supranational as well as national levels. Therefore, the discussed research design must include those two levels. Concretely, the broader national context of higher education policies and rules of doctoral education must be studied – especially in the light of European policies – in order to understand structured doctoral education, such as currently existing. It is unclear whether these international policies influence all European countries to the same extent. Therefore, it would be interesting to study this influence in at least two national higher education systems.

However, limiting the study to international and national levels would correspond to an oversimplification of the research problem. The implementation of international and/or national policies within HEIs happens rarely in a linear manner because HEIs may be characterised by variation concerning mission, size, disciplinary composition, funding mechanisms, governance forms, own interests and so on. In short, there may be a very complex diversity. These varying characteristics may also be sources of variation regarding structured doctoral education. Therefore, it is argued that a study with the ambition to understand doctoral education cannot neglect institutional and infra-institutional levels. The consideration of these levels is even more important if we consider them as the "operational centre" of structured doctoral education: presumably, doctoral students complete their doctorate essentially, however not always exclusively, in universities, doctoral training is mainly provided by university professors and other scientific staff, and doctorates are awarded by universities.

II.1.2. Research Objectives and Choice of Methods

As mentioned in the introduction, this study has two main objectives: to identify, characterise and analyse, first, changes in doctoral education's governance, and, second, changes *in practices* of doctoral education in Switzerland and Norway. The following paragraphs develop how those objectives can be dealt with.

Several elements plead for *exploratory research*: due to the phenomenon's relatively recent character, few studies have been carried out about structured doctoral education in Europe until now. Although they partly include some explicative power for the phenomenon,[8] there is still a need for further research: on the one hand, regarding other countries than those observed until now, because there may be other explanations, and on the other hand, regarding the degree of depth, in particular in relation to institutional and infra-institutional levels.

Lijphart's (1975) typology of scientific methods helps to develop the methodological choice. It firstly distinguishes between the experimental and the non-experimental method. The former method is certainly not applicable to exploratory research because in opposition to research in natural sciences, the objective is not to test hypotheses in order to confirm or reject them. In the present case, hypotheses should rather help to define the empirical field and find relevant explanations. Among the non-experimental methods, Lijphart lists three types, that is to say the statistical, case study and comparative methods. The statistical method can be used if sufficient cases are available. In the *trade off* between breadth (large number of cases with limited depth) and depth (small number of cases with large depth), preference is given to depth. This choice can be justified by the phenomenon's multi-level character. Consequently, the statistical method is not appropriated. According to Lijphart, the case study is limited to one case. Limitation to one case would have the same effect as the statistical method, yet regarding breadth, namely too strong reduction of the problem's complexity. In both methods, statistical and case study, possible explicative variables would be eliminated in advance. In contrast, the *comparative method* makes it possible to broaden to a certain degree the empirical basis and deepen it as much as possible. In fact, the comparative method seems to be most appropriate to the research problem and objectives. This is confirmed by Teichler (1996: 431) writing about comparative studies on higher education: "They are indispensible [sic] for understanding a reality shaped by common international trends, reforms based on

8 See for instance Kehm (2004), who compares 13 mostly European countries and identifies economic (for Europe and States) and strategic (for HEI) interests explaining the increased concern about more structured doctoral education in Europe.

comparative observation, growing trans-national activities and partial supra-national integration in higher education". Structured doctoral education seems to resemble the type of reality described. Therefore, a comparative research method is adopted.

The next step consists in the decision upon *what* exactly is to be compared. As structured doctoral education is often organised in the framework of *structured doctoral programmes* or *doctoral schools*, they are chosen to serve as units upon which comparison is carried out. In order to avoid choosing elements which do not correspond at all to the idea of structured doctoral education the following definition is applied: *a programme or school at the doctoral level, visible as such and applying certain minimal rules regarding issues concerning doctoral education such as its duration or recruitment, supervision or training of doctoral students.*

Given the adopted in-depth research design, an exhaustive study of all doctoral programmes in a given national higher education system is impossible. Therefore, a limited number of *cases are chosen.* Gerring (2004) discusses several definitions of the *case study*. He is not satisfied by them and formulates his own definition, which fits quite well with the research objective: "As a substitute for these flawed definitions, I propose to define the case study as *an intensive study of a single unit for the purpose of understanding a larger class of (similar) units.* A unit connotes a spatially bounded phenomenon – *e.g.* a nation-state, revolution, political party, election, or person – observed at a single point in time or over some delimited period of time (2004: 342)." In the given study, a unit is one structured doctoral programme or school observed in its current state. As they exist only since recently, their emergence and development is considered too. However, this also means that the considered overall time period may slightly vary from case to case.

II.1.3. Theoretical and Practical Aspects in the Selection of Case Studies

In an article about research in higher education, Tight (2004) asks the question whether the community of researchers in higher education is an *a-theoretical community of practice.* By analysing a large database of 17 specialist higher education journals, based outside North America, he notices that in the majority of cases, "any theoretical perspective is only implicit, and broader engagement with theory is absent" (Tight 2004: 409). Therefore, it is legitimate to raise the question whether theory is helpful for research in higher education. Tight shows that regarding this question, *the* higher education research community of practice does not exist as one single community but is strongly divided. He argues that this is due to different disciplinary backgrounds and departmental location of researchers working on higher education. "Researchers who do make their theoretical perspectives explicit tend to be based more often in social science disciplines or academic development units, rather than education departments or higher education research centres (Tight 2004: 409)." Tight thinks that there is a need for more theoretical engagement because that would allow the field to develop further and to gain credibility and respect.

Concerning theory and related hypotheses, more specifically in comparative higher education research, Kogan (1996) has a clear opinion: "Whilst we can certainly look for juxtapositions and thematic comparisons, and attempt to find causal explanations, we will be tying ourselves into an unnecessary bed of nails if we try to direct our research on the basis of pre-structured hypotheses. Where there are usable hypotheses let us enjoy them. Otherwise there is plenty of good work done at the third level, of thematic comparison (…) (1996: 398)." Teichler goes in the same direction when he writes that "most theoretically demanding and empirically successful comparative research on higher education *starts off from a semi-structured set of* [theoretical] *assumptions* (1996: 449-450)." In his opinion, the use of theory and hypotheses in combination with comparative studies is a strength that should not be missed. However, the adopted theoretical assumptions should not be handled too narrowly; otherwise, the study might arrive at simplistic conclusions ignoring the complex reality.

The introduction of theoretical aspects may also be useful in the study about structured doctoral education and university governance. Concerning variables, which may shape structured doctoral education, several hypotheses – partly built on theoretical foundations – emerge. Four variables appear in particular to be determinant for the features of structured doctoral programmes and schools. The *first variable* consists in the *type of scientific discipline or field.* In their book called "Academic Tribes and Territories. Intellectual enquiry and the culture of disciplines", Becher and Trowler (2001) convincingly describe specific characteristics of twelve different scientific disciplines and their respective communities. Differences related to these disciplines and their communities are demonstrated in a varied range of categories: They run from the validation process of results, deviations in language and style, nature and incidence of collaboration, recruitment and initiation to form of doctoral supervision. On this basis, the hypothesis that these differences among disciplines and their communities also create differences in the concrete design and management of doctoral schools can be made. Differences resulting from factors related directly to disciplines, like varying disciplinary needs and cultures in terms of supervision, training and its underlying governance patterns can be assumed.

A second variable consists of the size of disciplines and HEIs, for instance, in terms of numbers of doctoral students and supervisors. Regarding the politically and economically often evoked criterion of *critical mass*, not all HEIs may probably have "enough" doctoral students and teaching and supervisory staff in each domain in order to offer a specialised doctoral school. Therefore, solutions like inter-disciplinary or inter-institutional doctoral programmes may be expected. However, it can be assumed that such alternatives do not remain without consequences on content or steering aspects of doctoral programmes. For instance, in interdisciplinary programmes, content cannot be too specialised within a certain discipline, yet may be organised around a common thematic. In the case of inter-institutional programmes, involved institutions have to agree on elements like, programme content, (practical) organisation, funding and so on.

HEIs differ not only regarding structure but may also be distinguished between different *types of HEIs*. This *third variable* may refer to the distinction between academic and vocational HEI. From this point of view, once again the disciplinary variable may be of importance. However, there may also be other criteria related to the variable "type of HEI", like types of awarded degrees, degree of prestige, steering and/or funding mechanisms.

The *fourth variable* is related to differences of national *governance patterns*. Distribution of responsibilities in higher education on national and regional governments, funding agencies and other intermediary bodies and actors vary from state to state, especially between unitary and federal states. Consequently, policies in higher education and their implementation through respective reforms may vary too. Hence, this variable may also have an impact on concrete doctoral schools.

Thus, those variables might explain diversity in existing doctoral schools. The following points argue how these variables as well as other factors like feasibility, access to the field and existence of case studies are taken into account regarding the selection of the case studies: First, it appears to be preferable to choose cases on the base of certain variables rather than by ignoring theory and empirical reality. Taking into consideration these two factors allows the choice of "significant" rather than exceptional cases. Furthermore, diversity is preferred to similarity. Potential diversity can be achieved through the choice of national higher education systems. However, this is not simple for two reasons: first, no exhaustive comparative information exists regarding all enumerated variables in all European higher education systems, on which a choice could be based. Second, the possibility is not excluded that other important variables were ignored until this research phase. Therefore, the choice of countries always remains a little ambiguous or uncertain. Consequently, uncertainty might be reduced by choosing countries according to the hypothetical importance given to each variable but also by the empirical existence of cases, feasibility in terms of working charge and access to the field. Finally, considering certain variables in the case selection does not necessarily exclude the discovery of others. Empirical work that is not only concentrated on the chosen variables but generally open should allow surprising discoveries as well.

A first question within the tension between variables, existence of cases, feasibility and access to the field concerns the disciplines. As there are numerous different disciplines, it is impossible to consider all of them. Becher and Trowler (2001) demonstrate in their study one way of categorising disciplines. They distinguish between hard pure (*e.g.* physics), hard applied (*e.g.* mechanical engineering), soft pure (*e.g.* history) and soft applied disciplines (*e.g.* law). Although these distinctions are not that clear for all disciplines, they put some "landmarks" allowing the choice of doctoral schools in each of these four categories. This pragmatic way is a first possibility to reduce complexity somehow without ignoring it completely. Therefore, four structured doctoral programmes or schools per higher education system, one school in each of the four distinguished categories are chosen. In order to simplify comparison between countries, the chosen disciplines must be the same in both countries.

A next step consists of identifying higher education systems within which doctoral programmes are chosen. Again, there is the question of the number of higher education systems to consider. Here, it is important to underline that what is compared are not higher education systems as such but doctoral schools (within different higher education systems). Thus, higher education systems and the policies existing within them are not the compared object but a variable, hence, a potential source to explain diversity. Consequently, the *N-question* must be asked first at the level of the doctoral schools. Since four doctoral schools per higher education system are suggested, this number is multiplied with the number of national systems. The hypothesis related to the fourth variable supposes differences in doctoral schools due to varying governance patterns. The distinction between unitary and Federal states, respectively centralised and decentralised higher education systems requires *two* different higher education systems. However, this is not the only variable to consider as regards the choice of higher education systems. If further diversity is introduced with the second and third variables, that is to say the number of doctoral students per discipline and HEI as well as types of HEI, higher education systems offering the possibility to choose doctoral schools varying also from these points of view must be chosen.

Considering the four crucial factors in the selection of the cases, that is to say, first, hypothetical importance given to each potential variable, second, feasibility in terms of working charge, third, access to the field and forth, empirical existence of cases, higher education systems of *Switzerland and Norway* are chosen. The following elements support this choice:

1. As regards variables:
   a. *Governance patterns (4th variable):* They differ regarding the distribution of responsibilities among central and decentralised governments. The Swiss higher education system is strongly shaped by Switzerland's federal character. Hence, the three types of HEI are legally related to different types of authorities. Each of the ten cantonal universities has its own cantonal law

and, in addition, is subject to a federal law (LAU 1999)[9], whereas the two Federal Institutes of Technology (Zurich and Lausanne) are subject to only one federal law (LEPF 1991).[10] Differences also exist regarding funding of these two types of HEIs. In opposition to these existing differences in Switzerland, all Norwegian HEI types are put on the same legal and financial footing (Tjeldvoll 1999; NHEA 2005). Legally and financially speaking only the central government is competent.

b. *HEI types (3rd variable):* both higher education systems possess several types of HEIs. In Switzerland, Federal Institutes of Technology and cantonal universities are allowed to award doctorates, in Norway, apart from the seven universities and six[11] specialised university institutions, university colleges do award doctorates in certain fields. However, compared to (the large general) universities, university colleges award only a very small number of doctorates. Hence, in both countries two types of institutions mainly award doctorates and distinguish themselves more or less between generalised vs. specialised universities. However, Norwegian specialised university institutions have partly different disciplinary profiles to the Swiss ones.

c. *Differences of size (2nd variable):* Given the differences concerning doctoral students' numbers in HEIs and disciplines, diversity in terms of size is assured in both national systems. HEIs are roughly distinguished between small ones – less than 10,000 students – and large ones – more than 10,000 students.

d. *Disciplinary differences (1st variable):* A closer look at doctoral schools makes clear that a distinct choice according to Becher and Trowler's typology is quite difficult. Doctoral schools do not always necessarily respect these categories and are not

9 LAU: in French: "Loi d'aide aux universités".

10 LEPF: in French: "Loi fédérale sur les écoles polytechniques fédérales". Cantonal universities and federal institutes of technology are the two HEI types awarding doctorates. In the third type of HEI, the Universities of Applied Sciences are legally submitted to both, federal and cantonal, levels. As they do not award doctorates, they do not dispose of any doctoral programmes.

11 Since the study's start, the number of PhD awarding specialised university institutions has increased to eight institutions.

always simply allocable. Reasons may be that a school embraces both, theoretical and applied courses; doctoral students following the same courses (even if they are for instance exclusively theoretical) may do their PhD in differently oriented laboratories (pure or applied) and, hence, orient their thesis work correspondingly, independently from course work; a doctoral programme may be interdisciplinary. For all these reasons, the suggested categories act rather as an orientation point than as a strict typology. The choice of disciplines and related doctoral schools is addressed below.

2. Limitation of the study to two higher education systems allows in-depth research. Furthermore, two systems permit covering potential differences related to the de/centralisation of responsibilities in higher education. The integration of a third national system with again (at least) four doctoral schools would be certainly a gain for research about doctoral education and university governance in the given system. However, it is difficult to say whether it would go beyond the feasibility limits of a doctoral thesis. Therefore, the research is limited to two higher education systems.
3. In principle, the access to the field should be assured in both cases. Living in Switzerland as well as support from a Norwegian research team facilitates the realisation of the research project. Due to geographical reasons (long distances between certain HEIs), case studies in Norway are limited to two "university cities".
4. The last and most practical criterion to be considered is the existence of cases. The cases must cover simultaneously the same four disciplines (as far as possible being part of the respective disciplinary category) in both national higher education systems, the two HEI types principally awarding doctorates and differences between HEIs in terms of doctoral students' numbers. Doctoral students in the following scientific disciplines are chosen: molecular biology (hard pure category), materials science (hard applied category), interdisciplinary programme in humanities (soft pure category) and finance (soft applied category). Doctoral programmes of these four disciplines exist in both countries; however, due to different HEI profiles, they are not distributed equally in the two HEI types.

Table 1 summarises these choices and details them further, in particular regarding concrete doctoral programmes and doctoral/research schools. The case studies' characteristics regarding the four variables are described in Table 2. Besides the above-mentioned criteria a desk research about Swiss and Norwegian programmes and schools helped in the concrete choice:

	Switzerland	*Norway*
Scientific discipline	*Name of considered doctoral school and size (number of students) of mainly involved and considered HEIs (in 2009)*	*Name of considered doctoral school and size (number of students) of mainly involved and considered HEIs (in 2009)*
Hard pure	"PhD programme in Biomolecular Structure and Mechanisms" **(1)**	"Molecular and Computational Biology Research School" **(2)**
	Federal Institute of Technology Zurich: 15,071 University of Zurich: 25,815	University of Bergen: 13,042
Hard applied	"PhD programme in Materials Science and Engineering" **(3)**	"FUNMAT Research School" **(4)**
	Federal Institute of Technology Lausanne: 7,383	University of Oslo: 25,917
Soft pure	"Graduiertenprogramm Intermediale Ästhetik, Spiel – Ritual – Performanz" **(5)**	"National Research Training Programme - Text, Image, Sound and Space" **(6)**
	University of Basel: 12,088 University of Bern: 13,912	University of Bergen: 13,042
Soft applied	"SFI PhD programme in Finance" **(7)**	"PhD programme in Finance" **(8)**
	University of Lausanne: 11,581 University of Geneva: 15,014 University of Zurich: 25,815 University of Lugano: 2,704	Norwegian School of Business and Economics: 2,824

Table 1: Description of chosen case studies

Sources: www.bfs.admin.ch; dbh.nsd.uib.no ; accessed on January 2011.

Case study	*Type of discipline (Variable 1)*	*Size of HEI(s) (Variable 2)*	*Type of HEI(s) (Variable 3)*	*Type of political system (Variable 4)*
1	Hard pure	Large	Specialist/generalist	Federal
2	Hard pure	Large	Generalist	Centralised
3	Hard applied	Small	Specialist	Federal
4	Hard applied	Large	Generalist	Centralised
5	Soft pure	Large	Generalist	Federal
6	Soft pure	Large	Generalist	Centralised
7	Soft applied	Large	Generalist	Federal
8	Soft applied	Small	Specialist	Centralised

Table 2: Qualification of chosen case studies

II.1.4. Concrete Realisation

In order to realise the suggested research design, the following steps are proposed: The *first step* consists of understanding the emergence of *doctoral education as policy object* and of identifying the current state of art in legal and quantitative terms in Switzerland and Norway. It focuses on actors who put doctoral education on the political agenda and the arguments put forward. Means to realise this step is the analysis of existing scientific and grey literature, desk research, where necessary, interviews as well as the analysis of regulations and statistics.

Case studies build the *second step.* From a practical point of view, each case study begins with the analysis of the doctoral programme's regulation documents and grey literature about its development and current organisation. Then, interviews are carried out with actors closely related to each doctoral programme or school; for example, scientific and administrative leaders of the given doctoral programme, professors teaching in the framework of the doctoral programme and supervising doctoral students who participate in the programme, doctoral students, in addition to actors, who are related to the programme or school (perhaps) in a wider sense like (vice-)rectors and (vice-)deans for doctoral education, administrators responsible for doctoral education at the central university or faculty/department level. Questions are principally oriented around the programme's *development, steering, objectives and concrete activities.* Precise choice of interview partners and questions also depend on the accumulated information through the preceding document analysis. However, since only little information about concrete case studies is available, interviews are treated to a large extent as provider of factual information (see Annexe for interview guides). This also means that questions do not go beyond a certain degree of depth. This applies in particular to issues related to characteristics of disciplinary fields. Yet, the (sociological) study of scientific disciplines is not the study's goal either. Finally, with respect to data treatment it is worth underlining that personal opinions of interviewees are taken into consideration where relevant and, of course, declared as such.

II.1.5. Doctoral Education and University Governance

The following paragraphs explain the interest of scrutinising the steering of doctoral education as a concrete example to learn about university governance. At least four arguments can be put forward: *first,* doctoral education is a recent phenomenon, which has received attention on the political agenda only for a short time (Teichler 2006). Due to this recent characteristic, it seems to be particularly suitable to observe who, with which means and objectives occupies this relatively "new" field.

Secondly, university governance can be analysed through different topics or "entry points". For instance, one may raise the question about the steering of curricula or certain types of research projects within universities. However, both topics, curricula and research projects, cover principally one of the universities' core activities, that is to say respectively teaching or research. Yet, doctoral education has the advantage of being connected more clearly with both of them. On the one hand, it affects teaching on the highest possible level. On the other hand, it also relates to research to the extent that doctoral students carry out an important part of HEIs' overall research production (Enders 2002).

Thirdly, doctoral education is a particularly important mission of HEIs. Thus, changes in its steering may strongly affect the "mission doctoral education" as such. In other words, the character of doctoral education may be oriented in different directions, representing varying interests of different actors inside and outside of academia: rectors, deans, professors, doctoral students, European and national political actors, representatives of industry, finance, etc. The main question here is whether doctoral education should be oriented towards the required skills for an academic career (see Austin 2002; Shambaugh 2000) or the wider employment market requiring more general skills (see Harman 2002; Campell et al. 2005; Golde et al. 2006), like managerial skills. As mentioned, in some countries, doctorates are adapted to the required competencies of the non-academic labour market by creating "Professional Doctorates". According to Kehm (2004: 292), professional doctorates "are often related to projects carried out within an enterprise and jointly supervised by the home university and the according enterprise and the course work emphasizes more generic skills and interdisciplinary approaches." Behind these different options of doctoral education's content lie varying, for instance economical and strategic interests (Kehm 2006). Hence, among others, case studies will allow disclosing different actors' configurations and related interests.

Finally, as demonstrated above, doctoral education is a multi-level issue. Enders (2004) underlines that, in the light of Europeanization and globalisation, features of governance theory and its application in higher education studies must be rethought. Among others, he points to deficits like the "concentration on the single nation state (even where international comparisons are made), and a selective concern with domestic politics". Moreover, he indicates, "the concern with macro level policy-making and meso level organisational adaptation, neglecting to some extent the micro dynamics and effects in the actual practices and performances of academic work" (2004: 373). From this point of view, a study about the multi-level issue doctoral education represents a good opportunity to respond to the challenges of the integration of neglected levels.

II.1.6. Discussion of Choices

The study of European higher education is somehow ambiguous. On the one side, common developments or *trends*, often shared by most, if not all, European higher education systems can be observed at a macro level. These trends may be a consequence of a common policy formally established at European level, of informal idea diffusion, mutual influence and imitation or of a mixture of all these elements. On the other side, especially when it comes to the meso and micro levels, that is to say the levels of individual HEIs and their scientific disciplines, one does not talk anymore about common trends but *diversity*. Noticing this tension between common trends and diversity, existing also in the case of structured doctoral education, seems to be somehow trivial. Nevertheless, it raises large challenges concerning the concrete research design.

Structured doctoral education is put into place within an institutional, national and even European framework. However, the infra-institutional level can be considered the "operational centre". Therefore, a multi-level approach that considers not only the supra-national, national and institutional levels but also the infra-institutional level appears appropriate. This should take into account *diversity from a vertical point of view.* Starting from this assumption, theoretical and practical considerations help designing the study further. Becher and Trowler's study (2001), pointing out varying disciplinary characteristics, helps illuminating potential *diversity from a horizontal point of view.* Consequently, the consideration of the infra-institutional level, often neglected in higher education studies interested in governance, seems particularly worthy of being integrated in the study, both from the point of view of vertical and horizontal diversity. Subsequently, the choice of case studies is carried out at this level. However, it is precisely at this level, that one has to go on from theoretical considerations to practical ones. As in the case of structured doctoral education, it is not always easy to find theoretically defined cases in empirical reality. However, theory helps to orient more precisely the choice of the empirical field, which turns out to be particularly useful when the object of study is a recent and therefore under-investigated phenomenon.

This first section of the present chapter concludes with an evaluation of the developed research design by a SWOT (*S*trengths, *W*eaknesses, *O*pportunities, *T*hreats) analysis and some more general observations about the study of higher education. A first *strength* is made of the in-depth study of a European trend. The research does not settle for an analysis of a European policy nor a comparison of national policies, but, seeks to understand concrete examples of structured doctoral education. It takes into consideration statements of different actors at different levels in order to provide a most complete picture.

At the same time and to a certain extent, this strength may be considered a *weakness* because the price of this depth relies in the loss of breadth: a European trend is scrutinised, yet, limited to two national higher education systems. Consequently, possibilities for generalisation regarding the European level might be limited. However, the choice of two contrasted systems with respect to governance patterns brings some diversification which might be meaningful for other European countries as well. It is right to say that contrast between other systems might be even bigger. Yet, first, opinions about the "necessary" extent of contrast within comparisons vary and, second, although one objective consists of the observation of governance mechanisms by the example of structured doctoral education, governance patterns are not the only variable that leads to the choice of these two national systems. Another weakness may consist of the fact that suggested case studies are not easy to categorise in Becher and Trowler's typology. Nevertheless, the suggested four case studies seem to be sufficiently contrasty in order to observe potential differences in structured doctoral programmes due to the disciplines' respective characteristics. Finally, the big number of potential structuring variables may also be considered a weakness. However, the goal consists not of examining systematically each of these potential variables. This would require too many case studies, especially because there may be further variables to those suggested in this research design. By choosing case studies that consider a certain number of them, the potential variables' premature elimination is avoided. At the same time, this does not necessarily exclude the discovery of other (perhaps even more) structuring variables. This exploratory approach can be justified by the small number of studies carried out in this domain and the resulting necessity to illuminate the field of European structured doctoral education further.

Thanks to its relation to many varying issues, the chosen topic includes many *opportunities* and thus a rich potential from the point of view of higher education studies. First, the issue of the universities' missions is concerned. Until recently, doctoral education was almost exclusively an issue at the micro level, between the doctoral student and his or her thesis director. Given its gain in importance on the political agenda and its transversal character related to education and research, it might be expected to occupy permanently a more important and even stable place in universities' missions. Second, the question of its orientation towards the academic and/or wider employment market opens the debate about the university's role in the production of academic and/or non-academic workforce. Therefore, it is, thirdly, also connected to the relation between universities and economy or society. Finally, it is also an opportunity to enlarge studies about relatively small higher education systems with partly distinguished institutions. These issues remain for the moment all potential. The study will show which issue plays a role and to what extent. However, their diversity seems to be promising.

Mainly due to its exploratory character, the *threats* of this research may be as numerous as the mentioned opportunities. They are at least twofold: on the one side related to the topic as such, since its interest may be overestimated, and on the other side, due to the research design. Based on the study's objectives a comparative case study method is chosen. Of course, the selection of cases also implies the danger of choosing exceptional cases that are not very meaningful regarding the totality of structured doctoral programmes of the given national systems. However, with the decision to cover each of the four disciplinary types with a doctoral programme and to consider the different types of HEIs regarding their disciplinary profile and (more or less) their importance in terms of doctoral students' number, this threat should be reduced, at least to a certain extent. Finally, as each qualitative study, which is mainly based on interviews with a large number of actors, its outcome strongly depends on the potential interviewees' availability for interviews.

II.2. Collected Data and their Treatment

This section provides information about effectively collected data and their treatment. Six types of data have been used in this study:

1. Scientific literature.
2. Grey literature (reports, etc.) in particular concerning national developments but also regarding the chosen case studies.
3. Quantitative data provided by national statistics offices or HEIs' services.
4. Legal sources, regulating doctoral education in the corresponding HEIs and scientific fields.
5. Web-sites, especially of the corresponding HEIs and, where existing, of the examined doctoral schools.
6. Semi-structured interviews.

As expected only little information about the chosen case studies was available. Therefore, the most important source has been consisting of the semi-structured interviews. The following paragraphs describe the latter.

Totally, *89 interviews* have been carried out. In some cases, two or even three people participated in the same interview. Hence, the total number of interviewed people achieves exactly *100 participants*. 84 interviews have been carried out "face to face", recorded and entirely transcribed. In 5 cases, interviewees refused to be recorded, only wanted to answer in a written form or were only attainable by email. The average interview duration attains exactly *60 minutes*.

Since an important issue of doctoral education's reform consists of the overall duration, it might be interesting to calculate the number of hours and days invested in the completion of the interviews and their transcription. With an average interview time of 60 minutes, multiplied with 84 interviews, the total duration for all interviews corresponds to 5040 minutes, that is to say, 10.5 non-stop, eight-hour working days. That might look rather modest. However, considering that one hour has been used for transcribing 10 minutes of interview, 63 days or about three months were necessary for the entire transcriptions. One could add about at least one hour per interview for interview preparations, like designing and adapting the questionnaire, (sometimes multiple) demands for interviews by email and phone. Then, one could also add time for identifying interviewees as well as travelling time (and travel preparations) in order to get to the different cities and places…

		Norway	Switzerland
Molecular Biology	*Vice-/Rector*	1	1
	University administrator	1	4
	Vice-/Dean	1	-
	Faculty administrator	1	-
	Doctoral School leader	1	2
	Doctoral School administrator	1	1
	Involved professors	2	3
	Doctoral students	3	4
Material sciences	*Vice-/Rector*	1	1
	University administrator	1	-
	Vice-/Dean	1	2
	Faculty administrator	1	-
	Doctoral School leader	1	1
	Doctoral School administrator	1	2
	Involved professors	-	4
	Doctoral students	3	3
Humanities	*Vice-/Rector*	(1)	1
	University administrator	(1)	2
	Vice-/Dean	1	-
	Faculty administrator	1	-
	Doctoral School leader	2	1
	Doctoral School administrator	-	1
	Involved professors	3	2
	Doctoral students	3	4
Finance	*Vice-/Rector*	1	2
	University administrator	-	3(+2)
	Vice-/Dean	1	-
	Faculty administrator	1	-
	Doctoral School leader	1	3
	Doctoral School administrator	-	1
	Involved professors	2	3
	Doctoral students	4	3
Total per country		40	54
Total			**94**

( ) = interviews which are used in two case studies and therefore have already been counted once.

Table 3: Number of interviews per type of actor and case study

In principle, interviewees have always been chosen on the basis of their function and the corresponding relevance regarding the examined doctoral schools and the related research questions. All in all, 10 (vice-) rectors and (vice-)deans, 20 administrators at the central university, faculty and doctoral school levels, 34 professors out of whom 15 with leading positions within doctoral school as well as 30 doctoral students, out of whom 3 with administrative tasks in the framework of doctoral schools, have been interviewed. In addition, 6 people of national research funding agencies, the Swiss university rectors' conference as well as of a (Swiss) regional association of French-speaking universities have been interviewed. Since examined doctoral schools are organised in varying manners, the circle and number of interviewed actors varies from case to case. A certain number of potential interviewees declined to be interviewed. In most cases, those people could be replaced by other interviewees such that lacking data could nevertheless be collected. More in detail, 94 interviewees are distributed on the eight case studies like illustrated in table 3.

Figure 1 provides an overview on the number of interviewees per HEIs. However, it is important to remind that the choice of interviewees has been based on the case studies and their institutional environment and not the HEIs as such.

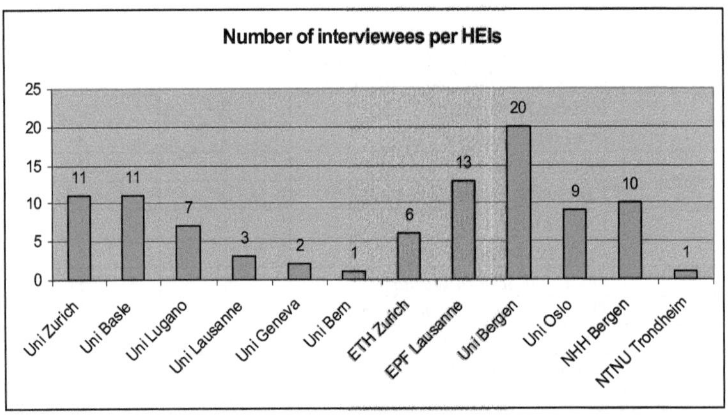

Figure 1: Number of interviewees per HEIs

A last statistic provides information about the languages within which those semi-structured interviewees have been carried out. Out of those

89 interviews, 45 have been completed in English, 22 in German, 17 in French, 3 in Italian and 2 in Norwegian.

The overall number of interviews may be suggestive of a difficult data treatment. However, since interviews are distributed on eight case studies, the effective number of interviews that had to be treated simultaneously was much lower, what has considerably facilitated data treatment. In addition, interview guides already pre-structured data to the extent that questions have been divided in sub-themes like the genesis of the given doctoral school, its activities, involved actors, funding, regulation, etc. Moreover, the transcription process contributed to the memorising of central statements and their origin in terms of interviewee(s), which accelerated the finding of particular statements.

Once the structure of the first case study has been defined in terms of thematic subdivisions, data of the other seven case studies has been selected according to the same subdivisions. Concretely, after their identification, the concerned interview sections have been regrouped thematically (and per case study) and then systematically synthesised. This way, central information could be prepared, without fearing that any important information would have been ignored. No IT programme has been used for the treatment.

III. Theoretical framework

This chapter aims at providing the main theoretical framework for the analysis of the empirical findings. It consists of four parts: based on the state of the art in higher education governance studies and the thesis' scrutinised object, the first section (III.1.) exposes a number of arguments for the theoretical framework's choice. The second section (III.2.) is dedicated to a presentation of the three narratives' central elements, the relationship between them and some considerations regarding their use in the analysis. On the basis of those narratives, three ideal-types of doctoral schools are developed. Built on previous studies, the third section (III.3.) gives a short overview of the narratives' presence within Swiss and Norwegian higher education and research. Finally, the fourth section (III.4.) develops the actors' framework used within this study.

III.1. Arguments for the Theoretical Framework's Choice

As mentioned in chapter II., Tight (2004) points out that, in the majority of 17 analysed specialist higher education journals, any theoretical perspective is only implicit and broader engagement with theory is absent. However, he also notices differences within the higher education research community, which mainly follow disciplinary logics: "Researchers who do make their theoretical perspectives explicit tend to be based more often in social science disciplines or academic development units, rather than education departments or higher education research centres (Tight 2004: 409)." We argue, that these disciplinary differences can also be considered as an indicator for the lack of "own" theories of the higher education studies' community. As a consequence, more generic concepts from disciplines which are part of this community need to be used. The choice for this study was made in favour of a theoretical perspective originating from administrative and political sciences, namely a *public management perspective*. More precisely, three public management "narratives" are used: New Public Management, Network Governance and Neo-Weberian-State. This section exposes a number of arguments for this choice.

The first argument concerns the term "public". European universities – among which also the Swiss and Norwegian institutions – are mainly publicly funded. Ferlie et al. (2009: 2) argue that "the state increasingly seeks to govern and "steer" higher education systems as it does for its other publicly funded services." From this point of view, a public management perspective offers the possibility to observe to what extent the state also steers doctoral education and schools.

Secondly, one has to underline the general importance to suggest more than just one narrative, in order not to build a too narrow analytical framework from the beginning which would neglect certain aspects of governance. The three complementary – but not necessarily mutually exclusive – suggested narratives[12] address in particular and to varying extents the instruments, actors and objectives of governance. Therefore, this theoretical framework is specifically suited to answer the questions of *"how"*, *"who"* and *"what for"* in the management of doctoral education (for further developments: see section III.2.4.). Hence, this complementarity should allow analysing a large number of aspects of the observed reform's steering on the basis of this theoretical background.

The emphasised consideration of actors through the Network Governance narrative deserves being a third argument for a public management perspective because, according to Enders (2004), taking into account an increasing number of actors at different hierarchical levels represents a particular challenge to higher education governance studies. When used within higher education governance studies, a public management perspective – in particular the New Public Management narrative – has often served to describe and analyse the changing role of the state (cf. for instance Braun and Merrien 1999; Braun 1999; Paradeise et al. 2009). However, that does not mean that this perspective

12 According to Paradeise et al. (2009a), "They are called narratives because they are not pure analytical and theoretical frameworks aiming at comprehension (in the Weberian sense): they both mix technical and also political and normative elements."

cannot be useful for examining the role of other actors than the state. In opposite, we argue that, especially through the Network Governance narrative, a public management perspective is open enough to examine the role of any type of involved actor.

A fourth argument consists in the hitherto existing higher education literature using one or several of those narratives in order to analyse higher education governance. In their study comparing several European and non-European higher education systems, Amaral et al. (2003) clearly notice that it would be exaggerated to talk of a multinational conversion towards a "Managerial Revolution". In contrast, a large diversity, "ranging from situations in which most of the key characteristics of managerialism are absent to situations where the managerial paradigm seems to have been largely adopted", could be identified (Amaral et al. 2003: 280). In their study about "New Managerialism" in British higher education, Deem et al. (2007) noticed that – even in a national system which is strongly shaped by New Public Management – other, often mixed forms of management appeared. In particular, they identified elements of "network-based forms of governance" (Deem et al. 2007: 19). In a recent comparative study of seven European higher education governance systems, Paradeise et al. (2009) enlarged the theoretical framework with the Network Governance and Neo-Weberian-state narratives. In this book, Bleiklie (2009) and Baschung et al. (2009) identified, besides New Public Management characteristics, also elements of Neo-Weberian-state and Network Governance in the cases of the Norwegian and Swiss higher education governance systems. Thus, it seems worth broadening the analytical framework and to apply it to further empirical research.

A last important argument is related to the innovative character of the chosen perspective within the existing literature of higher education governance. The latter can be broadly distinguished between those studies which focus on public policies and the role of the state, and those which pay attention to policy networks, their nature and the relationship between the actors who compose the networks. Only few studies combined both perspectives (Ferlie et al. 2009). The adopted public management perspective, with its three narratives, makes a combination of both types of studies possible. Paradeise et al. (2009) demonstrated this. With regard to doctoral schools, it can be examined for instance, what type of network of actors are behind them, which allows comprehending to what extent they are the result of a public policy. This represents a considerable advantage in the analysis of a phenomenon whose origin is not given *a priori*.

III.2. Three Public Management Narratives

This section starts by presenting the three public management narratives and their main characteristics. As mentioned in the introduction of this study, the three chosen public management narratives and their main characteristics are used – similarly to the "Governance Equalizer"[13] of de Boer et al. (2008) – as a *normative benchmark* in order to characterise and compare the university governance of the different case studies. In other words, by noticing the presence or absence of those main characteristics, each case study can be somehow classified and, thereby, compared. Therefore, the principal objective does not consist in providing an exhaustive overview and profound critical discussion of existing scientific literature about those narratives. This would go beyond the purpose of and relevancy for this study. However, this section mainly aims at introducing the central elements of each of the three narratives and to present some invented ideas about how the management story of a doctoral school shaped by the respective narratives might look like. In addition, their mutual relationships as well as some considerations about their effective analytical use are discussed.

13 The idea of the "Governance Equalizer" consists in the consideration that a change in one governance dimension does not necessarily directly influence a change in another governance dimension. For instance, less state regulation does not necessarily imply more market orientation. Hence, rather than suggesting a governance model which puts different dimensions in direct relation, de Boer et al. (2008) suggest an equalizer containing several dimensions which can increase or decrease more or less independently one from the other.

III.2.1. New Public Management

Many different views exist on what New Public Management is, where it comes from, why it diffused in so many countries and so on. Nevertheless, there is one common denominator: "NPM is a departure from the classic public administration paradigm" (Homburg et al. 2007: 3). In Europe, this paradigm was heavily influenced by the ideas of bureaucracy described by Weber, a paradigm which remained relatively untouched until the late 1970s (Homburg et al. 2007).

Since the end of the 1970s, New Public Management reforms diffused over many western countries all over the world (Kickert 1997). The origin of the term New Public Management comes from New Zealand and describes the reforms initiated there in the 1980s (Schedler and Proeller 2002). Changes took place in rhetoric and actual practice of public administration. However, that does not mean that reforms were similar in various countries, though they used the same label. Detailed analysis shows that underlying ideas and their implementation fluctuate enormously (Homburg et al. 2007). Rather than "buying" the whole New Public Management package, many continental European countries have made selective and limited use of its elements or instruments (Pollitt 2007). This selection or emphasis of certain elements has been made according to the respective countries' challenges (Schedler and Proeller 2002).

Actual reforms have not only varied but the opinions held by public management scholars about the central elements of New Public Management have also differed. The following classical definition is Christopher Hood's (1991: 4-5), who talks about *doctrines of* New Public Management, when he summarises the narrative's main elements and their meanings:

1. *"Hands-on professional management"* in the public sector: Active, visible, discretionary control of organizations from named persons at the top, "free to manage".
2. *Explicit standards and measures of performance*: Definition of goals, targets, indicators of success, preferably expressed in quantitative terms, especially for professional services.

3. Greater Emphasis on *output controls*: Resource allocation and rewards linked to measured performance; breakup of centralized bureaucracy-wide personnel management.
4. Shift to *disaggregation* of units in the public sector: Break-up of formerly "monolithic" units, unbundling of U-form management systems into corporatized units around products, operating on decentralized "one-line" budgets and dealing with one another on an "arms-length" basis.
5. Shift to greater *competition* in public sector: Move to term contracts and public tendering procedures.
6. *Stress on private-sectors styles of management practice*: Move away from military-style "Public service ethic", greater flexibility in hiring and rewards; greater use of PR techniques.
7. Stress on greater *discipline* and *parsimony* in resource use: Cutting direct costs, raising labour discipline, resisting union demands, limiting "compliance costs" to business.

More explicitly, concerning the idea of "control of organisations from named persons at the top" (cf. point 1.), Christensen and Lægreid underline that "NPM is thus a doubled-edged sword which prescribes both more autonomy and more central control at the same time (Christensen and Lægreid 2007: 8)." In other words decentralisation means "let the managers manage" whereas centralization stands for "make the managers manage" (Christensen and Lægreid 2007: 8). Thus, there is a desire for a stronger hierarchy where management is entrepreneurial rather than collegial. The centre defines the strategic framework and governance instruments. Instead of tacit or self regulation, strong performance measurement, monitoring and management systems with increased audit systems are established (cf. points 2 and 3). The periphery has operational freedom (cf. point 4.) but only within the given strategic framework. The goals of public management consist in efficiency, value for money and performance (cf. points 7.) rather than democracy or legitimacy (cf. point 6.) (Ferlie et al. 2009). Finally, greater competition in the public sector (cf. point 5.) shall be achieved through the principle of quasi-markets. The latter are an alternative to the privatisation of complete functions, as it took place for instance in certain British public sectors. Concretely, quasi-markets mean that "public funding is no longer allocated solely through planning or through formula funding, but instead through such devices as competitive bidding, or an earmarked budget which can be given to users, or to agents acting on their behalf. They then allocate the budget between competing providers (Ferlie 1996:57)."

On the basis of the New Public Management elements developed above, we suggest an ideal-type of a management story of a doctoral school shaped by the New Public Management:

HEI governing bodies are encouraged by the state to make doctoral education more efficient – that means more value for invested resources – within their respective HEI. In-/effectiveness is sanctioned by de-/increase of funding awarded to the HEI. Therefore, each HEI governing body defines a certain number of goals related to doctoral education and corresponding performance measurement instruments. Overall goals may be an efficiency improvement in the "production" of doctors and an increase in quality of their research. Accordingly, defined instruments measure indicators like the ratio between numbers of doctoral students and those finishing their degree or the number of publications which result of doctoral research and figure in highly cited journals. Traditional units of the public activity "doctoral education", like the "doctoral student-supervisor unit", are disaggregated and reorganised in new organisational units focusing on the product "doctorate". A person, free to manage, is named at the top of this new organisational unit. He or she is responsible of the operational implementation of the defined goals. In order to bring in more competition, doctoral positions are advertised on a broad public basis. The employment of doctoral students is handled in a flexible way.

Before dealing with the second chosen public management narrative, some criticism about the implementation of New Public Management reforms, formulated by public management scholars, is developed. Indeed, those managerial principles and instruments are not neutral. They constitute an ideology about how government should work (Minogue 1998) and even may transform the objectives and values of state action (Giauque 2006). Regarding the manner government should work, that is to say – if formulated in a New Public Management logic – in a rational, efficient and effective way, several authors contest the applicability of this paradigm. Dunn and Miller (2007) argue that rationality based incentives do not necessarily have the wished effect because actors react in varying manners to them. Indeed, in his sociological study of New Public Management's implementation in two different administrative units of a Swiss canton, Bühlmann (2005) noticed opposition from some of the concerned administrators towards such managerial reforms. As a consequence, the reform's implementation was only partial and its presumed rational character could not unfold. Also Lienhard et al. (2005) underline that not all performances and even less their impact can be measured. Gregory (2007) argues that, in addition, the striving for precision in performance measurement accentuates bureaucratic mechanisms instead of diminishing them. Thus, this contradicts the rationality argument. Furthermore, Kickert (1997) identifies a conflict between the efficiency paradigm and the nature of national political systems. He cautions against transposing American public management methods onto other parts of the world, especially onto continental Western Europe. He argues that "States, societies, politics, governments and administrations differ too much between the Unites States and Europe and within Europe itself, to be able to simply imitate and transpose the American theories and methods of public management onto the various European administrations" (Kickert 1997: 37). He especially sees potential conflicts between efficiency and democracy. Respecting that efficiency and effectiveness are certainly of great importance in the public sector, Kickert nevertheless argues that other norms and values such as liberty, legality, legitimacy, equity and social justice play a role as well. It is also at that level that strong criticism came up for instance in Switzerland, whose administration is not only strongly based on law, but whose laws, at least in some cases, have to be accepted, and hence legitimised, by popular votes. In addition, there is a strong tradition to integrate interest groups in the preparation process of new laws (Knoepfel 1995; 1996). Also from an actors' perspective, Lienhard et al. (2005) emphasise that the parliament cannot be assimilated to a supervisory board (*Führungsgremium*) because its steering activities are often specific instead of long-term strategic.

As mentioned, besides the manner government works, New Public Management may also have an impact on the actual content of state action. Often, financial considerations have led state governments to examine their fields of action. For instance, in the United Kingdom, this examination has provoked the privatisation of a series of previous public services. Thus, instead of assuming certain tasks by own public agencies, the state outsources them to private ones (Kickert 1997). In the case of Switzerland, Giauque and Emery (2008) observed the displacement of certain public services from the Swiss Confederation to the lower levels of cantons and municipalities. However, these displacements only took place in terms of financial burden. Simultaneously, the Confederation strives to regulate an increasing number of political fields. Since cantons are not able or willing to assume this increased financial burden, the Confederation's contradictory procedure provokes the simple downsizing of public services. This could be noticed for instance concerning the amount of available students' grants (Giauque and Emery 2008).[14]

III.2.2. Network Governance

Building partly on a criticism of New Public Management, and partly on the basis of empirical observations in western European democracies for instance, several scholars developed the elements forming the framework of another public management narrative, the Network Governance narrative. The central argument put forward by those scholars consists in saying that a broader analytical framework is needed to understand public management. Thus, Kickert (1997) argues that public management cannot be isolated from its societal and political context, that it corresponds to governance in complex networks composed of a wide range of actors going beyond the public administration and that it works according to other forms of governance like negotiation – rather than for instance hierarchical top-down control – without any dominant actor. Similar or even identical ideas to the Network Governance narrative – which partly built the basis for the narrative's development – can be found in concepts and notions like the "hollowing out" of the traditional national-state (Rhodes 1997), "Multi-level Governance" (Bache and Flinders 2005; Hooghe and Marks 2003) or "whole-of-government" approach (Christensen and Lægreid 2007). According to Ferlie et al. (2009: 16), the following elements form the Network Governance narrative:

14 For further literature and criticism concerning New Public Management, we refer for instance to the following authors: Lane (2000), Jones et al. (1997), McLaughlin et al. (2002), Hablützel et al. (1995), Christensen and Lægreid (2001).

1. A greater range of actors and interactions emerge.
2. The central state plays more of an influencing and less of directing role. It works as relationship facilitator.
3. There is a shift from vertical to lateral forms of management.
4. There is devolution of power downwards from the centre of the nation-state to lower tiers and also upwards to higher tiers, including European ones.
5. Coordinating power is shared among social actors, possibly operating at multiple levels of analysis.
6. Knowledge and "best practices" spreads across the network.
7. The network develops self-organising and self-steering capacity.
8. Accountability relationships are a way of "giving account" to local publics and not an ex-post state-driven system of checking.

Similarly to the ideal-type developed concerning the New Public Management narrative, an ideal-type-like management story about a doctoral school shaped by the Network Governance narrative is developed in the following paragraph:

A broad range of actors from inside and outside of HEIs come together in order to tackle and reform certain issues of doctoral education. This network of higher education and other social actors functions through negotiation, rather than according to clearly established hierarchical steering mechanisms. It develops self-organising and self-steering capacity, independently from traditional steering structures within higher education and HEIs. Within those networks, actors at European tiers and lower ones than the nation-state take an important place in the decision making about elements of reform and in the diffusion of "best practices" concerning doctoral education, like doctoral training or supervision. Without directing the reform, the state tries to influence it and facilitates the relationships between the various involved actors.

III.2.3. Neo-Weberian-State

Both critical study of New Public Management elements and the observation of their concrete implementation especially within continental European countries contributed to further debate on the appropriate conceptual definition of public management reform. On the one hand, Gregory (2007) argues that New Public Management is rather a means of refining the bureaucratic form of governmental organisation than an attempt to abolish it. He considers New Public Management as "the latest and most significant manifestation of what Weber called the process of 'rationalisation', the quest for greater calculability and precision in the management of human affairs" (Gregory 2007: 222). Hence, from his point of view, the dominant organisational form remains Weberian. On the other side, Pollitt (2007) notices that with respect to New Public Management, the dominant Anglophone literature has tended to overlook the possibility of other, alternative models of public management being implemented. He especially concentrates on continental Europe to draw attention to an alternative model called Neo-Weberian-state. He argues that in the case of those countries, "the story has been one of a *modernisation* of the Weberian tradition, not its outright rejection in favour of the market model. The process has been one of addition, not demolition" (Pollitt 2007: 21). Compared to the New Public Management and Network Governance narratives, it is particularly the state's role which is considered differently: changes in public management are not to be interpreted as weakening of the state but as a sign of *adaptability* of the state to a changing environment (Paradeise et al. 2009). Based on Paradeise et al. (2009a), the Neo-Weberian-state narrative can be summarised in the following way: as a reaction to new activities within a field of the public sector (e.g. higher education), the state adapts by formalising new aspects of those activities through new policy instruments. Thereby, the state makes those aspects accessible to outside administrative and political control. The objectives consist in the stabilisation of the field's function, a more efficient control of its costs and a tighter steering of it.

Again, based on the Neo-Weberian-state narrative, a third ideal-type-like management story is developed here:

Changes related to doctoral education happen: for instance, doctoral education is increasingly internationalised (e.g. an increasing number of doctoral students are recruited from abroad), new training offers for doctoral students are established and so on. Simultaneously, doctoral education's importance for the state goes beyond the supply of academic labour force to the provision of labour force for the knowledge based economy which plays a fundamental role regarding economic competitiveness. As a consequence, the state adapts to those developments by introducing new policy instruments aiming at a tighter administrative and political control of doctoral education. Thereby, activities related to doctoral education like recruitment of doctoral students, their training and supervision as well as the production of doctoral research are formalised. As a consequence, doctoral education becomes more cost effective and assures its enlarged function.

III.2.4. The Relationship between the Narratives and Considerations of their Use

Before using those three narratives in order to characterise and compare the individual case studies, the relationship between them as well as their status has to be clarified. As mentioned in the previous sections, those narratives have not been developed simultaneously but one after the other, and, partly, as a reaction to each other. In addition, several authors have contributed to their development. Therefore, it is not astonishing that they do not focus to the same extent on the same dimensions of public management (and, of course, not with the same ideas). On the basis of the narratives' main characteristics developed above, this section characterises and discusses the dimensions of public management the narratives focus on. Thereby, it underlines the narratives' complementary but also competing character. In addition, it critically discusses their concrete use in the analysis of empirical data.

Considering the narratives' elements, developed above, four main dimensions can be distinguished: instruments of governance (I), actors of governance (A), objectives of governance (O) and types of decision-taking (D). Elements attributed to the dimensions "instruments" and "decision-taking" tell something about the "how" of governance, those attributed to the dimension "actors" about the "who" and those with the label "objective" indicate the "what for". On the basis of the four chosen dimensions, a classification of the narratives' individual elements is suggested on table 4.

Although all three narratives possess elements which have been attributed to (as good as) all four dimensions, each narrative emphasises one dimension in particular. The NPM narrative contains a large number of elements focusing on instruments of governance, the Network

Governance narrative underlines the actors' dimension (and decision-taking), whereas the New-Weberian-State narrative puts forward the objectives of governance. Hence, from this point of view, the narratives have somehow a complementary character. Also from an ideological point of view, some elements of varying narratives seem to be compatible and could be used in a complementary manner. For instance, the New-Weberian-State objective of a "more efficient control of a public field's costs" would probably fit with the New Public Management's doctrine. In contrast, regarding other elements, the narratives seem to be mutually exclusive or, in other words, competing. For instance, the NPM element of "hands-on professional management" and "discretionary control trough persons at the top" is clearly competing with the Network Governance element consisting of a "shift from vertical to lateral forms of management".

Besides their respective emphasis on the one or the other governance dimension, the narratives and their composing elements also vary with respect to their degree of preciseness in the description of a given situation. This directly influence on its use in the analysis of empirical data.

Some of the enumerated elements like the Network Governance element of "the central state as relationship facilitator" are clearly attributed to two dimensions (here to the dimensions "actor" and "decision-taking"). Thanks to this relatively clear description, those kinds of elements can quite easily be identified within empirical data. However other elements are only one-dimensional – like the NPM "instrument" of greater emphasis on output control – or formulated in quite a vague manner – e.g. the Network Governance element of "coordinating power is shared among social actors at multiple levels". Perhaps, this partly unclear definition is the result of an (over-) simplification of the narratives' content into a presentation consisting of bullet points. However, two possible consequences may result of these partly unclear definitions: on the one hand, there is a certain risk of "over-interpretation". In other words, the narratives' elements might be considered as existing in empirical data although they do not. On the other hand, new insights in the functioning of public management may emerge. For instance, the application of NPM instruments at unexpected levels of governance or decision-taking through new kinds of actors' networks might be found.

In conclusion, the use of non-uniform and not completely mutually exclusive qualitative frameworks for the analysis and comparison of case studies certainly poses some challenges. Yet, notably due to their consideration of a large range of public management stories and dimensions, they offer a rich analytical framework.

Dimension	Narrative	Element
D + A	NPM	Hands-on professional management: discretionary control through persons at the top
I	NPM	Explicit standards and measures of performance
I	NPM	Greater emphasis on output control
A	NPM	Shift to dissagregation of units in the public sector
I	NPM	Shift to greater competition in public sector: term contracts
I	NPM	Stress on private-sectors styles of management: greater flexibility in hiring and rewards
A	NG	A greater range of actors and interactions emerge
A + D	NG	The central state plays the role of a relationship facilitator
D	NG	Shift from vertical to lateral forms of management
A	NG	Devolution of power from the nation-state to lower and higher tiers
A	NG	Coordinating power is shared among social actors at multiple levels
I	NG	Knowledge and "best practices" spread across the network
A + D	NG	The network develops self-organising and self-steering capacity
I +O	NG	Accountability relationships are a way of "giving account" and not a ex-post state-driven system of checking

A + D	NWS	The state reacts to new activities within a field of the public sector
A + I	NWS	The state formalises new aspects of those activities through new policy instruments
A + O	NWS	The state makes those aspects accessible to outside administrative and political control
O	NWS	The objective consist in the stabilisation and tighter steering of the field's function
O	NWS	A more efficient control of its costs are aimed at

Table 4: Classification of the narratives' elements in terms of governance dimensions

III.3. Norwegian and Swiss Higher Education and the Narratives

New Public Management ideas have clearly showed up in the reform of Norwegian higher education during the 1990s (Askling and Stensaker 2002). In line with the ideas of the university as a "corporate enterprise" (Bleiklie 1998), a double measure of decentralisation and centralisation process has been, at least from a legal point of view, implemented. It is given expression in the new Act on Universities and Colleges, which came into effect in 1996. One central intention of this Act consisted in the strengthening of academic and administrative leadership (Dimmen and Kyvik 1998). If certain doubt a real reinforcement of the academic leadership (idem), there seems to be a common view about the strengthened position of administration within HEIs. Administrative staff has been professionalised (Gornitzka and Larsen 2004) and has got new competences among others in strategic planning and budgeting (Bleiklie 1998). Bleiklie considers these developments not only as "an efficiency drive" but also as a "demystification or *entzauberung* of academic affairs" (Bleiklie 1998: 308). "Academic work can be administered as any work in any service-providing agency (idem)." Besides those changes related to law and internal administrative structures, further indicators for New Public Management policies can be detected concerning research funding and doctoral education. However, no traces would suggest changes from traditional hierarchical to a network structure. Hence, at least in the context of doctoral education and research funding, state regulation remains strong, what conduces to an interpretation of Norwegian higher education management as corresponding to the Neo-Weberian-state narrative rather than to the Network Governance narrative (Bleiklie 2009).

Like in Norway, New Public Management ideas undoubtedly appear in Swiss higher education during the 1990s. All cantonal university laws as well as the principal federal university law – the Federal Act on the funding of cantonal universities and co-operation in higher education[15] – have been revised according to New Public Management ideas during this period (Perellon 2006). The position of the university management has been strengthened and the number of professional staff has been increased (Weber 1999). Moreover, New Public Management is given expression by the instrument of contractualisation, which has been introduced in the beginning of the 2000s. Higher education activities, like teaching, research publications, etc. are increasingly perceived as services or products which have a cost. Those activities are defined in a service level agreement (*Leistungsvertrag*). The implementation of this agreement or contract contributes to progressively and partially orient the funding of HEIs on the basis of their quantified results (outputs), measured through performance indicators. However, the existing contracts between public authorities and the research funding agency – the Swiss National Science Foundation – and/or HEIs strongly vary concerning their degree of constraint or flexibility (Leresche and Benninghoff 2006; OECD 2003). Higher education funding instruments, especially those of the Confederation, do not only integrate New Public Management principles. In the name of efficiency in terms of public money's use, new instruments including conditions of cooperation between HEIs have been put into place (Perellon and Leresche 1998). From this point of view, HEI governing bodies cannot act in a vacuum but have to negotiate with other HEIs. Furthermore, their autonomy varies also within their own HEI according to the funding instrument:

15 Loi sur l'aide aux universités et la coopération dans le domaine des hautes écoles (LAU).

this is illustrated for instance regarding the Confederation's three special programmes aiming at the promotion of the young academic staff, where the Confederation attributes varying degrees of autonomy to HEI governing bodies, academic professions and individual academics (Baschung et al. forthcoming). Hence, although reinforced by legal changes, HEI governing bodies are operating within an environment shaped both by New Public Management and Network Governance principles (Baschung et al. 2009).

In summary, considering the existing public management literature on higher education within Norway and Switzerland, we notice that both countries depict clear elements of New Public Management. However, those elements seem to be combined with Neo-Weberian-state elements in Norway, whereas they are supplemented rather with Network Governance elements in Switzerland.

III.4. Redefining the Actors' Framework

As mentioned in the introduction, this study uses – compared to a large number of previous studies focusing on university governance – a slightly redefined actors' framework. This section develops this actors' framework and the underlying rationales. The development of such an actors' frameworks aims at providing a clear basis for the analysis of empirical data, complementing thereby the analytical basis consisting of the three public management narratives.

As most of the studies cited in the previous section, much research on university governance concentrates on actors at the macro-level, that is to say the state and HEIs (as a whole). This "macro-view" is sometimes complemented by categories of actors from within the HEIs like groups of academics, often based on scientific disciplines (e.g. departments or Faculties) (see e.g. Musselin 2001).[16]

Keen to bring in differentiation in analytical frameworks for university governance, Clark (1983) distinguishes six *authority levels*: the lowest academic unit (department or chair); the aggregate of those

16 Musselin uses the French term "profession universitaire".

units (colleges or faculties); the individual enterprise; the multicampus system; the state, provincial, or municipal government; and the national government. He further distinguishes between academic, bureaucratic and political *forms of authority* and stresses that that they spread into and across different levels of authority. It is important to underline that, with his famous "triangle of co-ordination",[17] he adds another category of actors, namely the one of the market (Clark 1983). On the basis of Clark's distinctions, the "Actors' Framework A" is deduced (see below).

Although already quite differentiated, it is argued that – at least in this study – a slightly redefined actors' framework could be more appropriate to shed light on university governance. The resulting "Actors' Framework B" contains two essential changes: first, it integrates intermediary bodies like public research funding agencies and rectors'/presidents' conferences. Second, the internal actors of HEIs are partly relabelled and slightly enlarged. For instance, instead of speaking of "the academic profession", deans and professors are first of all looked at individually, without assuming *a priori* that they simultaneously form a homogeneous body. In addition, doctoral students and other doctoral students' supervisors than chair-holders are taken into consideration.

---

17 For Clark (1983), advanced industrial countries have developed different forms of "co-ordination" of higher education: co-ordination is carried out between the market, the state and the academic oligarchy.

"Actors' framework A":

State
- National government
- National bureaucracy
- Regional governments
- Regional bureaucracies

Higher Education Institutions
- Presidents/Rectors, institutional bureaucracy
- College (aggregated chair-holders)
- Professors (chair-holders)

Market
- Companies
- Students

Actors' framework B

State
- National government
- National bureaucracy
- Regional governments
- Regional bureaucracies

Intermediary Bodies
- Public research funding agencie(s)
- Rectors'/President's Conference(s)

Higher Education Institutions
- Presidents/Rectors, institutional bureaucracy
- Deans, Faculty bureaucracy

Market
- Companies
- Students
- Individual professors and other formal supervisors
- Doctoral students

Part 2:
Empirical Results

IV. Doctoral Education in Switzerland and Norway

This chapter aims at presenting knowledge about the specific Swiss and Norwegian contexts with respect to doctoral education. Thereby, the following individual case studies can more easily be situated, understood and interpreted. The chapter is divided into four main sections.

In the first section, reforms and issues of reforms in relation with doctoral education of the approximately last twenty years – varying according to the country – are dealt with. Within these elements, the upcoming of the idea of doctoral and research schools is particularly stressed. In the second section, the varying legal situations of doctoral education in the examined countries are shortly presented and compared. The third section quantifies doctoral education of both countries. Besides illustrating the role of doctoral education within both national higher education systems, this section also allows introducing some wider implications dealt with in the fourth section. The latter points to some broad issues of Swiss and Norwegian higher education with which doctoral education and the related reforms are in tight interplay.

IV.1. Reforms and Issues of Reform

The following section provides an overview of reforms and reform issues with respect to doctoral education, which have come up over the last decades. Particular emphasis is put on the role of the national governments. Besides depicting the upcoming of doctoral education as an issue on the national reform agendas of Switzerland and Norway, this focus gives also the opportunity to illustrate the (partly changing) role of the national governments in higher education.

IV.1.1. Fostering the New Generation of Academics

As we will see, compared to Norway, the Swiss government began to intervene quite late in organised doctoral education. Until the second half of the 1990s, it was as a non-issue on the national policy agenda. Also among the HEIs, only some isolated institutional initiatives, explicitly targeting doctoral students, existed. For instance, within the HEI network CUSO (Conférence universitaire de Suisse occidentale) universities of the French-speaking part of Switzerland[18] invested some money in a common pot, in order to offer common courses to doctoral students. These courses were thought as a support without any formal obligation for doctoral students. Until a few years ago, only very few HEIs or single Faculties and institutes obliged their doctoral students to follow courses as part of the doctorate's requirements. As we will see later, there is still no general regulation about coursework in doctoral education as opposite to Norway.

The non-existence, both, of an explicit public policy regarding doctoral education and of common national regulations, can partly be explained by the federal structure of Switzerland and its impact on the Swiss higher education system. Indeed, the competence of the Confederation had been traditionally limited to the two existing federal HEIs, *i.e.* the Federal Institutes of Technology of Zurich (*Eidgenössiche Technische Hochschule Zürich* – ETHZ) and Lausanne (*Ecole Polytechnique Fédérale de Lausanne* – EPFL), all other HEIs being regulated by their respective cantons. It was only in the late 1960s that the Confederation gained a clear competence of (co-)funding of the cantonal universities, through the Federal Act on Financial Assistance to Universities (LAU).[19] The revision of this act in 1999 transformed the Confederation further from a mere payer to a proactive actor (Perellon 2001). Among others, the revised act allows the Confederation to fund special programmes of limited duration that target cantonal universities. A decisive element of the special programmes consists in the fact that

18 Universities of Neuchâtel, Geneva, Lausanne and Fribourg as well as the Federal Institute of Technology Lausanne.

19 For an analysis of the Confederation's role as a promoter of research and research training (among others within cantonal universities) before the LAU's introduction, we refer to Joye-Cagnard (2007).

the Confederation does not only pay but that it also defines the related rules.

It was still in the framework of the "old" LAU – hence before 1999 – that the Confederation funded a project that was not directly being thought as a promotional instrument for doctoral education but more generally as a fostering measure for the "new academic generation". Worried about the predictable retirement of many university professors, federal parliamentarians decided to fund this programme called "promotion of the next academic generation" (*Encouragement de la relève académique*)[20] which finally[21] lasted from 1992 to 2004. During this period, it funded supplementary working places of teaching and research assistants, young doctors doing teaching and research[22] and assistant professors in all cantonal universities (proportionally to each university's number of graduates). Official goals resided in the promotion of the next academic generation, the improvement of the supervision of undergraduate students, the researchers' mobility as well as in the increase of women's proportion in academic working positions (Felli et al. 2006). However, this programme did not include any special measure for doctoral education like particular training activities.[23] During this programme, more precisely in 1997, a research team, commonly mandated by the Swiss Science Council (CSS),[24] the Swiss National Science Foundation (SNF)[25] and the Swiss University Council (CUS),[26] published a detailed report about the so-called "intermediate body", comprising doctoral students and young doctors employed at universities (Lévy et al. 1997). According to the study's authors, doctoral students were suffering, on the one hand, from insufficient supervision

---

20 In German: *« Akademische Nachwuchsförderung ».*

21 Its duration has been lengthened twice, the second prolongation concerning the period 2000-2004.

22 In French called *« Maître-assistant »*, in German *« Oberassistent »*.

23 Moreover, doctoral students were not anymore sustained in the framework of this programme during the programme's last four years (out of twelve).

24 *Conseil Suisse de la Science.* The CSS was the counselling body of the Federal Government in the domains of science.

25 *Fonds national suisse de la recherche scientifique.* The SNF is Switzerland's leading scientific research funding agency.

26 *Conférence universitaire suisse.* The Swiss University Conference is the joint organisation of the cantons (represented through their respective ministers) and the Confederation for university policies.

by their official supervisor and, on the other hand, from work overload (especially the doctoral students working as teaching assistants in disciplines with many undergraduate students), which led to too little time being left for their thesis doctoral research (Lévy et al. 1997). Later reports and case studies focusing on individual universities confirmed these general problems concerning the working conditions of doctoral students. The situation has been especially alarming in social and human sciences (see Young et al. (2009); Maurer and Zeltner (1997); Fluder and Hildbrand (1997)). Different experts, beneath the Swiss Science Council, recommended, among others, the establishment of doctoral schools. As we will see, the Confederation followed this recommendation only hesitatingly and, from the end of the 1990s, has been developing several actions.

IV.1.2. The Norwegian Doctorate: From an Honorary Title to an Asset for Society

In Norway, the doctorate was traditionally no formal requirement to do research. Rather it was carried out when an opportunity for tenured professor- or readership emerged (Bleiklie and Høstaker 1994). Hence, "the needs of the university as an institution rather than the needs of scientific development determined when the doctoral degrees were completed" (Bleiklie, Høstaker and Vabø 2000: 245). During the expansion period in the 1960s and 1970s, the significance of the doctorate was becoming even smaller: universities reacted to the increased number of students by hiring lecturers – first provisionally, then on a tenured basis – without doctorates. Thus, the *ius docendi* was not anymore linked to the doctorate.

However, this temporarily low significance of the doctorate does not mean that there were no attempts to change the doctorate as such during this period. After discussions during the 1950s about the disconnection of the university degree system from the needs of the higher secondary schools[27] in order to satisfy other, particularly scientific, needs, the

27 During this period, students were often educated in order to teach at secondary schools.

Rosenquist Commission[28], proposed the introduction of the Anglo-American PhD model in 1963. This proposition is no surprise to the extent that, generally, the Norwegian research community was being internationally oriented towards the USA during this period. This can be illustrated by the foreign doctorates awarded to Norwegians: between 1960 and 1966, 53% of all foreign doctorates were American, 35% European (Kyvik and Tvede 1998).

Yet, the enthusiasm for the American PhD was not shared by all disciplines. Representatives of humanities and social sciences rejected the proposal. Nevertheless, the breakthrough of a structured doctorate succeeded in 1974. The Norwegian Institute of Technology managed to introduce the Dr.ing. degree (in engineering) and opened hereby the formalisation of this new doctorate also for other disciplines: in 1978, the natural sciences followed this trend by introducing a new doctorate based on organised educational programmes. Later, humanities and social sciences followed the movement but maintained the possibility to do a "free" degree, *i.e.* according to the old, "unstructured" doctorate (Bleiklie and Høstaker 1994). All in all, eleven different doctoral degrees, having varying titles according to the respective discipline, developed according to the new doctorate (Heen 2002). In the framework of the "quality reform"[29], a standardised PhD degree replaced these eleven titles in 2003. However, the *dr.philos.* degree continued to exist as an alternative to organised training (Broch and Hillseth 2004). During the 1980s and especially from 1985 on, the total number of doctorates increased thanks to the new doctorates. However, this success was limited to doctorates in engineering and natural sciences. Most doctorates in social sciences and humanities were still being carried out according to the traditional *dr. philos.* mode (Bleiklie and Høstaker 1994).

After the beginning of this bottom-up movement – initiated by engineers and natural scientists and only hesitatingly followed by social sciences and humanities – the government began to intervene

28 A commission from the School of Sciences at the Universities of Oslo and Bergen.

29 The principal goals of the « Quality Reform » consisted in the quality improvement of teaching and research, higher intensity in teaching and stronger internationalisation. Source: http://www.regjeringen.no/en/dep/kd/About-the-Ministry/Minister-of-Education-and-Research/taler_artikler/2006/Kvalitetsreformen-mellom-malsetning-og-virkelighet.html?id=445053. Accessed on 3rd August 2009.

increasingly. Seeking to enhance the flow of students through the system, it made an important measurement factor of the master-level candidates' and doctors' production. Moreover, in 1990, the doctorate was declared a *sine qua non* condition for a tenured position which put the doctorate at the very centre of the reproduction process at the university (Bleiklie et al. 2000).

As a consequence of these governmental interventions, university leaderships were put under pressure and reforms had to be implemented. One main reform objective resided in the improvement of the national coordination of doctoral education. Three main measures have been taken since 1990: firstly, the University Council[30] has been made responsible for the national coordination of doctorate programmes; secondly, boards of postgraduate education (*forskerutdanningsutvalg*) have been established at each university and; thirdly, national disciplinary councils (*nasjonale fagråd)* have become responsible for the coordination of the so-called national postgraduate courses. Formal regulations, largely based on a "hard research mode" and a "logic of schooling" (Bleiklie and Høstaker 1994: 316), were related to these measures (Bleiklie et al. 2000). For instance, the joint national regulation for the new doctorate degree, introduced in 1993, have scheduled a length of three years (or four years with 25% added duties).

These new government policies – putting universities and especially social sciences and humanities under pressure – are a sign for change for the doctorate's role: "The production of doctors is no longer an internal affair of academia, because availability of competent personnel in all disciplines is regarded as an asset for society at large" (Bleiklie et al. 2000: 258-9).

30 « The Council of Norwegian Universities is a body of cooperation between Universities and Scientific Colleges that was based on the former Rectors' conference and is charged with the co-ordination and promotion of national level initiatives by the institutions (Bleiklie et al. 2000: 313)." Since its merger with the Norwegian Council of University Colleges in 2000, this body is called « Norwegian Association of Higher Education Institutions (UHR) » (*Universitets- og høgskolerådet*).

IV.1.3. The Confederation's Reinforced Interventions

If the Confederation's first intervention, targeting the promotion of the new academic generation was rather a programme for doctors and future professors than for doctoral students[31], further federal programmes were more tailor-made for the latter. Furthermore, more and more regulations are related to those programmes. The politically oriented programme "Switzerland: Towards the Future", launched by the Swiss National Science Foundation (SNF), sought to promote topic-oriented research and networks for research as well as to strengthen structurally social sciences. This latter goal should have been achieved by several measures, among others, through the establishment of eight doctoral schools in social sciences, run during three years. The first of these doctoral schools started in 1998, the last in 2000. According to the evaluator of this programme (Schreitener 2002), goals have not really been achieved, among other reasons, because of the training programmes' low quality and lacking incentives for students (e.g. formal obligation and related financial support) and lecturers (e.g. diminishment of teaching charge).

Almost during the same period, that is to say around 2000, a new type of politically oriented programmes – the so-called "National Centres of Competence in Research (NCCR) [32]" – was started and has been implemented. Besides the creation of national research networks, one important goal of these programmes resides in the "promotion of talented young researchers at doctoral and post-doctoral levels and the advancement of women in research careers (SNF 1999: 5)". According to a manager of the National Science Foundation[33], special attention should be paid to professional perspectives inside and especially also outside the academic job market. Generally, NCCR regulations leave a lot of room for structural experiments as regards concrete doctoral

31 As mentioned, promotion was limited to the positions' funding.

32 The 20 currently existing National Centres of Competence in Research (NCCR) are large research projects organised in networks of several universities and non-academic partners. Selected by the National Science Foundation (SNF) and the Swiss Federal Council, they are one type of currently existing "targeted research projects". Their funding is assumed by the SNF and participating HEI. The NCCRs' maximum life duration is twelve years.

33 Interview in June 2007.

training's organisation. "Graduate schools"[34] are mentioned as possible special measures for training (SNF 1999). Each NCCR being composed of different HEIs' researchers and doctoral students, the latter are in principle obliged to follow courses either in mono-institutional based training programmes of their "home university" or in common inter-institutional training programmes. However, there are no written minimal requirements in terms of training volume.

Among the ten NCCRs, chosen in the first selection process in December 2000, no proposal coming from social sciences and humanities was accepted, except the one in Finance,[35] what created some polemic debates. According to the SNF responsible for the NCCRs' training aspect, the emerging polemic as well as the – since the end of the 1990s – regularly returning discussions and reports around doctoral schools, might have contributed to the Confederation's next action in the field of doctoral education. The SNF has again been mandated to implement a programme, this time exclusively targeting doctoral education and research. This programme called Pro*Doc was, in a first stage, principally targeting social sciences and humanities. It has been implemented since the end of 2006. Seven projects, comprising a common training module organised around a precise subject and several so called research modules (each corresponding to a research topic), were selected in the first selection round. Maximally 20 doctoral students, of whom ten receive a salary through the project, are part of one project. Possible course structures are again quite flexible. However, at least two HEIs as well as 40% women must be included in projects.

The SNF stays not the only actor on the national level being actively involved in the reform of doctoral education. From 2006 on, the Rectors' Conference of Swiss Universities (*Conférence des Recteurs des Universités Suisses* – CRUS) makes it also one of its issues. CRUS' involvement is made possible through its enlarged role, among others, thanks to a new competence of perennial strategic planning for the Swiss higher education system from 2001 on. Moreover, CRUS is designated as being responsible for the implementation of the Bologna reform in Switzerland. In the framework of the planning period 2008-2011, CRUS makes doctoral education and its standardisation one of its four priorities

34 Translated from the German « Graduiertenkolleg ».

35 NCCR Finrisk.

(CRUS 2006). According to its vice-secretary general,[36] this can be seen as the consequence of two elements: first, after a four-year period principally dedicated to teaching, it is the universities' second mission's turn, namely the research mission. Second, due to the doctoral education's integration in Bologna, it must also be modernised. Like NCCR doctoral education, it should include skills qualifying people for working positions inside and outside the academic job market. With its priority setting, CRUS asked the Confederation for a particular funding in the framework of a special programme in order to gradually implement doctoral programmes for *all* doctoral students. In its message for education, research and innovation 2008-2011, the Federal Council (Schweizer Bundesrat 2007) allocates indeed a credit for new doctoral programmes. However, three elements diverge from initial demand and intention. First of all, the allocated credit is lower than asked and, second, as in Pro*Doc, ten doctoral students per programme shall receive a salary related to the programme, although that has not been thought in this manner in the original proposal. In its first proposal, CRUS doctoral programmes would have been gradually addressed to all doctoral students, but without any related funding for doctorate as such (CRUS 2006a). Third, as a consequence, only part of doctoral students instead of their totality is targeted.

Besides those conceptual changes, CRUS doctoral programmes contained already during their planning phase a number of rules, which were quite similar or even identical to the ones of the SNF's Pro*Doc programme. For instance, each programme must involve several HEIs and training activities and were planned to be more or less distributed on the whole doctorate's duration. Announcing signs or not, before the actual implementation of CRUS doctoral programmes, CRUS took the decision to join the Pro*Doc project and to add the obtained funding to the Pro*Doc budget in order to reinforce the already started initiative.

Considering the CRUS' objectives for the period 2008-2011, which included among others the standardisation of doctoral education, its statement in 2008 may look like a step back. At that moment, CRUS took position on current developments of doctoral education and, more particularly, on the integration of doctoral education as third level into the Bologna process. In a joint position paper, the rectors of all Swiss

36 Interview in July 2007.

universities state that "they reject extending the Bologna Model to the doctoral level (Bologna III) – regarded as a "harmonisation" of the doctorate (CRUS 2008: 2)." By contrast, they underline that "each Swiss university organises and plans the doctorate in keeping with the institution's profile and under consideration of the particularities within a certain discipline (CRUS 2008: 1)". This statement does not specify whether the consideration of differences between disciplines means the maintenance of "old traditions" like for instance the renunciation to organised training programmes. However, the following citation also shows that this statement does certainly not correspond to a negation of any reform into the direction of more organised training: "The universities guarantee that all doctoral degrees meet the same demands of excellence and achieve the same high quality by creating the necessary conditions (guidance, educational offers, etc.) (CRUS 2008:1)." In other words, it looks like the rectors want to keep room of manoeuvre without obliging themselves to implement any formally binding reforms.

The next turning point, occurring in November 2009, illustrates that the rectors increasingly want to take control over doctoral education's reform. At this moment, the Rectors' Conference of Swiss Universities published its decision according to which universities will put the emphasis on the promotion of doctoral education for the funding period 2012/2013-2016. This way, universities should get the possibility to fully assume the responsibility for the doctoral level. Within this context, the CRUS decided to cease the common project with the Swiss National Science Foundation, Pro*Doc, at the end of 2011.[37]

IV.1.4. The Evaluation of Norwegian Doctoral Education: Towards a Network Model?

An evaluation of Norwegian doctoral education in 2002 brought new inputs for changes in terms of doctoral education's organisation. Mandated by the Norwegian Association of Higher Education

37 Source: http://www.snf.ch/d/aktuell/seiten/default.aspx?NEWSID=1319&WEBID = 22739AD6-FC54-4EC7-8825-3B708058CE3E; accessed on December 2009.

Institutions (*Universitets- og Høgskolerådet* – UHR),[38] the Research Council of Norway (*Norges Forskningsråd* – NFR)[39] and the Ministry for Education and Research (*Utdannings- og forskningsdepartementet* – UFD), a group of professors under the direction of a NIFU[40] researcher evaluated hitherto existing doctoral education. Three main problems of current doctoral education have been identified: first, too few doctorates compared to the other Nordic countries are completed, second, doctoral students are too old when they finish their doctorate, and third, they work for too long on their thesis. These problems are explained by the fact that certain disciplines have still not made a clear cut with the *dr.philos.* tradition. As solutions, the authors suggest, first, a new study structure within which doctoral education begins after the first year of master studies, yet, lasts one year more. Hence, a complete study cycle for doctoral candidates would consist of three years of Bachelor, one year of Master and four years of doctoral studies. Secondly, the one-year duties (*pliktarbeidsdelen*) should be replaced by only a half-year educational programme about teaching, scientific communication (*vitenskapelig formidling*), etc., as well as a practical part. These measures would leave a supplementary half year for the doctoral thesis and contribute to a broader doctoral education qualifying doctoral students for jobs within the HEI system, the institutes sector, administration and the economic sector. Thirdly, doctoral education should take place in so-called research schools (*forskerskoler*) with the following features: a research school is based on an internationally recognised research environment, has a broad training offer, is focused on topics, nationally and internationally visible, has many doctoral students, post-docs and senior researchers, enough resources, covers a broad spectrum of candidates and has a good infrastructure as well as a

38 UHR facilitates co-operation and co-ordination among Norwegian HEI and advocates shared positions on central issues concerning higher education and research policy towards the Norwegian government, parliament and society at large; Source: www.uhr.no.

39 "The mandate of the [Research] Council [of Norway] is to promote and support basic and applied research in all areas of science, technology, medicine and the humanities." Source: Research Council of Norway, accessed the 26th September 2007: http://www.forskningsradet.no/servlet/Satellite?c=Page&cid=113878583253 9&pagename=ForskningsradetEngelsk%2FPage%2FstandardSidemal.

40 Norwegian Research Institute in Studies for Innovation, Research and Education.

good social environment. Such research schools should be established in all disciplines, even though it cannot be for all doctoral students. They should develop a high standard as an example for the other doctoral programmes (Kyvik 2002).

The idea of research schools is appreciated both by the UHR and the Ministry (UHR 2003; UFD 2005). In a first statement, UHR recommends the establishment of research schools as an attempt and in addition to ordinary research education. They should be established as flagships or networks. On the one hand, flagship research schools may be established within internationally recognised research environments. On the other hand, the network-model may contribute to the strengthening of small disciplinary environments scattered on individual institutions. By relating them, resources would be put together in order to achieve a better course offer and study environment for doctoral students. All involved institutions should be represented in a steering council. In its position paper "Commitment to Research" (*Vilje til forskning*) (UFD 2005), the government indicates that it wants to establish a scheme for national research schools. This should be one element among several, targeted to make Norway a leading research nation. Furthermore, the number of PhD fellowship positions at universities and colleges should be increased and a scheme for industrial doctorates should be established in order to strengthen collaboration between enterprises and research institutions. The Ministry of Education and Research mandates the UHR and Research Council to examine schemes for national research schools and PhDs in industry.

Concerning national research schools, the Ministry includes in its mandate several premises, among which the stimulation of the collaboration between several institutions and fragmented fields is underlined. Finally, the mandated working group suggests the establishment of national research schools in a clear network organisation with a scientific leader, responsible for relating doctoral students and other researchers to the school and for developing the scientific activities of the research school. Institutions should channel both people and positions to research schools but the admission to a degree awarding institution is a precondition for doing a doctoral degree. One research school should normally be composed of at least 20-30 doctoral students and 4-8 supervisors. 20 schools, each with a yearly funding base of up to three million Norwegian Krones, should be established for eight years. The scheme should be opened for all disciplines (UHR and NFR 2006).

In May 2006, the Norwegian government appointed a committee who got the task to propose measures for the next 10-20 years in order to ensure that the structures of Norwegian HEIs would meet the society's needs and that corresponding resources would be well used. This committee, bearing the name of its leader – *Stjernø-utvalget* – also suggested measures concerning doctoral education, within which the idea of research schools occupied an important place. Among others, it points to positive experiences in relation with research schools – in particular with respect to the completion rate –, made by Danish higher education. Generally, it agreed on the ideas launched by the working group of the Norwegian Research Council and the Association of Higher Education Institutions, especially with respect to certain minimal standards in terms of numbers of doctoral students related to research schools. Furthermore, it underlines that several types of research schools should be possible but favours a network based model, in particular in order to relate small research environments. Considering the high objectives for Norwegian research and the importance of high quality doctoral education with regard to those objectives, it suggests a comprehensive approach consisting in research schools for all doctoral students. Estimated costs are around 300 million Norwegian Krones (~35,57 million €) per year (Stjernø 2008).

However, the idea of a comprehensive approach has not been followed. Instead, a call for applications for a limited number of national research schools has been launched by the Norwegian Research Council in 2008. Norwegian HEIs could apply in order to get funding for the establishment and running of such national research schools. Five applications have been selected. The resulting national research schools started operating in 2009. Until today, it is not clear whether further calls will follow.

Regarding PhDs in the economy, another working group of the UHR and NFR (2006a) suggests essentially two measures: on the one hand, the government should fund half of doctoral students' salary, because enterprises are often not able to pay the whole amount. However, only enterprises having already R&D staff and pursuing the ambition to increase their scientific competence level should be eligible for doctoral students and the corresponding financial support. On the other side, government shall also fund special research courses for doctoral students oriented towards applied questions (*e.g.* interdisciplinary collaboration, project management, communication, etc.). Indeed a special programme has then been planned and is being carried out during the period 2008-2011. Companies can apply for (maximally two) fellowships. Approximately 40 million NOK (~4,75 million €) have been set aside for the industrial PhD scheme for the year 2009.[41]

IV.2. The Legal Framework

Those reform developments are also reflected in the legal frameworks that regulate current doctoral education. Yet, as demonstrated, major changes in Norwegian regulations have occurred a few years ago, whereas an important part of Swiss regulations only are about to change at the moment of the writing of the present doctoral thesis. Therefore, the analysis of the Swiss legal framework such as carried out below may be not anymore completely accurate in the near future. Thus, occurred changes are taken into account until a certain moment which is March 2008.

Currently, the legal frameworks of doctoral education in Switzerland and Norway vary to quite some extent. Two types of variation can be distinguished: on the one hand, variation regarding the general regulation principle, and on the other hand, variation with respect to individual issues. The first type of variation opposes a principle of rather unified regulation in Norway to a principle of strongly diversified regulation in Switzerland. Concretely, the Norwegian Council for Higher Education agreed on a common legal framework for doctoral education of all Norwegian HEIs, whereas this regulative power is delegated to and exercised by the individual Swiss HEIs, what has a considerable impact in terms of legal diversification. Norwegian HEIs also have their own doctoral regulations either at the central institutional

41 Source: www.forskningsradet.no; accessed in November 2009.

level or at the Faculty level. However, they respect the agreed common framework.

The Norwegian Council for Higher Education, respectively the previous Norwegian Council of Universities, elaborated two varying legal frameworks, one for "unorganised" doctoral education – the dr.philos. degree – (Norwegian Council of Universities 1996), and one for "organised" doctoral education – the degree of Philosophiae Doctor (PhD) – (UHR 2003a). The dr.philos.' "unorganised" character consists in its small number of prescribed rules. The latter essentially limit to some minimal requirements in terms of admission, thesis characteristics and final evaluation. The Norwegian Agency for Quality Assurance in Education – NOKUT – announced that the old degrees (dr.juris, dr.theol., dr.techn., etc. and also dr.philos.) would be completely phased out by the end of 2007.[42] However, statistics show that such old degrees were still awarded in 2008. In addition, in its recently elaborated guidelines for the evaluation for candidates for Norwegian doctoral degrees, the UHR still refers to both, the PhD and dr.philos. degrees (UHR 2007). However, since the number of awarded dr.philos. degrees clearly decreases in favour of the "organised" PhD degree, further analysis concentrates on the latter degree.

The issue of "unorganised" or "organised" doctoral education is a useful variable in order to compare the varying legal frameworks. However, in order to become more operational, it has to be demultiplexed in individual indicators. Six different indicators are examined and compared: admission, content, duration, supervision, follow-up, final evaluation.

Regarding admission, Norwegian legislation generally contains more organisational elements. Besides the shared basic requirement of a master or equivalent degree, Norwegian legislation requires an application containing a project proposal for the thesis, a detailed plan of completion including deadlines, the name(s) of proposed supervisor(s), an account of project funding, a description of necessary infrastructure, possible plans for extended stay in other research institutions as well as a plan for publication and dissemination of results (UHR 2003a). A good part of Swiss regulations also ask the prior agreement of supervisors to

42 Source: http://www.nokut.no/sw21671.asp, accessed on July 2007 and November 2009.

advice the applicants. Yet, only some individual Swiss regulations require the formulation of a thesis project already at the moment of the application (Baschung 2008). All other listed information is generally not asked. The organisational dimension of the Norwegian admission procedure is even more reinforced by the signature of a written "Agreement upon admission to doctoral program" (UHR 2003a) by the doctoral student, the supervisor(s) and the institutional unit. Several elements like employment duration, funding conditions, place of work, a series of advisory activities through the supervisor(s), equipment and the right to use research results are specified and sealed in this agreement.

Two main elements potentially organise the content of doctoral education, namely training and research. The research component, which has to be an independent and original piece of research, is uncontested in all doctoral regulations. A training component corresponding to 30 credits is a compulsory requirement of Norwegian legislation (UHR 2003a). However, a training component is by far not part of all Swiss regulations (Baschung 2008). In addition, organised training programmes do only exist for a limited part of Swiss doctoral students (Groneberg 2008).

The general Norwegian legal framework does not define any overall duration. However, in its regulations about the employment of scholarship holders, the Ministry of Education and Research (UFD 2003), defines the doctoral students' length of employment on four years with 25% teaching duties or three years full-time. Most indications about duration in Swiss regulations mention a duration between three and five years. Yet, the manner those indications are formulated – e.g. minimal, general, maximal duration – leaves some leeway for interpretation (Baschung 2008).

In both countries, supervision through one supervisor is the formal norm. Yet, legislation, especially in Norway, also mentions the possibility of supervision through more than one person. As mentioned, the agreement upon admission also defines a series of advisory activities to be exercised by the supervisor(s). Swiss regulations remain rather vague regarding more precise descriptions of such activities. Norwegian regulation adds that supervisor(s) and the corresponding institution are responsible of facilitating the doctoral students' regular participation in "an active research community involving senior researchers and other doctoral candidates" (UHR 2003a: section 8). Such prescriptions do generally not exist in Swiss regulations either.

Concerning the organisation of follow-up mechanism, Norwegian regulations are also much more systematic than Swiss ones. Norwegian doctoral students and their supervisor(s) are obliged to separately write an annual report about progress and supervision. In case of for instance major delays in the research project or the training programme, doctoral students can be forced to abandon their doctoral education (UHR 2003a). Such mechanisms, both in terms of reporting and forced abandonment, only exceptionally exist in Swiss regulations (Baschung 2008).

Finally, the organisation of the final evaluation which leads to the award of the doctoral degree also varies to a certain extent, both between countries and between varying Swiss regulations. A common first step consists in the thesis' evaluation through a committee (yet, composed of a varying number of members). Then, regulations of both countries define a sort of (oral) exam dealing with the doctoral thesis. However, in some cases it is public (Norway and some Swiss regulations), in others not. Some Swiss regulations add a further – always – public defence. An element which does only exist in Norwegian regulation, is the so called "trial lecture" on a given topic (UHR 2003a; Baschung 2008).

IV.3. The Quantitative Framework

After this rough legal overview, this section provides a quantitative overview of doctoral education in Switzerland and Norway. It starts with a first macro indicator, namely *the number of doctorate holders within the national population.* In an international comparison of seven OECD countries[43], the number of doctorate holders within the 25 to 64 years old Swiss population, is at the top of the ranking. 23 out of 1,000 inhabitants hold a doctorate. The number is even higher among per thousand of labour force, namely 27.5. Thereby, Switzerland is ahead Germany (15,4/20,1) and even more clearly ahead other countries like the USA (8,4/10,7) and Canada (6,5/7,8) (Auriol 2007). In comparison, the share

43 According to the country, numbers are from the year 2001, 2003, 2004 or 2005.

of all Norwegian employees holding a doctorate from a Norwegian HEIs[44] is rather low. In 2003, it achieves 0.4% and it is estimated to attain 0.5% in 2007 (Olsen 2007). A further comparison of 15 OECD countries, which however is limited do doctoral degrees in Science and Engineering, again places Switzerland clearly ahead, followed by Finland and Sweden. Among the examined OECD countries, Norway fills a middle position, slightly over the OECD average (Moguérou 2005). Thus, from an international point of view, the Swiss (labour) population of doctorate holders is extremely high.[45]

This high share of doctoral holders among the Swiss and, to a lesser extent, Norwegian (labour) population may partly be explained by the constant increase of doctoral degrees within both countries. Between 1990 and 2008, the number of yearly awarded doctoral degrees increased more than 50% in Switzerland (from 2175 to 3209), whereas it even tripled in Norway (from 393 to 1244)!

---

44 No statistics including all Norwegian doctorates, thus also those who carried out their doctoral degree abroad, is available. However, considering that some Norwegians carried out doctoral degrees especially in other Nordic countries as well as in the USA (Olsen 2004), the overall share of doctoral holders might be estimated a little higher.

45 A recent parliamentary initiative asks to modify the „Law on foreigners" and thereby to facilitate the access to the Swiss labour market for foreigners coming from outside of the European Union and European Free Trade Association (EFTA) and who graduated in a Swiss higher education institution. The Swiss National Science Foundation comments on this initiative in a favourable manner (SNF 2009). Thus, if this legal modification is accepted and considering the already very high part of foreigners among doctoral students in Swiss HEIs (see in later chapter), the number of doctorate holders on the Swiss labour population may raise even more in the future.

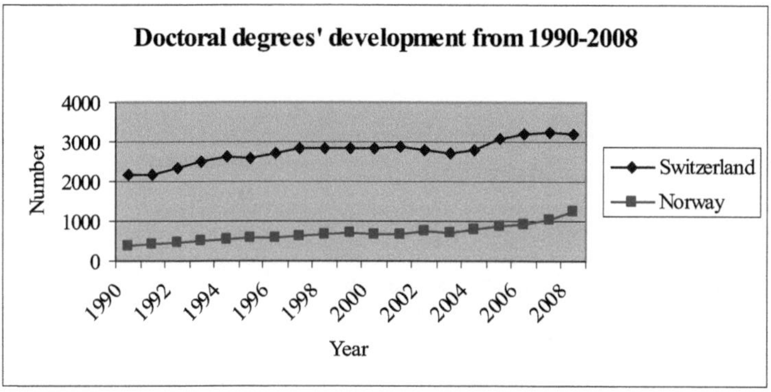

Figure 2: Doctoral degrees' development from 1990-2008

Sources: Swiss Federal Statistics Office, 2009, www.bfs.admin.ch; NIFU-STEP, 2009, www.nifustep.no

In international comparison, Swiss doctorate graduates' age at the moment of completion is quite low (between 32 and 33). German graduates are situated at the same level, whereas graduates from Australia, Canada or the United States achieve in average 35 to 37 years (Auriol 2007). In the 2000s, the Norwegian average age at graduation is also rather high, namely between 37 and 38 years.[46]

To come back to the number of awarded degrees, it is important to underline that this spectacular growth of the number of awarded doctoral degrees is also reflected in the number of doctoral students of both countries. Again between 1990 and 2008, the latter almost doubled in Switzerland (from 11,670 to 19,076) and almost tripled in Norway (from 2,840 to 7,914).

46 Source: www.norbal.no/norbal.

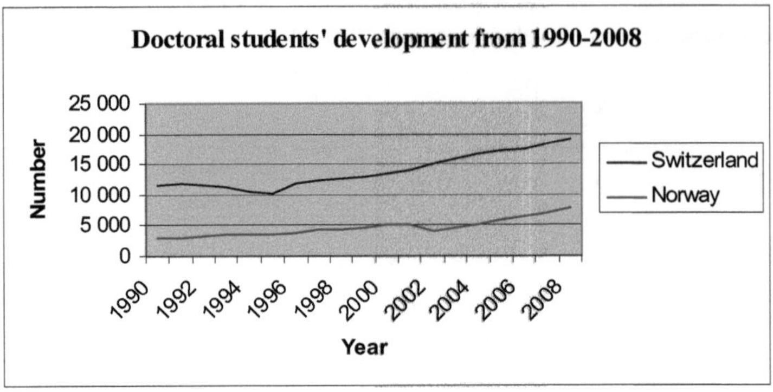

Figure 3: Doctoral students' development from 1990-2008

Sources: Swiss Federal Statistics Office, 2009, www.bfs.admin.ch; Norwegian Social Science Data Services, 2009, www.nsd.uib.no

As the next table shows, this increase more or less proceeds in parallel to the overall increase of undergraduate students. There is a difference between Switzerland and Norway to the extent that the former's share of doctoral students compared to undergraduate students (including master level) slightly decreased during the period 2000-2008, whereas the opposite is the case for Norway. However, a much more striking difference between both countries concerns the ratio as such: the Swiss ratio between doctoral students and undergraduate students is between three and four times as large as Norway's! A report of the Federal Office of Statistics confirms that the share of doctoral students among the total student population is exceptionally high. In international comparison, Switzerland is situated at the top (Bundesamt für Statistik 2006). In other words, it seems much more "usual" to carry on studies at doctoral level in Switzerland than in Norway. This statement can be relativised to the extent that a large part of doctoral students of Swiss HEIs come from abroad (see chapter X).

		NO			CH	
Ratio	Undergraduate (incl. master)	Doctoral	*Ratio*	Undergraduate (incl. master)	Doctoral	Types of student (in thousands)
2.9%	176,1	5,2	*13.6%*	99,3	13,5	2000
2.5%	204,8	5,1	*13.3%*	105,3	14,0	2001
2.0%	208,4	4,1	*12.8%*	116,7	15	2002
2.1%	208,2	4,5	*12.6%*	125,6	15,8	2003
2.4%	208,5	5,0	*12.6%*	132,0	16, 6	2004
2.9%	209,5	6,0	*12.5%*	137,4	17,2	2005
3.1%	208,9	6,5	*12.3%*	143,0	17,6	2006
3.5%	205,4	7,1	*12.3%*	148	18,2	2007
3.8%	209,1	7,9	*12.4%*	153,5	19,1	2008

In the Swiss case, also undergraduate (bachelor, master, licence) students from Universities of Applied Sciences have been included.

Table 5: Ratio between doctoral and undergraduate students (including master level)

Sources: www.bfs.admin.ch; www.norbal.no; www.nsd.uib.no

Obviously, it is interesting to ask which scientific fields contribute which part to the overall doctorates' production and whether certain disciplines contributed more than others to this overall increase. These questions are here examined with respect to the period 2000-2008, which can be considered as second wave of increase since 1990. In the case of Switzerland, mathematics and natural sciences are currently clearly the main producer of doctorates. Over the whole period, about a third of the overall doctorates' production can be attributed to them (32% in 2008). The share of the second producer, medicine and health sciences decreased since 2000 to about 25%, whereas the social sciences steadily come closer (22% in 2008). Over the whole period, the role of the remaining disciplines is significantly lower: in 2008, technical sciences attain 12%, humanities 7% and agricultural sciences and veterinary medicine 5%.

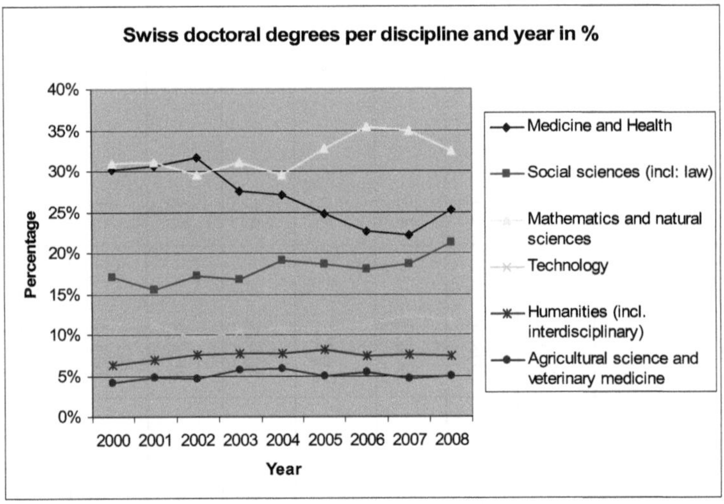

Figure 4: Swiss doctoral degrees per discipline and year in %

Sources: Swiss Federal Statistics Office, 2009; www.bfs.admin.ch

The same distinction between two groups of scientific fields can also be made in Norway, although it is less clear-cut. In addition, unlike in Switzerland, the first group is not dominated by mathematics and natural sciences, which are barely on the second place (23% in 2008), but by medicine and health sciences (27% in 2008). The former is tightly followed by social sciences (22% in 2008). Interestingly, the share of technical sciences constantly decreases since 2000, whereas humanities (11% in 2008) and agricultural sciences (6% in 2008) are situated at relatively constant low level.

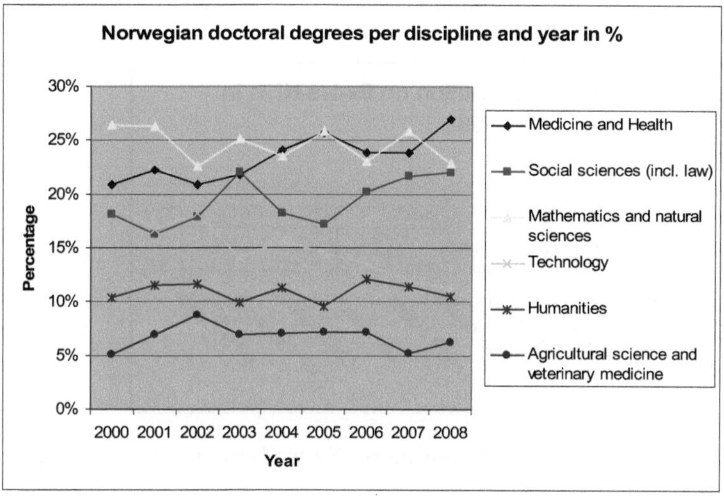

Figure 5: Norwegian doctoral degrees per discipline and year in %

Source: NIFU-STEP, 2009, www.nifustep.no

Last but not least, it seems also interesting to have a look at the doctoral degrees' distribution on the different types of HEIs and individual HEIs. Swiss Universities of Applied Sciences are until today not allowed to award doctoral degrees. Therefore, all Swiss doctoral degrees are distributed on the remaining two types of HEIs, the two Federal Institutes of Technology (*Ecoles Polytechniques Fédérales – EPF; Eidgenössische Technische Hochschule – ETH*) and the ten cantonal universities. Among them, the two HEIs of Zurich – University of Zurich and ETH Zurich – are clearly situated at the top and cumulate together more than a third of the overall number of doctoral degrees (University of Zurich: 671; ETH Zurich 581). Universities of Bern and Basle follow with respectively 496 and 365 awarded doctoral degrees. After a next step downwards, University of Geneva (272) is tightly followed by the EPF Lausanne (266). The last middle size university, the one of Lausanne awarded 186 degrees. Among the smaller HEIs, University of St.Gallen appears as leader (165) before University of Fribourg (106), whereas the remaining small institutions are clearly below the boundary of 100 awarded degrees: University of Neuchâtel (64), University of Lucerne (22), University of Lugano (15).

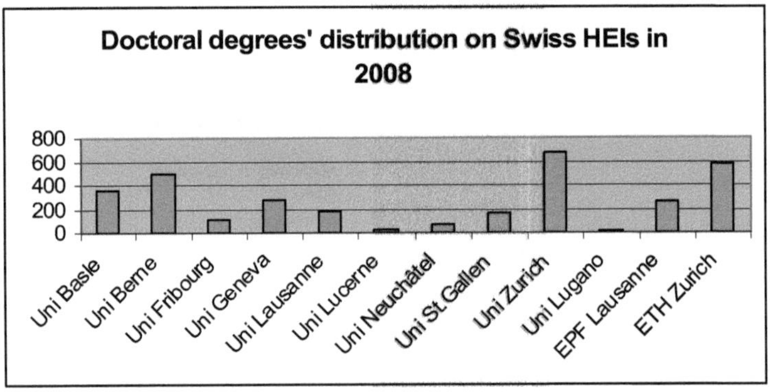

Figure 6: Doctoral degrees' distribution on Swiss HEIs in 2008

Source: Swiss Federal Statistics Office, 2009, www.bfs.admin.ch

The general result is similar in Norway, to the extent that the largest HEIs concentrate most of awarded doctoral degrees. However, in contrast to Swiss Universities of Applied Sciences, Norwegian HEIs with educational profiles which are more oriented towards professional directions also award doctoral degrees in certain scientific fields, though to a limited extent.

Type of Higher Education Institution[47]	*Higher Education Institution*	*Awarded doctoral degrees*
Universities *(Universiteter)*	University of Oslo	435
	University of Bergen	233
	Norwegian University of Science and Technology (NTNU)	314
	University of Tromsø	104
	Norwegian University of Life Sciences UMB	67
	University of Stavanger	12
	University of Agder	3
Specialised University Institutions *(Vitenskapelige høgskoler)*	Norwegian School of Veterinary Science	19
	Norwegian School of Economics and Business Administration NHH	15
	Norwegian School of Sport Sciences	6
	Norwegian Academy of Music	4
	The Oslo School of Architecture and Design	6
	Norwegian School of Management	7
	Norwegian School of Theology	5
	School of Mission and Theology	2
University Colleges *(Akkrediterte høgskoler)*	Bodø University College	6
	Molde University College	5
	Oslo University College	1
	Total	1,244

Table 6: Doctoral degrees' distribution on Norwegian HEIs in 2008
Source: NIFU-STEP, 2009, www.nifustep.no

47 The typology, the related terminology as well as the attribution of the individual HEIs to the three types of HEIs has been adopted from the Norwegian Association of Higher Education Institutions (UHR).

In 2008, the Norwegian higher education system awarded a total of 1,244[48] doctorates, out of which 1,168 were awarded by the seven existing universities, 64 by the eight specialised university institutions, and 12 by three university colleges.

IV.4. Wider Implications for Higher Education Institutions and Systems

Like most other countries, the Swiss and Norwegian higher education systems have been undergoing profound transformations during the last decades. It is argued that qualitative and quantitative developments in doctoral education such as described above (may) play an important role in the framework of such transformations. In the present section, three of such transformations and their link to (reforms of) doctoral education are developed. Those three transformations consists in first, differentiation, second, stratification, and third, massification.

Although with a considerable temporal difference of about thirty years, both national higher education systems have been *differentiated* through the integration and further development of a vocational education sector into the national higher education system. Besides their role as supplier of a new type of educational programmes, these vocational higher education institutions also entered the field as a new actor in research. Already before their merger in 1994 into state colleges, Norwegian regional and professional colleges have carried out some research. However, it is only in 1995 through the Act on Universities and Colleges that state colleges get the explicit mandate to engage in research (Kyvik and Skodvin 2003). Almost simultaneously, namely in 1997, Swiss former upper-secondary colleges have been upgraded to formal higher education institutions, called Universities of Applied Sciences (Perellon 2003). In opposite to their Norwegian counterpart, they received the research mandate from the beginning. In both cases, the political intention was to make those HEIs carry out applied research

48 48 doctorates were still awarded according to the "dr.philos. degree" and 242 according to the specialised dr.med, dr,juris, dr, theol., etc. degrees.

with particular use for the regional economies. Several authors argue that this distinction between basic and applied research is difficult to maintain, especially in certain (non-technical) scientific fields. In other words, a convergence tendency seems to threat the binary system to some extent. However, if it is argued that there is a clear tendency towards an academic drift in Norway – due to the staff's ambition and the national reward system –, such an assessment is not shared with respect to the Swiss case. Instead, a lack of competence in research is identified for the human resources of the latter case (Lepori 2006; Kyvik and Skodvin 2003). As demonstrated in the quantitative section of this chapter, some Norwegian university colleges awarded the *same type of doctoral degree* as universities. In addition, university colleges have the possibility to get the status of a university, among others under the condition to award doctorates in at least four different scientific fields (Lauglo et al. 2004). Thus, also from this point of view, the binary divide in Norwegian higher education seems to be quite fluid. In contrast, a large distinction between Swiss Universities of Applied Sciences on the one side and cantonal universities and federal institutes of technology on the other side consists in the non-award of doctorates through UAS. Thus, potential future developments, like either the maintenance of the current development or the creation of different types of doctoral degrees might have an impact on the binary system of those two higher education systems, either in the direction of a complete abandonment or reinforcement of the binary divide. Among the alternatives to the conventional disciplinary based doctoral degree, the following two types of doctoral degrees are mentioned for instance by Usher (2002). On the one hand, a *professional doctorate* which brings more closely together academy and the (non-academic) workplace, and on the other hand, a *doctorate by project* which Usher defines in the following way:

> In doctorates by project, the workplace becomes the site of research. Knowledge production takes off from specific problems or issues in the workplace. The research is action-oriented in the sense that it sees to make a difference in the workplace. It is collaborative either because the "student" is actually a member of that workplace or because the research is conducted with the full participation of members. This doesn't mean that there are no disciplinary elements but it does mean that they are not the starting point or the structuring agency. In all likelihood, the research will be multi- or trans-disciplinary. The outcome of this form of doctoral education is not a thesis but a short written exegesis. More significant is

> the "artefact" produced through the project. This is the outcome of the project with direct tangible benefit to the workplace. Its significance also lies in the fact that it subverts the primacy of the written thesis as the dominant assessable outcome. (Usher 2002: 150)

Hence, according to the non-/development of such alternative application oriented doctoral degrees – among which might range the Norwegian governmental initiative for industrial PhDs started in 2008 as well as more industry based doctoral research which, however, is run under the conventional doctoral degree label – and according to the type of HEI within which such alternative degrees would be developed, the binary divide of higher education systems may move into one or another direction.

It can be argued that a second movement, called *stratification*, is about to transform both higher education systems. Various political but also institutional funding instruments are aimed at specially supporting certain selected research fields in order to attain higher levels of quality and thereby outstand at national and/or international level. This can be observed for instance by the examples of the "National Centres of Competence in Research (NCCR)" in Switzerland or "Centres of Excellence" in Norway.[49] Such policies, aiming at the promotion of strategically important research fields, have been implemented since the beginning of the 2000s (Bleiklie 2009; Braun and Benninghoff 2003). Since only part of scientific fields and HEIs of a national higher education system benefit of such funding instruments, stratification between disciplines and HEIs is automatically promoted from a quantitative point of view. However, funding alone does not yet guarantee increase in quality. The latter obviously also depends on the quality of the research staff. Thus, as it can be assumed that doctoral students form a large part of this research staff, the attraction and training of *many high quality doctoral students* appears to be a crucial

49 Delamont et al. (1997) describe the same type of stratification through selective promotion of research and research training in centres of excellence for the British higher education system. According to Gumport (2005), American Federal research funding has also been distributed on the basis of a "logic of excellence" during the post-war period, what equally had a strong stratification impact on American higher education, especially at the expense of humanities.

element in the promotion of research within certain fields and HEIs that stands out compared to competitors.

As noticed, alike the number of undergraduate students, the number of doctoral students strongly increased during the last twenty years in Switzerland and Norway. Although the demonstrated increase in the number of doctoral students and degrees of the last twenty years does not attain a level which would be considered by the classification of Trow (1973) as *massification*, it remains nevertheless spectacular. The fact that, since 2000, the increase of doctoral students approximately corresponds to the increase of undergraduate students (see Table 4), underlines this impressive growth, especially in Switzerland, where the overall increase of undergraduate students has been particularly strong (~50%) due to the "explosion" taking place in the Universities of Applied Sciences. As a consequence of this impressive increase, the same question as for undergraduate students arises, namely of whether the high number of graduates is in adequacy with the *labour market*. Both studies about the Norwegian as well the Swiss contexts affirm that there is no oversupply of doctors on the labour market. Although with differences between individual scientific fields, doctoral education generally seems to be "worth" in Switzerland: graduates with a doctoral degree have higher income, their degree of unemployment is lower and they are happier with their type of work than their counterparts with lower university degrees (Engelage and Schubert 2009; Engelage and Hadjar 2008; Bundesamt für Statistik 2010). There can be no question of oversaturation either in Norway. Graduates have no problem to find relevant jobs. At the latest one year after graduation 90% got a position. In addition, 59% of them found a position in HEIs (41%), research institutions (18%) or R&D enterprises (*FoU-bedrifter*). Among the remaining graduates, 15% work in the social and health sector, 10% in industry, 9% in the service sector and 6% in public administration (Olsen 2007; Kyvik and Olsen 2007). To the extent that doctoral graduates find appropriate and satisfying positions on a diverse labour market, those results, both concerning Switzerland and Norway, go into the same direction as those of a German study (see Enders 2002). Thus, the question to what extent claims for doctoral education's adaptation to the needs of the broader non-academic labour market are justified can be launched.

V. Doctoral Schools in Biology[50]

V.1. PhD Programme Biomolecular Structure and Mechanism[51]

After this national overview, the announced eight case studies are developed. This first case study focuses on the PhD programme Biomolecular Structure and Mechanism (BSM). This PhD programme is one out of nine PhD programmes, which currently constitute the Life Science Zurich Graduate School (LSZGS). Both, the BSM and the LSZGS have been founded in December 2005. Three years later (November 2008), LSZGS includes over 300 faculty members and 946 doctoral students from the University of Zurich and the Swiss Federal Institute of Technology Zurich (*Eidgenössische Technische Hochschule Zürich - ETHZ*) (LSZGS 2009). At the same moment, BSM reunites 34 doctoral students from both HEIs as well as the Paul-Scherrer-Institute, which is a part of the domain of the Swiss Federal Institutes of Technology.[52]

---

50 The order of presentation of the individual case studies is based on the typology of Trowler and Becher (2001), which distinguishes between hard pure, hard applied, soft pure and soft applied scientific disciplines.

51 A general methodological note regarding the anonymity has to be placed at this stage: since Swiss and Norwegian higher education systems are rather small, concrete case studies and part of interviewees could easily be identified even if they would be anomysised. Therefore and because anomysisation would prevent the use of precise references to case studies' documents, it is renounced to the invention of artificial names for the case studies and related higher education institutions (as sometimes practiced in higher education studies). In contrast, instead of interviewees' names, their functions are indicated as they are crucial from a scientific point of view. Moreover, since several interviewees explicitly asked to remain anonymous, no index of names is added to this doctoral thesis.

52 www.structuralbiology.uzh.ch/phd, downloaded August 2009.

V.1.1. Building a Training Hot Spot in Life Sciences[53]

The reform story of this case study can be divided into three different episodes. The first episode can be called *pioneer episode*, the second one, *corporation episode* and the third one, *institutionalisation episode*.

The pioneer episode began in 2003 with the foundation of a PhD programme in Molecular Life Sciences (MLS). This episode has brought three types of changes to doctoral education within this disciplinary and institutional environment: the increasing and collective attraction of high level doctoral students, the provision of a training programme for the selected doctoral students and the introduction of thesis committees. The increasing and collective attraction of doctoral students has resulted in the following developments: in the first formal application round of fall 2003, 186 applications have been submitted out of which nine candidates finally began their doctoral education in the framework of the Molecular Life Sciences programme at ETHZ or University of Zurich. In the selection round of June 2005, 335 candidates applied, out of which 25 effectively found a "match", which means an agreement with a supervisor and a related position as doctoral student.[54] The collective character of the doctoral students' attraction consists in advertisement in the name of the PhD programme containing several positions belonging to several supervisors, rather than in the name of one single supervisor. The second issue, the provision of a training programme for selected doctoral students has essentially been consisting in three types of training activities: an about four-week introduction course dealing with specific topics related to molecular life sciences, a one to two-day course on scientific writing and presentation and a one to two-days course on laboratory ethics. Since its first edition in 2004, this training programme

53 Unless other sources are indicated, used data always originates from interviews with the pro-rector of ETHZ, the head of ETHZ doctoral administration, the University of Zurich's head of study reforms, two further collaborators of University of Zurich's central administration, the head of LSZGS, the administrator of LSZGS, the head and three further professors of the PhD programme BSM as well as four doctoral students participating in the PhD programme BSM.

54 A supplementary number of doctoral students, who have not been recruited in the framework of this formal application process but individually by their respective supervisors, has to be added to the total number of doctoral students enrolled in the PhD programme (cf. VI.1.2. Instruments of Management).

has been modified to some extent. On the one side, the course offer has been expanded, which provides more choice to students. On the other side, a forth type of activity, a retreat (in the Swiss Alps) with presentations through doctoral students and invited scholars, has been added (MLS 2003; MLS 2005; MLS 2008). Doctoral students' performances in the framework of this training programme are examined in a way or another and are rewarded by credit points. The third activity of the Molecular Life Science PhD programme concerns doctoral students' supervision and follow-up. During his doctoral education, each doctoral student has to be accompanied by a thesis committee composed of three members, that is to say, his main supervisor, an external member – coming from another HEI than the University of Zurich or ETHZ – and a third internal or external member. During their annual meetings, doctoral students present their progress and, together with the committee members, discuss occurred problems and further work.

The corporation episode has started in December 2005. It consisted in the creation of an umbrella organisation called Life Science Zurich Graduate School. The following double movement led to this development: on the one side, additional and more specialised PhD programmes have been created in the field of Life Sciences at ETHZ and the University of Zurich. Those new programmes work according to the same principles as the Molecular Life Sciences PhD programme. Accordingly, several interviewees spoke about "cloning". The actual first case study, the PhD programme Biomolecular Structure and Mechanism is one of those "clones". A difference between the clone "Biomolecular Structure and Mechanism" and the original "Molecular Life Sciences" consists in the volume of the compulsory course, which in the case of the clone only lasts three days.[55] Additional courses may be taken in the framework of other training programmes, in particular the training offer of the NCCR "Structural Biology". On the other side, further PhD programmes specialised in other domains of Life Sciences – but also situated within the two HEIs – have already existed before 2003. Thus, they have been offered the possibility to join a broader initiative in the field of Life Sciences, together with the Molecular Life Sciences and

55 This three-day programme consists of intensive courses in structural biology, biophysics and biochemistry. Source: http://www.structuralbiology.uzh.ch/phd/overview002.asp#; accessed on December 2009.

the “cloned” PhD programmes. Those older PhD programmes accepted the offer and the new umbrella organisation was born.

Concrete changes related to this corporation episode have essentially been consisting of two issues, namely first, the coordination of the attraction and recruitment of doctoral students as well as of the training offer and, second, the further dissemination of the practice of thesis committees in most other LSZGS PhD programmes. The coordination of the training offer mainly concerns the common offer of transferable skill courses. Instead of offering and funding the same courses in each of the nine programmes, the offer is more centrally coordinated and offered. In 2008, twelve, mostly one to two day lasting courses in the field of study design and data analysis, statistics for biologists, efficient literature search in the Life Sciences, scientific communication, self marketing and career planning have been offered at the level of the LSZGS (LSZGS 2009). With respect to the attraction and recruitment of doctoral students, coordination takes place regarding two aspects: besides previous advertisement measures in the name of the individual programmes, advertisement is also carried out in the name of the corporate identity “Life Science Zurich Graduate School”. Thus, this broad label should help attracting supplementary candidates. The second aspect concerns the concrete application procedure. In order to avoid multiple applications, candidates have to submit their application centrally to the LSZGS, by indicating one favourite PhD programme.

The name of the third episode, institutionalisation, refers to two distinct actions. One of them did not take place, the other one had not yet been completely carried out. The first (non-)action concerns the project “ETHZ Graduate School”, which involved the institution-wide introduction of PhD programmes (comprising curricular components). In spite of its setting on the agenda, this project as such has not been realised until today. In contrast, so called “fast-tracks” – essentially consisting in overall shorter education duration until the award of the doctoral degree – now exist at both HEIs in the field of biology. A second action in terms of institutionalisation may concern practices within LSZGS PhD programmes and the LSZGS’ administrative role within ETHZ and, particularly, within University of Zurich. Since their creation, the individual LSZGS PhD programmes developed more or less similar practices in terms of recruitment procedures (e.g. concerning entrance exam), training programmes (e.g. concerning volume) and supervision (e.g. concerning thesis committees). In the case of future possibly stable funding through their HEIs, the LSZGS administrator in turn expects requirements of formal institutionalisation of more standardised practises for all LSZGS PhD programmes. He also expects that LSZGS will be formally responsible of providing comprehensive numbers about LSZGS doctoral students – e.g. regarding enrolments, progress, etc. – to the HEIs' governing bodies. According to him, statistical information about doctoral students has been poorly developed until now at University of Zurich. Hence, the LSZGS would become a sort of central instance for the accumulation and provision of data about doctoral students in the field of life sciences at those two HEIs. However, currently, this second institutionalisation action has not yet been completely carried out.

Those three reform episodes have to be put into a certain context. First of all, it is important to underline that the initiatives which constitute the first and especially second episode, fall on generally fertile ground. The latter consists of an institutional environment which has been favourable to actions which aim at increasing the competitiveness of life sciences in Zurich. For instance, life sciences figure among the priority domains of the ETH Board's (*ETH-Rat*) strategic planning (ETH-Rat 2003). Furthermore, already in 2001, a broad initiative called "Life Sciences Zurich" has been started by the ETHZ and the University of Zurich. Initially, this initiative has two pillars – a "learning centre" and "communication and events" – which offer training opportunities for secondary school pupils and teachers, and organises popular scientific events for a broad public. Although not directly related to those two initiatives, the graduate school officially became the third pillar of this "Life Science Zurich" initiative. However, if the institutional environment has been favourable from an ideational point of view, this did not mean that the necessary funding automatically followed. In opposite, an interviewee involved in LSZGS' creation evoked that it was not easy to always convince *two* HEI governing bodies to financially contribute in an *equal way*. Often, HEI governing bodies wanted to wait until the other one makes the first step…

Such inter-institutional cooperation problems did not really occur at the level of the academic profession, when it came to the question of building a new common PhD programme in the field of structural biology. Thanks to their common NCCR "Structural Biology", the involved academics were already used to this type of collaboration and even already disposed of a certain training offer in the field. Interviewed professors also underline that a specialised programme in structural biology would provide a better framework for the attraction of doctoral candidates who were explicitly interested in structural biology. From this point of view, the creation of the PhD programme aimed at several objectives: on the one hand it was – together with the other newly created PhD programmes – a mean to avoid an "explosion" of the constantly growing PhD programme in molecular life sciences. Indeed, involved initiators became worried about the quality of the training activities, since the number of participating doctoral students has gone beyond an efficient "class size." On the other hand, it represented an opportunity to improve the visibility of a domain, which would be "a different world" compared to other domains within life sciences.

Also with respect to the third reform episode, further contextual elements must be developed. One among them is related to the confusion about the term "Graduate School".[56] Indeed, the ETHZ pro-rector indicates that the internal refusal of an institution-wide introduction of doctoral programmes may have been related to a misunderstanding induced by the term "Graduate School". Apparently, many professors interpreted this term in the American sense, which means that a graduate school would also integrate the master level. According to the ETHZ pro-rector, such an idea has been considered as a devalorisation of the master degree because students who finish their studies with a master degree would take the risk to be perceived as students who did not make it to finish the graduate school, which means including the doctoral degree. Such an assumption would compromise the traditionally high recognition of ETHZ master degrees on the non-academic labour market. Thus, the ETHZ pro-rector thinks that if the idea of a comprehensive introduction of doctoral programmes would have been suggested under the label of "doctoral programmes" instead of the one of a "Graduate School", it would have been less criticised.

Finally, it is also worth adding that the idea of an institutionalisation of certain standards, for instance concerning the admission to doctoral education, training components and supervision, has also been fostered

---

56 Misunderstandings about reform in doctoral education due to American forms of doctoral education have also been observed by Enders (2004a).

by the broader context. An administrator of the University of Zurich underlines in particular the influence of recommendations formulated in the framework of the Bologna meeting of 2003 in Berlin and the Salzburg seminar of 2005, the rectors' conferences of Switzerland, Germany and Austria, by the European University Association and the League of European Research Universities, of which the University of Zurich is a member.

V.1.2. Three Types of Management Instruments

Three types of management instruments have been used in the framework of the identified three reform episodes: a new recruitment procedure for doctoral students, normative elements, and conditioned funding.

The new recruitment procedure concerns two elements of paradigmatic change. The first element consists in the collective advertisement, which does not anymore exclusively take place per individual position, but is carried out and in the name of the Life Science Zurich Graduate School or of one of its PhD programmes for a number of doctoral positions. This is done on a broad basis, namely in worldwide diffused journals like "Nature". The objective is to attract a pool of candidates for a pool of doctoral positions. As a second change, applications of potential candidates are evaluated by an admission committee composed of three to four supervisors, belonging to the PhD programme chosen by the candidate, instead of the direct recruitment of doctoral students through individual supervisors. After a first selection round based on written applications, a limited number of candidates is invited to interviews in Zurich. Interviews essentially consist in the candidates' presentation of their previous research (usually their master research) and of their main research interests, discussions with potential supervisors and the visit of corresponding laboratories. Once a "match" between a candidate and a supervisor has been found, the candidates have to formally enrol as doctoral students at the corresponding institutional administration. The latter examine whether the candidates respect the formal requirements, especially in terms of previous degrees. However, the administrators underline that possible doubts about the degrees' value would be usually examined before the invitation of candidates to the interview round. As a consequence, this last step of the recruitment process, the formal enrolment, does hardly represent any obstacle. This new recruitment procedure – called "Track I" – takes place twice a year. In addition to this Track I recruitment procedure, doctoral students can still be directly recruited by supervisors, without undergoing the two selection rounds but still with the obligation to formally enrol as doctoral student in the institutional administration.[57] This "Track II" recruitment procedure partly[58] reflects the logic of what Musselin (2005) calls internal academic labour markets (Musselin 2005), namely to the extent that it mainly concerns doctoral students who already did their previous studies in one of the two concerned institutions.

Among the normative elements, one has to distinguish the more or less informal regulations of the LSZGS and each PhD programme from the formal PhD regulations of the according HEI. Those normative elements are here examined with respect to training and supervision activities. Regarding doctoral students' duties in terms of training, the respective institutional PhD regulations define the general framework, which consists of a training volume equivalent to at least twelve credit points (ETHZ 2000; ETHZ 2008; Mathematisch-naturwissenschaftliche Fakultät der Universität Zürich 2002). This formal requirement of a curricular component within doctoral education is a novelty. In the case of the ETHZ, at least a third of those credits has to be acquired outside of the research domain. Furthermore, the more recent regulations precise that credits are only awarded in case of a "personal contribution" through the doctoral student. In addition, credits have to be gained either in the framework of a regulated PhD programme or an individually composed programme. Finally, the recent regulations also mention possibilities – but not requirements – for supervision through additional supervisors than only the main one as well as for yearly progress reports. In case of a demand coming from either the supervisor or the doctoral student himself, the doctoral student writes a report which the supervisor has to

57 In the case of certain PhD programmes, doctoral candidates nevertheless have to pass through the interview round, even though they already got a „match" with a supervisor before.

58 The other characteristic Musselin (2005: 138) attributes to internal labour markets, namely that "rules and incentives organize such a development", does not necessarily apply to this case study.

immediately comment in a written form (ETHZ 2008). PhD regulations at the Faculty of Mathematics and Natural Sciences at University of Zurich vary compared to the ones of ETHZ especially regarding three points: first, decisions about the composition of the curricular component are delegated to the individual disciplines; second, thesis committees of at least two members are compulsory; third, follow-up reports are not mentioned, neither as an obligation nor as an explicit possibility (Mathematisch-naturwissenschaftliche Fakultät der Universität Zürich 2002; 2002a).

Thus, besides the general requirement of a curricular part with a certain volume, formal requirements remain quite unrestrictive. As a consequence, the LSZGS as well as the individual PhD programmes have all the more freedom in defining their own *internal requirements.* A first internal LSZGS requirement concerns the doctoral students' obligation to participate in a PhD programme's training activities. Here, a distinction between Track I and Track II doctoral students is made. In principle, the LSZGS internal rule says that doctoral students who were recruited through the Track I are obliged to participate, whereas Track II doctoral students can decide themselves where and how to acquire their training component. Other internal requirements are more or less formally defined according to the LSZGS PhD programme. The Molecular Life Sciences PhD programme disposes of a written regulation defining certain activities as compulsory, whereas this is not the case for the PhD programme in Biomolecular Structure and Mechanism. Nevertheless, the latter's introductory course is declared compulsory for each doctoral student. In the same vain, no written statement currently exists concerning the functioning and composition of the thesis committee. The LSZGS administrator underlines that many regulations still have to be elaborated. Many things have been done in a precipitated way. Accordingly, certain elements often work on the basis of "gentleman agreements". Gentleman agreements also determine the supervisors' engagement within the individual PhD programmes. Instead of being formally obliged to contribute to the PhD programmes in terms of course teaching or candidates pre-selection, they have rather a moral obligation: both the heads of the LSZGS and of the PhD programme in Biomolecular Structure and Mechanism emphasise that it would not be judged correct if a supervisor would recruit his doctoral students through the PhD programme without contributing through course teaching or other types of activities.

Two instruments which apply to this case study can be considered as constituting the third type of instruments, namely the one of conditioned funding. The different LSZGS PhD programmes have varying types of mostly ad hoc funding. In the case of the PhD programme Biomolecular Structure and Mechanism, the funding base comes from the NCCR Structural Biology. As each NCCR, the latter has to respect the formal condition of providing training possibilities for doctoral students who are financed through the NCCR project. However, no further requirements are specified in relation with this condition. This opens possibilities for synergies between the NCCR and the PhD programme. Among others, the NCCR funding can be used for the funding of the PhD programme training activities, since most of them are simultaneously considered as NCCR training activities. Hence, costs related to the recruitment procedures – like the invited candidates' flights and hotel accommodation – as well as the PhD programme's retreat can be funded through this source. However, as every NCCR is only funded for a limited period of time, this source will sooner or later dry up. Thus, like in the case of the other LSZGS PhD programmes as well as the LSZGS itself – a certain number of costs are covered by the entity LSZGS[59] – a new funding source has to be found.

Confronted to this generally unstable financial situation, the LSZGS asked, in the name of all its PhD programmes the governing bodies of both the ETHZ and the University of Zurich for stable funding. The University of Zurich succeeded in getting supplementary funding of their cantonal government for the further implementation of the Bologna declaration, namely the reform of the doctoral level. However, instead of simply redistributing the obtained money on the different faculties, the University Board decided to relate the funding's distribution to concrete reforms. Thus, only faculties who revise their doctoral regulations to a certain extent – e.g. by introducing clear admission criteria, the obligation for thesis committees, a minimal training component, a doctoral agreement between doctoral student and supervisor, etc. – get

59 The LSZGS's administrator's salary, the invited lecturers' salaries, web page, etc. (LSZGS 2009).

related funding.[60] Furthermore, supplementary possibilities, like a fast-track for the best master students, might be part of the reform, without, however, being a funding condition.[61] The supplementary funding of the canton Zurich is provided for the period 2008-2012. One consequence of this is that funding for the year 2008 had to be attributed to programmes under the anticipation of future changes in doctoral regulations, since time was not sufficient for the necessary legal change. Indeed, LSZGS PhD programmes got a certain amount of money (LSZGS 2009). Another consequence concerns the a priori – again – limited period of funding. The current supplementary funding is unstable project funding. In other words, if the according amount will not become part of the ordinary cantonal university budget, new solutions have again to be found. The situation is slightly different with respect to ETHZ. The latter HEI also decided to co-fund the LSZGS and its programmes (until 2010), though with a proportionally significantly lower amount of money (about a third of the University per capita contribution). However, ETHZ holds out a long-term funding in case of positive evaluation of the LSZGS and its member programmes (MLS 2009).

V.1.3. A Federal System

All interviewed actors underline that the initiative, which led to the first and second reform episodes, has been taken in a bottom-up process by a group of professors, without any influence from the central HEI governing bodies. LSZGS' first leader states that, arriving from American higher education in Switzerland, he found it "a bit strange" that no PhD programmes with curricular components and own

60 Such elements are developed in the University Zurich „model PhD regulation" (Universität Zürich Fachstelle Studienreform 2007).

61 Fast-tracks, essentially consisting in an overall shorter education duration until the award of the doctoral degree, are also figuring as a possibility in the revised ETHZ doctoral regulation (ETHZ 2008). In the case of biology, both HEIs give this possibility to outstanding master students who accomplish a certain number of criteria. Time saving is planned at the master level to the extent that the master thesis can be replaced by components belonging to the doctoral degree, like the writing of the doctoral project.

recruitment procedures existed. He met some other professors at the University of Zurich and ETHZ who agreed to take the initiative.

Confronted to their own success in terms of steadily growing numbers of applying and recruited doctoral students, this group of professors also decided by itself to clone the PhD programme in Molecular Life Science and to found the LSZGS.

LSZGS is managed by a steering committee which is composed of the heads of all LSZGS PhD programmes. This steering committee meets in order to discuss and decide about the strategic development of LSZGS, the advice and support for the PhD programmes and the graduate school administration, the development of common criteria for quality assurance of the PhD programmes, the promotion of relevant contacts within the scientific community of life sciences, the identification of common course needs, the development of a transferable skill curriculum and the identification of joint funding initiatives (LSZGS 2009). Still at the graduate school level, the individual PhD programme administrators meet in order to discuss administrative implications of the graduate school's activities. One involved professor underlines the importance of the graduate school's organisation through the immediately participating people. This would make possible that the needs of the respective disciplines can be taken into account. According to the LSZGS administrator power is mainly situated in the individual PhD programmes:

> It's perhaps also a bit like in a federal system as in Switzerland. Most power remains in the programmes and then they decide about how the graduate school shall function. [...] One would like to interfere as few as possible. They shall do what they want to do and somehow those programmes shall also be in contrast to each other.[62]

According to the LSZGS head, the PhD programmes' autonomy concerns in particular the content of their curricular components. In the case of the PhD programme in Biomolecular Structure, this autonomy seems to be delegated to the individual teaching academics: the interviewed professors declare that they are autonomous regarding the content of the courses they teach in the framework of the programme.

62 Many quotes are translated from other languages. In order to facilitate the lecture, we renounce to a systematic indication of the quotes' original text.

Since each of them basically teaches topics of his respective speciality, no overlap would be produced.

Interviewees mention a number of objectives which they relate to the LSZGS and the individual programmes' activities. A first overall objective can be qualified as strategic, a second series of objectives rather as practical. As a representative statement for the interviewees we here quote the LSZGS head's definition of the overall objective:

> To bring the best and most promising students to Zurich and to give them the best possible education at the level of research and curricular development. More or less, we would like to create the next generation of leaders in life sciences.

He also specifies that this objective has to be understood in a broader sense going beyond academia. Thus, the objective would be achieved if their candidates become leaders within academia but also industry. From a student's point of view, he defines as objective that a doctoral student learns how to become an independent researcher. More practical objectives are mentioned in relation with the concrete activities of the LSZGS and PhD programme Biomolecular Structure and Mechanism. First of all, the collective form of the recruitment process aims at a certain rationalisation. Instead of inviting certain candidates for one certain position, candidates are, at least in theory, eligible for several different doctoral positions. Thus, if it turns out during the interview process that an invited candidate does not fit into the originally planned position, he may better fit into another position of another supervisor.[63] Another thought related to this objective of rationalisation concerns the distribution of good candidates among supervisors. Thanks to this collective recruitment process, younger, less well known supervisors have a better chance to get good doctoral students. A second operational objective, related to the curricular component, concerns the teaching of discipline-specific competences: according to interviewees, significant publications in the aforementioned field require many different techniques. Therefore, courses with the purpose to teach such techniques are of importance. Furthermore, courses shall also help achieving the third objective, namely to give doctoral students the possibility to have a

63 In this case study, doctoral positions (and their funding) are mostly strongly related to a certain more or less predefined research project.

look beyond their immediate doctoral research project and to qualify them for the broader non-academic job market. A supervisor mentions a fourth objective, also relating to the curricular activities, which can be qualified as socio-scientific. In a first rather social sense, programme activities may be an opportunity of foreign doctoral students to quickly build a social network going beyond the doctoral students of their research group, which might be important especially in the beginning of their doctoral education. In a second more socio-scientific sense, more social event like activities like a retreat may also foster scientific exchange among doctoral students about for instance varying scientific techniques. In the same sense, contacts with invited academics may lead to the same exchange effect: in case of necessity, doctoral students know who to address to. In addition, an interviewed supervisor also underlines that exchange with invited academics may help doctoral students reducing possible inhibitions towards "scientific stars" and building networks. Finally, a fifth objective consists in enlarged supervision through supervision committees.

The first and second reform episodes have almost exclusively been shaped by the involved academic profession, whereas international actors and central HEI governing bodies of ETHZ and the University of Zurich became more central regarding the third reform episode, thus, what we called institutionalisation. According to a central administrator of the University of Zurich, the implementation of the next reform step of "Bologna", hence, the reform of the doctoral level, has been immediately set on the institutional agenda after the ministries' meeting in 2005 in Bergen. In 2007, the enlarged University Direction[64] recommends to implement the reform at doctoral level according to the suggestions made by the Rectors' Conferences of Switzerland, Germany and Austria (2004) as well as by the European University Association (2005), which have been elaborated shortly before the "Bergen communiqué" and built its basis. The attraction of outstanding doctoral students is also defined as an objective at the central university level (Universität Zürich Erweiterte Universitätsleitung 2007). However,

64 *Erweiterte Universitätsleitung*. This body is composed of the rector, three vice-rectors, the administrative director, all deans and respectively two representatives of the private-docents, assistants and students. Further members without voting right are part of it (Universität Zürich 1998).

according to the interviewed administrator, this objective could – mostly for financial reasons – not be pursued in a comprehensive manner. Therefore, it would concern in particular scientific domains, where the University is particularly strong, among others in biology. Also in 2007, the League of European Research Universities (LERU) put the reform of doctoral education on its agenda. As a LERU member, the University of Zurich saw its reform efforts as reconfirmed. However, it was already in 2006 that the responsible vice-rector of the University of Zurich addressed the cantonal government concerning supplementary funding for the reform of the doctoral level. Once accorded, the University Board, which is composed of the responsible member of the cantonal government as well as other appointed personalities of science, culture, economy and politics (Universität Zürich 1998) got the responsibility to distribute the obtained money. Thus, it is also this body, which can judge whether the faculties' new doctoral regulations correspond to the formulated requirements in a sufficient way. According to the central University administrator the overall objective of those reform efforts consists of structuring doctoral education regarding two aspects, namely supervision and training. Supervision shall be optimised through the introduction of regular meetings with the thesis committee composed of three supervisors. Structured training shall give deepened discipline-specific but also broader competences to the doctoral students.

At the central governing level of ETHZ, interest for a certain reform of doctoral education became already visible in the introduction of a compulsory curricular component in its doctoral regulations of 2000. In its strategic planning for the period 2004-2007, the ETH Board – i.e. the strategic management and supervisory body of the ETH-Domain – launched the idea of introducing graduate schools at ETHZ and its sister institution in Lausanne. The ETH Board even defines the establishment of a world class graduate school[65] as target (ETH-Rat 2003: 33). According to the ETHZ' pro-rector, the ETHZ president of the period 2005-2006[66] was determined to achieve this goal and suggested the

65 In German: *"Die ETH Zürich baut eine Graduate School von Weltformat auf"* (ETH-Rat 2003: 33).

66 Due to the strong resistance of the group of professors towards his plans of changes in the institution's organisational structures, the president resigned after only eleven months.

comprehensive introduction of “Graduate Schools”. Also his successor ad interim relaunched the idea of an “ETHZ Graduate School”, among others also by referring to “Bologna” (Osterwalder 2006). However, according to the interviewed ETHZ pro-rector, this idea has been rejected by the departments. Therefore, the introduction of structured PhD programmes has become voluntary.

V.1.4. Network Managerialism and a breeze of the Neo-Weberian-State

What is the management story behind this case study and to what extent can it explain the occurred three reform episodes? The first and second reform episodes, that is to say the pioneer and corporatisation episodes, are essentially shaped by elements of the Network Governance narrative as well as to a lesser extent by the New Public Management narrative. In contrast, the third reform episode, institutionalisation, is mainly characterised by the Neo-Weberian-state narrative.

Regarding the first and second reform episode, elements of New Public Management are principally visible in the new recruitment instrument and the normative framework regulating the curricular component. Though not formulated in quantitative terms, the increasing attraction of good candidates can be seen as a measure of performance. Private-sector styles of management are applied by increasingly using PR techniques. The latter are visible in the broader advertisement forms for doctoral positions. As a concrete result of this new recruitment instrument, the number of applications for doctoral positions – first in the case of the Molecular Life Science PhD programme, then in the overall LSZGS – increased significantly. The recruitment instrument expresses also two further New Public Management characteristics: on the one side, greater competition for doctoral positions can be noticed. However, the recruitment instrument is not applied in a comprehensive way. As a result, some “internal” doctoral students are still recruited according to the Track II procedure, that means individually by their supervisors, without going through the complete competitive selection process like Track I doctoral students. On the other side, the recruitment instrument also reveals stress on resource use. This efficiency concern is visible in the collective form of the recruitment instrument, which consists in the attraction of a pool of candidates for a pool of doctoral positions. Doctoral candidates, who did not find “a match” with a professor for a certain position, may find an agreement with another supervisor for another position. This way, high investments, which were carried out for the invited candidates’ flights, are less risky and losses may be avoided. Interviews with doctoral students show that such non-planned matches effectively take place. If the central New Public Management characteristic “explicit standards and measures of performance” does not completely apply to the recruitment procedure, it can be more clearly seen regarding doctoral training. Corresponding PhD regulations of both HEIs define a minimum of twelve credit points as a standard. In addition, doctoral students’ performances in the framework of their training activities are examined and awarded by corresponding credit points.

The establishment of organised PhD programmes and the LSZGS could be interpreted as another New Public Management element, namely as the disaggregation of units in the public sector into corporatized units around the product “doctoral education”. However, such an interpretation would be inappropriate to the extent that the PhD programmes and the graduate school do not disaggregate but complement old units. They are supplementary providers of training programmes, supervision opportunities and means to attract doctoral students. As a result, older units still go on carrying out their functions: the apprentice-ship model and the laboratory are still a basic unit for supervision and the institutional doctoral administration still examines applications for the enrolments as doctoral student from a formal point of view.

The fact that tasks like formal admission examination are not (yet) delegated to the new units of PhD programmes and the graduate school may also be related to the actors who initiated the new units’ establishment. In this case study, the latter are not the result of a for instance presidential top-down decision but of a bottom-up initiative coming from an informal group of supervisors. From this point on, the management story leading to the first and second reform episodes is strongly shaped by Network Governance characteristics. Indeed, the composition of the network of actors, which is central in this case study, corresponds to a certain extent to what a central Network Governance characteristic describes: a greater range of actors and interactions emerge. Supervisors and doctoral students from two different HEIs as well as invited, often foreign, academics form this network. Interaction between such types of actors in the framework of doctoral education is not necessarily new. However, what is new is that interactions are organised and more or less regular. Hence, they are less random. This network is quite strongly self-organising and self-steering. It defines its own main objectives – the attraction and training of an increasing number of good doctoral students –, which are implemented accordingly, since no other management instrument impedes their concrete measures. As a result, inter-institutional recruitment procedures, training programmes and supervision committees are established. Furthermore, the network organises its own steering structures, which consists of the LSZGS steering committee and autonomous individual PhD programmes, led by their respective heads. This "federal system" expresses two further Network Governance characteristics, namely the coordination of power between actors at multiple levels and lateral rather than vertical forms of management. Those Network Governance features have a concrete impact on the present case study: differences between individual PhD programmes, supervisors and doctoral students exist. For instance, individual training programmes differ regarding their volume and compulsory character, some professors in life sciences at both HEIs are engaged in tasks related to the running of the programmes whereas others are not, and Track I doctoral students are obliged to follow a training programme whereas Track II doctoral students of some programmes are free to decide themselves upon their participation. Finally, in the case of the PhD programme Biomolecular Structure and Mechanism, a further typical Network Governance characteristic appears. Through its research funding instrument NCCR, which conditions inter-institutional cooperation and the offer of a doctoral training programme, the state worked as relationship facilitator. The NCCR Structural Biology's start in 2001 contributed to the development of a cooperative climate, from which the PhD programme Biomolecular Structure benefits.

In contrast to the first and second reform episodes, the management story of the third "institutionalisation" episode is mainly shaped by features of the Neo-Weberian-state narrative. Indeed, public authorities react to new developments in the field of doctoral education: in the case of the ETHZ, the ETH Board, as a sort of representative of the Federal Government, took the initiative and defined the institutionalisation of graduate schools at ETHZ as strategic goal. As a reaction to "Bologna", the cantonal government of Zurich provides extra funding for the reform of doctoral education. Thus, in terms of Neo-Weberian-state language one can say that attempts of formalising new aspects of doctoral education have also been made in both cases. However, at least for the moment, the success of those attempts is rather modest: the ETH Board wanted the ETHZ to introduce graduate schools in all disciplinary domains. This objective has been rejected by parts of professors. Concerning the university, the cantonal extra funding will probably also require a certain formalisation and thereby increased institutionalisation of aspects which until now have been dealt with in "gentleman agreements". Such a formalisation would open the door towards an increased administrative and political control of those aspects. However, since this initiative is currently in the process of implementation, such assumptions remain for the moment hypothetical. The same applies to further potential Neo-Weberian-state characteristics like the stabilisation of the field's function, a more efficient control of costs and a tighter steering of it through the state. However, considering the generally increased institutional autonomy of Swiss HEIs towards their respective public authorities (Baschung et al. 2009), those last three Neo-Weberian-state characteristics seem rather unlikely to apply. In opposite, it is more likely that a certain formalisation of those new aspects of doctoral education – i.e. training volume, supervision committees, etc. – may lead to a New Public Management characteristic, namely more explicit standards and measures of performance. If this would be the case, differences between PhD programmes, supervisors and doctoral students such as mentioned above, might appear less frequently.

V.1.5. Managerial Power for a redefined "College" of Academics

If one examines the role played by the varying actors figuring in the "Actors' Framework B" (see III.4.) in the reform described above, three main statements can be made. First, the number of actors who intervene on doctoral education has indeed increased but this does not seriously threaten the reinforced power of professors. On the one side, public authorities – federal and cantonal ones – either "personally" or through intermediary bodies like the National Science Foundation and the ETH

Board step in, essentially by funding doctoral research and training. Yet, their degree of influence on concrete regulation of doctoral education is rather weak. On the other side, the desire of increasing intervention is also visible in the case of the ETHZ governing body. Yet, besides the definition of a minimal volume for doctoral training and the formal control of the admission procedure, attempts for further centralised and uniform organisation of doctoral education failed. Professors from a number of departments successfully refused the introduction of an ETHZ Graduate School. In contrast, thanks to a number of NPM instruments, professors have quite large control on many central aspects of doctoral education like the recruitment of doctoral students, the definition and evaluation of training programmes as well as the supervision of doctoral students. Thus, it seems fair to speak of managerialism – though not in an extreme form – through professors.

Besides this managerialism through professors, a second statement can be made: individual power of professors is complemented and even partly replaced by collegial power. Yet, this is not a simple return to collegialism in the sense of consensus based decisions among colleagues of a same discipline or department within one institution. The "college"[67] is redefined! On the one hand, only professors and other supervisors who engage in the doctoral programme are part of it. In other words, the ones who do not engage lose part of their power in favour of the "new college". On the other hand, the "college" does not anymore respect institutional boundaries but is trans-institutional! Thus, in this case, doctoral education is largely determined by a trans-institutional college of academics.

Finally, a third statement concerns the role of doctoral students. They have definitely been recognised as central "research producers". Their PhD project is not anymore considered as a personal life's work, but as a crucial piece for the success of a local scientific community on the world-wide scientific scenery. All identified NPM elements focus on doctoral students. This clearly expresses that doctoral students and their work are considered as being too precious (and expensive) to be left to chance. Hence, they are increasingly and more systematically selected, trained, advised and followed.

---

67 Here as well as in the further chapters, the term "college" is – unless specified – never used in the sense of a HEI but in the sense of a community of academics.

V.2. Molecular and Computational Biology Research School

This second case study deals with the Molecular and Computational Biology (MCB) Research School which has been founded in 2006. Its founding bodies are the Department of Molecular Biology, the Department of Informatics – both situated at the Faculty of Mathematics and Natural Sciences of University of Bergen –, the Computational Biology Unit at the Bergen Center for Computational Science and the Sars International Centre for Marine Molecular Biology. Those latter two research centres are organised under the Unifob research organisation.[68] One further unit, the Department of Biomedicine at the Faculty of Medicine and Dentistry has joined MCB Research School in 2007.[69] All those composing bodies are situated in Bergen. Currently about 60 doctoral students are following MCB Research School activities.

V.2.1. Establishing an Interdisciplinary Research School[70]

The reform story of this case study consists of two episodes. The first episode can be called *local networking*, the second episode *continuity*. The local networking episode brought three changes. The first change involves the creation of a training programme explicitly addressing doctoral students in the fields of molecular and computational biology enrolled at one of the units mentioned above. This doctoral training programme comprises, first, an introductory course to research in molecular and computational biology, second, a series of courses and workshops related to the disciplines of MCB Research School, third, a

68 Unifob is a non-profit research organisation, owned by the University of Bergen (85%) and the Foundation for University Research in Bergen (15%). Source: www.unifob.no; downloaded in September 2009.

69 Source: www.mcb.uib.no; downloaded in September 2009.

70 Unless other sources are indicated, used data originate from interviews with University of Bergen's vice-rector, University of Bergen's PhD administrator, the Faculty of Mathematics and Natural Science's dean and one administrator of the same Faculty, the head and two further professors of MCB Research School as well as four doctoral students participating in MCB Research School.

MCB Research School seminar series, a scientific communication module containing a course in scientific writing, and a MCB Research School PhD Forum, and fourth, a science theory, history and ethics course.[71] If this general pattern has been maintained during MCB Research School's creation, its concrete content and form might have slightly changed from year to year. In 2009, the introductory course is divided into two steps. In the first, two days lasting, step, MCB Research School is presented, the doctoral students introduce themselves and several general aspects of research like experimental design, "selling science", the popularisation of research, the dynamics of research and project management are dealt with. In a second step, composed of four individual half-day lasting sessions, the research activities of the different MCB Research School member laboratories are presented to the doctoral students. The training programme's second component consists in 2009 of three intensive one-week courses.[72] In the same year, the third component consists of a three-day course called "effective life-science writing in English", a one-day course in "experimental design and data analysis" and one "PhD Day" per term (PhD Forum) which aims at providing a platform for social and scientific exchange among all doctoral students affiliated to MCB Research School. In addition to those "pure" MCB Research School training activities, a few other courses from other Norwegian universities are explicitly open to doctoral students affiliated to MCB Research School.

The second change related to MCB Research School concerns the establishment of a local network of doctoral students and supervisors in the fields of molecular and computational biology. Several supervisors as well as doctoral students emphasise that in spite of intellectual and geographical proximity, the various units involved into MCB Research School were only weakly connected before MCB Research School's creation. Thus, thanks to MCB Research School activities, the awareness about the colleagues' research topics and techniques as well as the

71 This course figures on the official MCB Research School training programme. However, it is organised at the level of the Faculty of mathematics and natural sciences at UiB. In addition, it has been introduced before the creation of MCB research school, with the revision of the Faculty's PhD regulation in 2003. Thus, it is not really a novelty related to the creation of the MCB research school.

72 "Recombinant proteins – Expression, Purification & Interaction studies", "Fish as Models for Medical Research" and "Integrative Bioinformatics".

exchange among doctoral students and MCB Research School supervisors have increased. According to several interviewees, this has not only enlarged the various network members' scientific horizon but also accelerate the research process.

The third change involved by MCB Research School concerns the introduction of supervision committees, consisting of at least two supervisors. Interviewed supervisors and doctoral students attribute two functions to those supervision committees. On the one hand, it is seen as a possibility to add further scientific, methodological or technical expertise to the doctoral student's supervision, in particular in the case of interdisciplinary research projects. On the other hand, the additional supervisor(s) is seen as "security measure" in case of conflicts between the doctoral student and his main supervisor. In the latter case, the main supervisor could be replaced by an additional one.

The second reform episode, the one of continuity, concerns the Norwegian Research Council's initiative for National Research Schools. Considering that MCB Research School's profile would not fit with the criteria given by the Norwegian Research Council, the MCB board renounced to submit an application to the call for National Research Schools. According to MCB Research School's administrator, MCB Research School covers "a broad range of research which is opposed to the Research Council's wish for a more clear cut and focussed research profile." Thus, the MCB Research School did not become a National Research School and still remains organised at the local level of Bergen. However, two academics of the Faculty are involved in one of the five National Research Schools which have been selected in 2009, the Structural Biology Research School. According to the MCB leader, MCB doctoral students also have access to this National Research School thanks to the two academics' involvement.

Those varying changes have to be situated in a certain number of contextual elements. First of all, several interviewees mentioned the national evaluation report of Norwegian doctoral education as a major source of input directing to the establishment of research schools. However, compared to the other scientific disciplines, the Faculty of Mathematics and Natural Sciences did significantly better with respect to completion rates, overall duration and age of doctoral graduates.[73] Since, the establishment of research schools has been recommended as a sort of "medicine" to the problems experienced by the other disciplines several supervisors first did not feel urged to implement a research school. In addition, initial hopes that the creation of a research school would generate additional money from the national level had to be quickly abandoned. According to the involved supervisors' statements, they then realised that a Research School may nevertheless be a possibility to improve certain aspects of doctoral education. One aspect consisted in the Faculty's course offer at doctoral level. At least in the case of molecular biology, this course offer has been inexistent during several years until the establishment of MCB Research School.[74] Thus, doctoral students had either to find themselves course offers in other places or to attend regular courses at bachelor and master levels in order to fulfil the institutional requirement of 30 credit points.[75] The latter solution has been negatively judged both by supervisors and doctoral students. According to them, courses at bachelor and master levels were often irrelevant with respect to the doctoral students' research topics and, unlike intensive one-week courses, interrupted once or even twice a week the doctoral students' experimental work in the laboratories.

Interviewed supervisors also argued that MCB Research School represented an opportunity for increased collaboration between the different participating research units, not only among doctoral students but also supervisors themselves. They expressed their hope that such collaboration would lead to new interdisciplinary research. A final argument has been seen in connection with a broader national research policy issue, namely the recognition of certain research units as centre of excellence. A research school might be an added value which favours such achievements.

---

73 Between 1993 and 1997, 52% of all doctoral students in the Faculty of Mathematics and Natural Sciences finished their doctorate after 5.5 years, whereas only 35% did in the Faculty of Humanities. In the year 2000, the average age of the first group was situated at 33.5 years, whereas it was of 41.8 years for the second group (Kyvik 2002).

74 One supervisor underlined that one doctoral course existed on a regular basis some years before MCB Research School's creation.

75 According to MCB Research School's head, the new PhD regulation (2003) have lowered the number of required credit points for students in natural sciences.

V.2.2. Top-Down Requirements and Bottom Means

Two types of management instruments have been used in the framework of the reform MCB Research School is part of: on the one hand, financial instruments, on the other hand, legal instruments. Two instruments figure among those related to funding. The first one immediately concerns the funding of MCB Research School. No funding has been obtained from the national, central university or Faculty levels. According to the head of MCB Research School, the school's funding is composed of an equal contribution of each of the five partners. In 2008, the amount of money asked to each partner was 100,000 Norwegian Krones (NOK) (~12,000 €). He underlines that those various contributions are currently provided regardless of the number of involved doctoral students per MCB Research School member, an issue which he expects to be discussed in the future. The total amount of money is essentially used for the funding of a 50% administrative position, teaching activities from external lecturers, social gatherings and travel fellowships for doctoral students. The latter are provided in order to fund costs related to conference visits of doctoral students who are member of MCB Research School. In some cases, supplementary funding is sought by other funding sources like NordForsk[76] in order to fund certain courses. The second funding instrument is part of the result-based reallocation (*resultatbasert omfordeling*) of funding provided from the Norwegian Ministry of Education and Research (*Kunnskaps-departementet*). One component of this reallocation system, which has been introduced with the quality reform in Norwegian higher education in 2003, concerns the number of completed doctoral degrees per University. Thus, the Norwegian Ministry of Education and Research allocates a certain amount of money for each completed doctoral degree to the University of Bergen which is varying from year to year.[77] In 2009 it was 370,000 NOK (~44,000 €). The university then allocates this

76 "NordForsk is a Nordic research board with responsibility for cooperation on research and researcher training in the Nordic region." Source: www.nordforsk.org; downloaded September 2009.

77 The annual variation is due to the fact that the total amount allocated by the Ministry for completed doctoral degrees is stable from year to year. Thus, the allocated amount *per doctoral degree* depends on the total number of completed doctoral degrees.

amount to the Faculties. 75% of the allocated sum is determined by a stable basis, 25% is based on effective results in terms of completed doctoral degrees. In the case of the Faculty of Mathematics and Natural Sciences, 75,000 NOK (~9,000 €) of this amount remains at Faculty level in order to cover expenses related to the thesis defence, the evaluation committee (*bedømmelsekomite*) and the printing of the doctoral thesis. The remaining amount is allocated to the institutes within which the degrees have been completed.

Besides those funding instruments, two instruments of legal character determine a certain normative framework for doctoral education and MCB Research School. The first one consists in the PhD regulations of University of Bergen, which have been approved and entered into force in 2003. Among other elements, those PhD regulations deal with admission, follow-up, research training, compulsory termination, evaluation, etc. A certain number of those aspects are specified through a written contract or agreement between the admitted doctoral student, his supervisor(s), the corresponding department and the Faculty. In particular, this contract and the PhD regulations more clearly define the doctoral students', the faculties' and the supervisors' responsibilities: first of all, doctoral students are obliged to complete a training programme of at least 30 credit points. The only explicitly defined compulsory training component of those 30 credit points consist of a course in theory of science and ethics. Second, the Faculties have either to provide an appropriated training programme or to arrange the candidate's participation in programmes of other Faculties or institutions. Third, in the framework of their application for a scholarship, doctoral students had to define among others their research programme with a corresponding schedule comprising deadlines. The regulations state that progress with respect to the doctoral research, such as defined in the application, has to be yearly reported in separate reports, one by the doctoral candidate and another by the principal supervisor. These reports are to be sent to and approved by the Faculty or other units to which the Faculty has delegated this function. In case of non-respect of the doctoral student's duties like the delivery of the yearly reports or fundamental delay in research progress, compared to the defined schedule, which would raise doubts about a successful completion in time, doctoral students can be eliminated from the doctoral programme. Fourth, the supervisor ought to provide advice concerning the formulation and delimitation of the thesis and research questions in the research project, consider suitable hypotheses and methods, help the candidate to find specialist literature and basic data sources and discuss the plan and execution of the paper (University of Bergen 2003; 2003a).

The second instrument of legal character, which again concerns the whole University of Bergen, is called *action plan for doctoral education* (Universitetet i Bergen 2009). The document's subtitle, "From life-work to career start" (*Fra livsverk til karrierestart*), indicates doctoral education's new role, namely a step within a training period preparing the professional career, instead of being the career's culmination. A number of concrete measures of reform are defined in the report. Among others, each doctoral student should have at least two supervisors, have access to a research group and/or a research school, and be given the possibility of a sojourn abroad during doctoral education. Furthermore, a new regulation about intermediary evaluation and follow-up of the doctoral students' progress as well as the conditions of the doctoral students' elimination of doctoral programmes shall be established. In addition, information about training opportunities should be collected. This action plan has been decided upon by the university direction (*universitetsstyret*) of University of Bergen. According to the PhD administrator of University of Bergen, it has to be implemented by the Faculties until 2015.

Those two legal instruments define a certain normative framework. Simultaneously, they nevertheless leave some issues open. Most importantly, they clarify the responsibilities of each of the involved actors, but only to a certain extent. For instance, Faculties have the responsibility to provide doctoral students with an appropriated training programme or to arrange their participation in programmes of other Faculties or institutions. Furthermore, doctoral students have to complete a training component of 30 credit points, among which credits for a course in theory of science and ethics. However, such regulations do not oblige individual supervisors to get involved into activities of research schools, nor doctoral students to complete their curricular training component within a research school, even less within MCB Research School. This gives room for manoeuvre at a more individual level. Concerning the supervisors' involvement, only supervisors who are convinced of the added value of research schools engage in its running. With regard to the doctoral students' participation in MCB Research

School, the attitude of their respective supervisor(s) as well as their own conviction seems to be determining. Interviews both with supervisors and doctoral students showed that those attitudes and convictions vary in their degree. Some supervisors recommend MCB Research School to their doctoral students, whereas others make it a condition for recruitment. In other words, from a legal point of view, MCB Research School has no absolutely clearly defined status. To some extent, this unclear legal character is also reflected in the control of doctoral students' performance in the framework of MCB Research School's training programme. Although most of MCB Research School training activities imply the award of credit points, not all of them are evaluated through exams or other forms of control. Two main arguments are put forward by supervisors and doctoral students for this practice. On the one hand, the objective of MCB Research School training activities does not only consist in the teaching of knowledge whose memorisation by the doctoral students should be tested. An important part of the overall objective also concerns other issues like the doctoral students' familiarisation to a research environment. On the other hand, some interviewees also underlined that it should finally be the doctoral students' interest and own responsibility which makes them actively participate in MCB Research School activities. This argument reflects the idea according to which doctoral students are to be considered as early stage researcher rather than as students. Finally, still with respect to the attribution of responsibilities, it is worth underlining that the reporting of the doctoral students' progress is not carried out through MCB Research School but the Faculty's PhD programme. In other words, the training of doctoral students and their follow-up take place in two more or less separate organisational units.

V.2.3. Appropriation through the Academic Profession

According to our interviewees, the idea to establish research schools at University of Bergen is tightly related to the developments at national but also international levels. In the case of MCB Research School, the main background consists of the national evaluation report of doctoral education (see Kyvik 2002). However, the effective origin in terms of initiating actors who led to the creation of MCB Research School is somehow contended. The interviewed professors involved into MCB Research School perceived it rather as a top-down initiative. They stated having been strongly recommended by the vice-rector and Faculty to establish a research school. Interviewees at central university and Faculty levels spoke about a bottom-up initiative. They argued that their recommendation was of general nature and did not impose the establishment of research schools in particular scientific fields. That said the actors of the next steps on the way towards MCB Research School's establishment are uncontested. The posterior head of MCB Research School contacted the various heads of the partner units involved into MCB Research School in order to discuss the school's perimeter in terms of scientific disciplines, its types of activities and funding. They agreed to have a broader scope in terms of scientific disciplines then a research school focusing either on molecular biology or bioinformatics. However, according to the MCB Research School's head, the real problem concerned the funding question, since no additional funding came from the central university or Faculty levels. Finally, they agreed that every partner unit contributes 100,000 Norwegian Krones (~12,000 €). In early 2006, they submitted their elaborated proposition to the Faculty's committee for doctoral training (*forskerutdanningsutvalget*).[78] Among others, the committee of doctoral training deals with admission to doctoral education, acceptance of doctoral training plans of individual doctoral students, changes in complementary regulations and quality assurance in doctoral education. After a few modifications, MCB Research School has been accepted by the Faculty and the university board. A few months after MCB Research School's creation, the department of biomedicine at the Faculty of medicine and dentistry approached them regarding its participation. This demand has been accepted. Currently efforts are made to relate MCB Research School to other Nordic and international networks with the objective to widen the training offer. From the point of view of the interviewed professors,

78 This body is composed of the respective leaders of doctoral education of each institute (9), one representative of doctoral students, one representative of undergraduate students and led by the faculty's pro-dean. The faculty's head of studies is the body's secretary; Source: www.uib.no/mathnat; downloaded in September 2009.

MCB Research School's establishment period can be summarised by the following quote, stated by MCB Research School's head:

> Well, in the beginning of the discussion of research schools I was not really convinced of the necessity to have this system. Then, of course, the research school system was new to me. We didn't see what it was like or could become. So, it took a while to get over that feeling of another thing you have to do. So when we discussed it here, we made it kind of our initiative. We made it to our own thing. And I think this feeling is now part of the school. So it's our school and not something the university or faculty said we had to do.
>
> (Head of MCR Research School)

Today, MCB Research School is led by the MCB Research School board. The latter is composed of representatives of each involved unit – either heads of department or other members appointed by the respective heads of department – as well as two doctoral students. At the time of the interview, the MCB Research School board met about every second month. Issues of meeting essentially concern the school's training components as well as their funding. Initiatives for the creation of training activities come from the board itself but also individual lecturers. According to a MCB Research School board member, it would be no problem to mobilise lecturers for the introductory course, whereas it would be a bit more difficult to find people who volunteer for teaching additional intensive courses. Such courses are carried out by MCB Research School internal teacher but also by lecturers from external, mostly foreign, institutions. Since May 2008, the MCB Research School board has an own administrator who focuses on the organisation of the school activities and the development of the school in a larger Nordic and international network.

Several MCB Research School board members emphasised that MCB Research School is in a blurred situation from an organisational and functional point of view. On the one hand, MCB Research School is neither integrated into the usual institutional structures, nor is it an independent body. On the other hand, it is not dealing with all issues of doctoral education, but only with part of them. In particular, MCB Research School is not dealing with the recruitment and admission of doctoral students, and, neither with their follow-up concerning their progress. Those are responsibilities of the Faculty based PhD programmes and departments. The following quotes of two MCB Research School board members express those ambiguities:

> So where is the border between the activities of the school and the departments' responsibility because we are talking about a new structure in the system which is both between the departments and the Faculty. The school is under the Faculty, so it's the Faculty who has established the school but we are established by partners which are departments and units and funded by these departments and units. So we are in a way in between and on the top of the departments but we are under the Faculty. Our contents or our customers, I guess, are PhD candidates who are also at the same time hired by the department to take a PhD programme. Well there is a contract between the student and the department and the Faculty. So the research school is not a part of this contract. Our faculty staff is hired at the department level and we are taking part of this time to do activities within the research school. So it's always this kind of boarder discussions. Where goes the line between this, what we can do within the school, what should the purpose be, you see, we have a new construction which is very loosely built.
>
> (A professor involved in MCB Research School)

> Therefore, it's less of a school if you compare to other systems that might be outside, abroad, [where] the school is really a school that handles both, the admission to the programme checking it out at the end, and even they organise the thesis defence and everything.
>
> (A professor involved in MCB Research School)

The various involved actors were quite unanimous regarding the objectives related to MCB Research School. The first objective which has been underlined concerns the provision of a course offer specifically dedicated to doctoral students in the given scientific fields. This course offer should provide doctoral students with relevant courses – instead of less relevant courses at bachelor and master levels – and improve the quality of their overall doctoral training. A second objective is seen in the provision of an attractive learning environment consisting of a network of a considerable number of doctoral students and supervisors. Such a network should give doctoral students the feeling to belong to a wider network than exclusively the "network" composed of the doctoral student, his supervisor and possibly his laboratory colleagues. This especially applies to doctoral students who are completing their doctoral education in research units which are not in a department but in for instance Unifob but nevertheless are awarded the degree by the University of Bergen. In addition to the elimination of possible isolation, this widened network should also facilitate social and scientific exchange between its members. Through MCB Research School and in particular its introductory course such exchange gets an initial spark. Since the beginning, doctoral students are conscious of the research topics and techniques dealt with in other laboratories situated in Bergen. Thereby they know who to contact in case of interest or necessity linked to their own research project. A third objective goes into the same direction but considers this network from a more institutional point of view. Generally speaking, the local network between the various research units located in Bergen should be improved. Still in the same vein, a fourth objective mentioned by some interviewed professors consists in the stimulation of interdisciplinary research. By meeting doctoral students from other complementary research fields – thus, in the case under consideration, for instance a doctoral student in molecular biology meeting a doctoral student in bioinformatics – interdisciplinary cooperation should emerge. The interviewed dean also considered such interdisciplinary developments as particularly desirable since a lot of the groundbreaking research would take place between disciplines. According to him, an interdisciplinary research school is a good instrument for fostering such developments. Finally, some interviewed professors also mention the objective for MCB Research School as a meeting place for supervisors where they could mutually exchange their experience as supervisors. Thereby they could improve their practices as supervisors.

Two further potential objectives for MCB Research School are considered by the interviewees as rather ambiguous. The first of those two additional potential objectives concerns the attraction and recruitment of doctoral students through MCB Research School. On the one hand, one professor sees in MCB a potential for attracting talented doctoral students, in particular thanks to its particular combination of molecular biology and bioinformatics. On the other hand, all interviewees underline that the actual recruitment process takes place at the level of departments and faculty. Thus, MCB Research School as such is not dealing with the doctoral students' recruitment and therefore has no particular strategy regarding this issue. The second ambiguous objective concerns the doctoral students' preparation for the non-academic job market through MCB Research School. Some doctoral students consider in particular MCB Research School's network building activities as a plus, also with respect to the opening of opportunities on the non-academic job market. Supervisors also report that their former doctoral students would have found jobs in many varying job markets, among which also in public administration, management and industry. However, simultaneously, they state educating their doctoral students as future scientists. One supervisor argues that this is due to doctoral students' uniform motivation to do research and the fact that they are not so numerous that reflections about possible adaptations in their education to the non-academic job market would have imposed. Another supervisor argued that, being a "hard-academic" researcher, he would simply not be able to explicitly prepare doctoral students for jobs in industry. This apparent contradiction between the supervisors' academic background and their recently required task to educate doctoral students for non-academic jobs has also been raised by Dahan (2007).

V.2.4. Network Governance constrained by New Public Management

This section analyses the management story behind the occurred changes in the language of the three public management narratives of New Public Management, Network Governance and Neo-Weberian-state. Simultaneously, it is pointed out to what extent the described changes in doctoral education of this case study can be explained by this management story. The latter can be summarised as the one of a research school which is essentially amalgamating Network Governance characteristics but moving within an environment shaped by New Public Management features which constrain the school's freedom of action to a certain extent.

This story can be developed more in detail by the following illustration: the Network Governance part of the story begins with the state's role. Confronted with the results of the national evaluation report of doctoral education, the Ministry for Education and Research (2005) does not immediately decree concrete measures but contents itself by mandating the Norwegian Association of Higher Education Institutions (*Universitets- og Høgskolerådet* – UHR) and the Research Council of Norway (*Norges Forskningsråd* – NFR) to elaborate a scheme for research schools. Through those developments, the idea of research schools has definitely been launched and influenced the governing bodies of the University of Bergen and its Faculty of Mathematics and

Natural Sciences. Thus, the state's role corresponds to the one defined within the Network Governance narrative, namely that of an influencing instead of a directing state. Although this influence seems having been transmitted to the departments with a certain insistence, it would probably go to far to interpret it as a New Public Management characteristic like "Hands-on professional management", since neither the university nor the Faculty governing bodies imposed the precise scientific fields within which research schools had to be established. However, once dealt with at the department levels, MCB Research School definitely essentially depicts Network Governance characteristics. A new body composed of a number of various actors emerges and interacts. Within a lateral form of management and by sharing its coordination through the MCB Research School board, this body decides to develop a network for doctoral students and supervisors in an interdisciplinary field. The diffusion of best practices in terms of supervision within this network is also defined as an objective. In a self organising manner, the body decided to give itself certain financial resources by building an own budget and to create a training programme for interested doctoral students. Besides the idea of supervision committees and examinations for certain training activities, this network renounced to a large extent to defining explicit standards and measures of performance. Neither professors nor doctoral students of the corresponding scientific fields are obliged to get involved into this network as participant or teacher.

However, MCB Research School's environment is quite strongly determined by New Public Management features. Such a first feature can be seen in the fact that MCB Research School could not emerge in a completely autonomous manner but it had to be accepted by the Faculty body which is responsible of doctoral education, namely the committee for doctoral training, as well as by the University board. To a certain extent, the creation of the committee for doctoral training – which already took place in 1993 in the framework of the dr.scient. degree's introduction – can be considered as a New Public Management like change, that is to say a shift to a disaggregation of units in the public sector towards corporatized units around products. If one can disagree on whether disaggregation took place or not, the creation of a unit responsible of a number of aspects related to doctoral education certainly can be interpreted as a development towards a corporatized unit around a product, namely the product "doctoral education". Furthermore, the University of Bergen's PhD regulations determine standards and measures of performance regarding admission, training and follow-up procedure of doctoral students. Its action plan adds a further standard, namely the idea of multiple supervision through the compulsory introduction of supervision committees. Finally, the University's reward through the Ministry of Education and Research for each completed doctoral degree stands for a further typical New Public Management feature, that is to say a greater emphasis on output controls.

This management story can explain to quite some extent the occurred changes in doctoral education of this case study. Since the general idea of establishing research schools has been emphatically diffused from the national level downwards to the Faculty level, without, however, defining disciplinary and institutional boundaries, the initiating actors behind MCB Research School had the possibility to choose their partners in a self-organising manner, namely beyond usual administrative boundaries. Considering that cooperation with colleagues from other disciplinary specialisations would make sense from a scientific point of view, they have tried not only to improve various aspects related to doctoral education, but also to foster research within an interdisciplinary field. Thus, this Network Governance feature of self-organisation has been translated into certain autonomy in terms of institutional and disciplinary organisation. However, the other side of the coin of this autonomy has been consisting of their reliance on own funding, without any further financial support coming from the institution or national actors. In addition, their loose organisational character implicates a personal involvement of doctoral students and supervisors which depends on their respective conviction of MCB Research School's relevance. Possibly as a consequence of the limited funding and commitment of individual doctoral students and supervisors, MCB Research School's actual training activities are relatively modestly developed. The already existing institutional framework of doctoral education within the given case has also an impact on MCB Research School, especially with respect to MCB Research School's central missions. Several issues related to doctoral education – in particular admission and follow-up – have already been shaped by a central New Public Management principle, namely by explicit standards and measures of performance. Therefore, only less explicitly standardised issues could become a mission of MCB Research School. This concerns in particular the offer of an appropriate research milieu, supervision and training activities: an active research milieu is mentioned but not more precisely defined in PhD regulations, they define supervision by several supervisors as possible but not compulsory, and the overall required volume of training activities is defined to 30 credits, however, not their content (except the course in theory of science and ethics). Finally, one can say that, with respect to multiple supervision, MCB Research School was somehow ahead of time, but is currently caught up by overall university regulations comprised within the action plan. However, since those changes currently induced by the central university level go into the same direction as what has already been changed in the framework of MCB Research School, the according management instruments like the action plan have no concrete impact on MCB.

V.2.5. Informal Implementation vs. National and Institutional Managerialism

Two observations related to university governance can be emphasised on the basis of this case study. First, compared to the previous case study, the political and institutional influence is more strongly visible. A number of doctoral education's elements like admission, training and follow-up are defined in national and thereof deduced institutional legal frameworks. Besides such clear standards, measures of performance like the number of yearly awarded PhDs have an important financial impact on Norwegian HEIs and their disciplines. However, not only the national government's influence is quite strong. The central institutional level composed of its rectorate and administrative unit dedicated to doctoral education underlined its ambition to intervene on doctoral education by its "action plan". In the light of these rather "heavy-looking" instruments of governance, professors at the "research front" appear quite weakly equipped at first sight. Yet – and this is the first important point – the national and institutional governance instruments predetermined the reform to a certain extent, but they still left some important leeway regarding the more concrete content of reform. Thus, if some legal changes as well as the idea of research schools may have come from upper levels, the concrete content of reform – i.e. the type of the research school's activities – has been determined by a college of academics. Thereby, the involved college of academics nevertheless succeeded in quite an informal way to initiate and implement some changes in doctoral education which they judged relevant and meaningful.

As a second point, it is again the redefined character of the college of academics which has to be mentioned. Thus, the implementation of those concrete reform elements is again the result of a collective action. A number of voluntary academics joined in order to form this informal college, which is not only trans-institutional but – and this is particularly interesting – interdisciplinary! In other words, the college is not anymore necessarily defined in terms of disciplinary boundaries but can cut them across.

VI. Doctoral Schools in Materials Science

VI.1. PhD Programme in Materials Science and Engineering

This third case study focuses on the PhD programme in Materials Science and Engineering (MSE) of the Federal Institute of Technology Lausanne (*Ecole Polytechnique Fédérale de Lausanne* – EPFL). This PhD programme is one out of 19 PhD programmes, which currently constitute the EPFL Doctoral School. The MSE PhD programme has been founded at the same time as the institution wide EPFL Doctoral School, namely in 2003. Currently, 35 thesis directors (out of which 29 professors) and 114 doctoral students (end of 2008) are associated to MSE PhD programme. The total number of doctoral students at EPFL at the end of 2008 is of 1,629 (EPFL 2009).

VI.1.1. From the German to a more Anglo-Saxon Doctoral Education Model[79]

The reform story of this case study can be divided into two different episodes. The first episode, lasting from 2001 to the beginning of 2006, can be best described as the one of *a school wide cultural change.* The second episode, beginning in 2006, corresponds to a period of *stagnation and adaptation.*

The school wide cultural change concerned in particular four issues. First, the recruitment process of doctoral students changes from an individual to a collective approach. It does not anymore exclusively happen between an applicant and an individual supervisor but has to be

79 Unless other sources are indicated, used data originates from interviews with the EPFL vice-president for academic affairs education, the dean, the former dean and two administrators of the EPFL Doctoral School, the head as well as four further professors of the PhD programme in materials science and engineering as well as three doctoral students participating in the PhD programme.

examined and accepted by an intermediary body composed of a number of supervisors situated at the level of each of the 19 doctoral programmes. Thus, a supervisor cannot anymore directly recruit his doctoral students without the consent of this intermediary body. For an applicant this means that he has to formally apply to a doctoral programme, with or without prior contact to a potential supervisor. Since the EPFL Doctoral School's creation in 2003 until 2008, the total annual number of applicants has increased from 826 to 1,576, whereas the number of admitted applicants has grown from 264 to 593 during the same period (EPFL 2009: 10).

The second issue concerned by this institution wide cultural change relates to the introduction of a compulsory curricular component for doctoral students. Before this change, doctoral students were considered having completed the necessary coursework for the accomplishment of a doctorate through their previous degree(s). Nowadays, they are obliged to complete some coursework during their doctoral education. To this end, each doctoral programme disposes of a certain number of doctoral courses. Currently, the PhD programme in MSE offers 23 different courses covering different topics and techniques of materials science.[80] Courses usually take place annually, every other or third year and only under the condition of a minimal number of participating doctoral students.[81] According to the head of MSE PhD programme, their scope of content goes from rather broad to very narrow topics.

A third change concerns the follow-up of doctoral students. Hitherto the examination of doctoral students' progress has been ceded to themselves and their supervisors. During this first episode, a formal follow-up has been added at the level of the PhD programme. In the beginning of their doctoral education, doctoral students have to clearly define their research project and deadlines for its various stages. In an annual rhythm, doctoral students have to report about their progress and to justify possible deviance to the initially defined research plan.

80 For instance, "3D Electron Microscopy and FIB-Nanotomography", "Effects of radiation on materials", Functionalized nanoparticles for biomedical application", "Material characterisation techniques", "Micro- and nano-machining of materials by lasers", "Tensorial properties of solids", etc. Source: www.epfl.ch; downloaded September 2009.

81 Unfortunately, the responsible administrative unit of EPFL was not able to provide information about the number of courses which really took place.

Finally, the last change of this first episode relates to the doctoral students' scientific and social environment. Their working environment essentially consisted of their laboratory and its members. Through the introduction of courses doctoral students automatically meet more people from outside of their laboratory. Interviews with doctoral students showed that this gives doctoral students a double opportunity: first, doctoral students more easily contact other doctoral students and professors for scientific questions than if they would not have known them. Thereby, they have facilitated access to other infrastructure and specialised knowledge. This seems to be especially relevant for doctoral students working on interdisciplinary research projects. Second, a foreign doctoral student underlines the importance of courses for foreign doctoral students in order to make first acquaintances and to better understand the new social environment, for instance regarding the relationship between doctoral students and supervisors.

The second episode, the one of stagnation and adaptation, essentially takes place in the years 2006 and 2007 and is shaped by debates and decisions upon a further reform of doctoral education at EPFL. One suggestion of reform consisted in the introduction of programmes combining the master and doctoral degrees. Such MS-Doctoral programmes could have been introduced on demand of individual doctoral programmes and should have facilitated the access for foreign candidates with bachelor degrees of four years. However, this suggestion has been refused. As a consequence, applicants with four-year bachelor degrees are still handled case by case. We qualify this development as stagnation because an introduction of such a degree would have opened the way towards further adaptation to the American Graduate School system and thereby potentially promoted further recruitments of applicants with such degrees.

In contrast, two other reform suggestions, which we qualify as adaptation, have been accepted and subsequently integrated in the PhD regulations and directives of EPFL (2008; 2008a). One of these two modifications engenders a certain flexibilisation of the curricular component at the level of each PhD programme. On the one side, PhD programmes can now ask their doctoral students to acquire between 12 and 30 ECTS instead of maximally 12 credits. On the other side, the hitherto existing limit of maximally four credits acquired through master courses has been eliminated in order to allow a course programme adapted to the individual needs of each doctoral student. Finally, the last modification involves the introduction of a "candidate's exam" after the first year of doctoral education, which decides about the definitive admission or refusal to the doctoral programme. The modalities of this exam are individually decided by each PhD programme. In the case of the MSE PhD programme, it essentially consists of the oral presentation of the research project and plan by the doctoral student to the PhD programme committee.

Those two reform episodes have to be considered in a certain number of contextual elements which illustrate the cultural change and the related tensions. First of all, the described elements of reform have taken place in a period of strong institutional changes initiated with the arrival of the new president in 2000. Among others, those changes consisted in the introduction of life sciences in a HEI which traditionally has been dominated by engineering sciences, a new organisational form replacing departments by Faculties and a huge growth in terms of students and staff. The latter was already strong before the year 2000. However, according to an interviewee, it has been accompanied by a cultural clash related to the hiring of a large number of tenure track professors coming from the Anglo-Saxon, particularly the American higher education system. Those developments at the institutional level have a double significance regarding the reform of doctoral education. On the one hand, for the present professors, the doctoral school's introduction was one more element within a series of changes. According to several interviewees, those changes, among which the doctoral school, have not been appreciated by all of the present professors, simply because it represented a change. On the other hand, in opposite to the tenure track professors socialised in the American Graduate School system, a lot of the present professors believed in a – what many interviewees called – "German" doctoral system. According to the former dean of the doctoral school, they criticised in particular four points: first, the collective form of recruitment, arguing that they would know themselves how to find and recruit good doctoral students; second, the coursework for doctoral students, which would be a waste of time. Doctoral students should use this time for their work in the laboratory; third, the increase of bureaucracy; fourth, the increase of the professors' working load related to the additional teaching of doctoral courses. Opposition also came from the side of doctoral students.

According to the former dean of the doctoral school, they disliked the idea of being obliged to attend courses, and even more, to be examined for getting the related credits. They argued that they were not anymore students. The former dean also underlined that attitudes towards those changes strongly varied according to the disciplines.

Interviews with actors involved in the two reform episodes also reveal a number of contextual elements conditioning the organisational form of the doctoral school, that is to say its construction on the basis of one only HEI rather than in collaboration with other HEIs: first, it has been argued that nothing comparable existed in Switzerland at the time. Thus everything had to be created from scratch. A central ambition was to create the doctoral school as fast as possible. Considering the internal opposition, it was already difficult enough to quickly progress. A collaborative action, in particular with even more "Germanic" HEIs, would have taken even more time. Second, some potentially interesting foreign HEIs already collaborated with other HEIs. Therefore, they were not interested in further collaborations. Third, the competitive character of parts of the related objectives, in particular the recruitment of the best doctoral students, interferes with inter-institutional collaboration.

Finally, two last contextual elements have been put forward regarding the second episode in particular. First, the introduction of the "candidate's exam" replaced the general exam which previously had to be completed by the doctoral students at the end of their doctoral education. This general exam included questions about the wider field of materials science. However, according to several interviewees, doctoral students often became very specialised in their doctoral topic and forgot more general knowledge which they acquired during their previous studies. As a consequence, doctoral students often failed this general exam in an embarrassing manner… Probably therefore, its elimination was rather appreciated by most of those interviewees. Second, some interviewees considered the potential introduction of a combined master-doctoral degree as a threat to the value of the present master degree. They argued that the HEI's reputation within the non-academic labour market traditionally relies to a large extent on the quality of its master degrees. Assuming that the best bachelor students would directly go into the combined degree, the introduction of such a master-doctoral degree could be seen as a devalorisation of the classical master degree and thereby deteriorate the HEI's reputation on the non-academic labour market.

VI.1.2. A Comprehensive Group of Governance Instruments

Two different types of governance instruments have been applied in order to accomplish the various reform elements described above, namely financial and legal instruments. Concerning the financial instruments, it is first of all noticeable that, since its creation, the EPFL Doctoral School disposes of a regular budget within the overall EPFL budget. In 2006, overall expenses were about 2,500,000 CHF (~ 1,600,000 €). The largest part of this budget is used for the salaries of secretaries employed at the doctoral school and each individual PhD programme as well as the so called "grants of excellence" (EPFL Doctoral School 2007). An important task of the respective secretary consists in checking and sorting out all the applications addressed to the doctoral programme. The grants of excellence were thought as an extra measure in order to attract the best doctoral students. A grant of excellence allowed to immediately hire an excellent applicant for whom no usual funding source was available at the moment of his application. This way, the probability that the applicant would be meanwhile hired by a competing HEI could be reduced and an appropriate funding source could be looked for during one year. The first doctoral school dean considered both – the secretaries' preparing work of the recruitments and the possibility to immediately hire excellent applicants – as incentives for professors to support the reform efforts related to the creation of the doctoral school. Since the end of 2007, the grants of excellence do not anymore exist. Instead, since 2009 and on the basis of the number of doctoral students, the doctoral school makes available funding to each PhD programme for inviting applicants to interviews in Lausanne and for organising other promotion and recruitment activities. In 2008, for the totality of EPFL PhD programmes, 200 candidates have been invited for interviews. In average, related costs were of 925 CHF (~610 €). In the same year, a relatively small part of the overall doctoral school budget, that is to say ca. 154,000 CHF (~102,000 €), has been used for expenses related to course teaching. With only 1,200 CHF (~800 €) the MSE PhD programme used an amount of money for course teaching which is well below the doctoral school's average (EPFL Doctoral School 2009: 7-8). This amount is generally used for salary of lecturers particularly hired for teaching certain courses at doctoral level.

To some extent, this relatively low amount of money expended for teaching activities can be explained by their partial payment through other funding sources than the budget line of the doctoral school. On the one side, ordinarily hired professors teach courses at doctoral level. Their teaching activities at doctoral level are not separately rewarded but integrated into their overall tasks as professors and thereby funded through their ordinary salary. However, interviews reveal that it is not yet very clear to what extent this new task is balanced through the reduction of other tasks. On the other side, academics invited by laboratories are often engaged to teach some courses, among which also at doctoral level.

Last but not least, it is worth underlining that EPFL got no additional funding by the ETH Board for the creation and development of EPFL Doctoral School as such. However, the number of doctorates is an indicator which is taken into account in the allocation of money through the ETH Board (EPFL 2007).

A large series of the described changes have been implemented and cemented by their integration into the principal legal basis related to doctoral education, namely the EPFL's doctoral education regulations (2008) and directives (2008a). It is noticeable, first, that this legal framework concerns the whole institution – what implies a certain standardisation –, and second, that the EPFL direction is authorised to decide upon possible changes. Among the issues dealt with in this legal framework, norms with regard to the curricular component, follow-up, candidate's exam and the recruitment of doctoral students are defined to a varying extent. First, the compulsory completion of a curricular component has been fixed to 12 credits. As mentioned, this rule has been made more flexible for individual PhD programmes, to an amount situated between 12 and 30 ECTS, through a corresponding legal adaptation in 2008. It is important to underline that those credits can only be acquired through courses and not by other performances like participation in conferences. In addition, ECTS are only awarded in the case of any form of control (oral or written exam, report and presentation, etc.). The form of control has to be individually determined by the corresponding lecturer. As mentioned, since 2008, those courses can be taken at other levels than only the doctoral level, but they have to represent the acquirement of new knowledge for the doctoral student. Finally, individual PhD programmes are allowed to define compulsory courses. In the case of the MSE PhD programme, no compulsory or core-course exists. Interviews showed that doctoral students are generally free to choose, but often get some advice by their supervisors. Interviewees also underlined that, due to materials sciences' interdisciplinary character, courses are often taken outside of the MSE programme, either in other EPFL PhD programmes or other HEIs.

EPFL PhD regulations also define the compulsory follow-up procedure of doctoral students. The concrete instruments consist in an annual report and in the "candidate's exam". The follow-up mechanisms related to the annual report include several steps. In a first step, doctoral students have to write this report and to send it to their supervisor. In a second step, the supervisor is obliged to answer by commenting the doctoral student's report towards the PhD programme head within one month after having obtained the report from the doctoral student. In case of unsatisfactory work or progress, the PhD programme's head and the supervisor discuss about the doctoral student's situation. The PhD programme's head then informs the doctoral student about the noticed problems and the required improvement measures and the related deadlines. Finally, on written demand of the supervisor and the PhD programme's head, PhD regulations allow the doctoral student's exclusion of the PhD programme. With the introduction of the "candidate's exam" in 2008, a further follow-up instrument has been institutionalised. Each doctoral student has to pass this exam after the first year of doctoral education. The exam's precise content is to be determined by each PhD programme. As mentioned, in the case of MSE, it essentially consists of the oral presentation of the research project and plan by the doctoral student to a jury, which is composed of a member of the PhD programme committee, the thesis director and an additional EPFL supervisor (of another laboratory). Again, if the doctoral student fails twice, he is excluded from the PhD programme (EPFL 2008; 2008a; 2008b). An interviewee emphasised that this entrance exam is also an opportunity to examine whether the planned doctoral research project is feasible within the usual four years of doctoral years. Certain supervisors impose projects on doctoral students which take significantly more time.

Therefore, the exam also provides an occasion for an outside control avoiding such practices.

Finally, EPFL PhD regulations also define to some extent the recruitment procedure for doctoral students. Formally, the latter have to apply to the PhD programme's head for admission to the doctoral programme. On the basis of the PhD programme commission's assessment, the applicants' level of excellence, the availability of the supervision resources and logistic means necessary for the realisation of the thesis, the head decides upon the applicant's admission. Finally, PhD regulations also require letters of recommendation, however, without specifying their number (EPFL 2008; 2008a). The rest of the procedure depends on the individual PhD programmes' implementation. In the case of MSE PhD programme, three official deadlines of application exist. Applicants have to send their CV, the grades of the passed studies, three letters of recommendation and a letter of motivation as an online application. They also more or less indicate their research interests. According to the MSE PhD programme's head, applicants formally apply after or before having been in-/formally accepted by a supervisor. Thus, to a certain extent there are two tracks of application. However, the programme commission examines *all* applications in one of the three meetings taking place a year. In each case they try to assess the quality of the applicant. The further proceeding depends on the number of available positions and the candidates' profile. As a consequence of previous informal exchanges, some matches between applicants who later have been considered as good by the commission, and supervisors with available positions may already have happened. The applications of all other candidates who have been favourably assessed are circulated among potential supervisors. In case of available positions and interest from the side of potential supervisors, the latter may contact the given applicants. Further procedures depend on individual supervisors. Some invite applicants to interviews in Lausanne others are content with alternative forms of interaction like by phone. Applicants who have been positively assessed but not immediately allocated a position – which should be the case for a minority – have the possibility to contact themselves potential supervisors in order to find a position. Several interviewees emphasised that this balance between accepted applicants and available positions is not always easy to find…

VI.1.3. Top-Down Decision, Collegial Implementation

Varying actors and modes of decision taking are related to the initiation, implementation and current running of the EPFL Doctoral School and the MSE PhD programme. First of all, all interviewees involved in the doctoral school's emergence underline that the initiative for the doctoral school's creation came from the presidency. Both the president and one of the vice-presidents have been mentioned as strongly pushing this initiative at an institution wide level. However, the presidency delegated the doctoral school's implementation to a professor who previously worked within a renowned American university. According to the charged professor, the president's words were "to make a graduate school". The charged professor specified that what has been done does not really correspond to a graduate school in the American sense since the EFPL Doctoral School does not include the master level. Yet, he also emphasised that his subsequent actions – in particular the introduction of a new recruitment procedure and the grants of excellence – have been largely inspired by his experience in his former American university.

If the initiative had a strong top-down character, the charged professor emphasises that he got large freedom in the manner he realised the doctoral school's implementation and that he had clear ideas about the changes to be carried out. According to him but also other involved interviewees, the largest part of the implementation process happened in a democratic manner. Concretely, he proceeded by calls for the submission of PhD programmes. In other words, he invited all supervisors from the whole institution to suggest PhD programmes defined in terms of collaborating laboratories, related objectives and a head. Then, in a first step, an "ad-hoc commission" composed of "experts" has examined the suggested PhD programmes. According to an administrator involved in this process, 12 out of 14 or 15 suggestions have been accepted in a first round. Further PhD programmes have been added later in the process. In a second step, the accepted PhD programmes had to be submitted in a more elaborated form, in particular in terms of course offer, pedagogic objectives and the composition of the PhD programmes' commission. Simultaneously, the doctoral school commission, composed of the heads of each accepted PhD programme, has been created. From this moment on, the latter decided by vote about a series of issues like general changes in PhD regulations – including the initial norm of 12 credits for the curricular component – but also course offers suggested by the individual PhD programmes. According to the charged professor, this implementation process within the Commission of the doctoral school lasted for two years. All decisions taken within this process had to be approved by the presidency. The charged professor underlined that no supervisor had been forced to adhere the varying PhD programmes during this emergence phase. Those who did not join could simply not benefit from the grants of excellence or preparing work of the secretaries in terms of preliminary checking and sorting out of all the applications addressed to the doctoral programme. However, according to the vice-president, a large majority of all doctorates have been carried out in the framework of the PhD programmes after about one year and a half. Subsequently, in December 2004, the presidency decided to limit doctoral education's completion in the framework of the PhD programmes. In other words, from this moment on, the reform such as formalised in the PhD regulations concerned every doctoral student and supervisor.

In the case of the supervisors in materials science, it seems that the invitation to suggest a PhD programme has met neither grand enthusiasm nor fundamental opposition. The PhD programme's implementation has been realised in quite a collegial way. Confronted to the call, full professors met in order to discuss about the person who should take the responsibility to take care of the PhD programme's creation in material science and engineering. Considering the availability and experience of all of them, a first head has been determined (with his consent). Together with other colleagues the newly named head tried to convince the sceptical colleagues of the importance of the courses. He then asked certain colleagues to suggest courses. Some among them accepted the suggestion and proposed a course, whereas others rejected. According to the first head, everything happened on voluntary basis, nobody has been obliged. Since they wanted to offer specific doctoral courses – which until this moment did not exist – related work was quite demanding and the first course offer was relatively small, which has been corrected since then. The first and current MSE PhD programme heads indicate that they have not pursued any strategy in terms of development of a particular, standardised course programme. Rather courses are offered on the basis of the individual teachers' research areas. One supervisor also argues that, that way, the level of courses can be significantly higher than if somebody would teach a course which is not directly related to his specialised field of research. The PhD directors also point to two factors which have an impact on the shape of their course programme. Both are related to the character of materials science and engineering as a scientific field. On the one hand, its interdisciplinary feature – and the corresponding course offer of the other PhD programmes at EPFL – increases the effective range of available courses. On the other hand, its alikeness over national boarders makes it also easy for doctoral students to follow courses abroad.

The tasks of the EPLF Doctoral Commission described in the initial phase remain the same for the doctoral school's current running. Under the lead of the doctoral school dean, it deliberates and decides on the admission of new PhD programmes, the general philosophy of doctoral education, changes such as happened in the second reform episode described above as well as the course offer. Regarding the latter, weight is put on coordination of the varying course offers of the different PhD programmes, especially in order to avoid duplications. Although those competences are basically delegated to the EPFL Doctoral Commission, the presidency has the final word about it.

As mentioned, the examination and decisions about the selection of applicants for doctoral positions usually take place at the level of the individual PhD programme commissions. In the case of MSE PhD programme, this commission is composed of three full professors, one assistant professor, one internal MER[82] and one external supervisor. In practice, yet, the final word depends on the individual supervisors' will and availability of resources to fund doctoral students' positions. Finally, it is also at a more individual level, namely between the PhD programme's head and the individual supervisor, that possible discussions and decisions related to the doctoral students' progress take place (EPFL 2008a). In case of serious disagreements with respect to for instance the intermediary evaluation of a doctoral student, the final deciding instance is situated by the doctoral school dean.

Finally, what about the role of the ETH Board (*ETH-Rat*) in this process? On the one hand, the latter did not mention at all the reform of doctoral education or the establishment of a doctoral school in its

82 Maître d'Enseignement et de Recherche. This status usually corresponds to a stable position for doctors without the title of professor.

strategic planning for the period 2000-2003 (ETH-Rat 1997). In addition, the first actions towards the doctoral school's creation in 2001 coincide with the period after the new president's arrival in 2000. On the other hand, the vice-president states that the doctoral school was a topic of discussion between the presidency and the ETH Board before, during and after the doctoral school's creation. Moreover, he notices a certain enthusiasm from the ETH Board concerning the doctoral school. Thus, the ETH board seems to have played rather a supportive than influencing or even determining role in the initiation and development of the EPFL Doctoral School.

Interviewed actors identified a series of objectives related to the doctoral school and the MSE PhD programme. First of all, much weight is put on an improved management of doctoral students as research staff. The vice-president underlines the central role of doctoral students for the institution's innovative research force. As a consequence, he as well as the former and current doctoral school deans call attention to the importance of a guaranteed uniform quality in doctoral education throughout the whole institution. They point in particular at the recruitment procedures as a domain where quality control needs to be systematic and standardised. One of the interviewees mentions that before the doctoral school's creation, recruitment procedures sometimes have been quite random to the extent that some supervisors contented themselves to announce available doctoral positions by posting announcements on the corridors' walls... In connection with the objective of an improved staff management, both doctoral school deans as well as MSE PhD programme's head consider the attraction of the best doctoral students at the international level as important objective. Last but not least, according to the vice-president, the increased attraction of doctoral students shall not only contribute to achieve a qualitative but also a quantitative objective, namely to increase the overall number of doctoral students from currently about 1,500 to about 2,000 to 2,200. However, he also underlines that this objective in terms of numbers is not absolute but also depends on available resources. An improved training through the course offer constitutes a further important objective. Those course activities should also help avoiding the isolation of doctoral students. Concretely, they should improve doctoral students' opportunities to meet people from other laboratories in the field of materials science or related fields. Finally, meetings in the framework of the courses are also considered as an opportunity to build networks which would be useful in future professional activities. Interviewees also mentioned an objective with respect to doctoral students' preparation for the labour market. Some interviewees mention the objective according to which those improvements shall lead to an improved preparation of the doctoral students as leaders in academia, but also in private economy and public service. All interviewees underline the universal character of doctoral education regarding the varying positions on the academic and non-academic labour markets. The doctoral school dean emphasised his opposition against a possible distinction between a title of "academic doctor" and "practical doctor". If all interviewees agreed on doctoral education's universal character in terms of career preparation, some disagreement could be identified when it comes to the question of the determinant factor for a successful preparation in particular for non-academic careers. One points in particular at the generic skills of an independent researcher, another at the specific doctoral research topic and a third at the added value of the curricular component, in particular related to more generic courses like in management and Chinese culture. The role of the later is most contested. On the one hand, as good as all supervisors underline that the curricular component is very small compared to the research component. Therefore, they argue that, in comparison, its impact is very weak (by underlining that they do not want the curricular component to become larger). On the other hand, doctoral students are not obliged to follow more generic courses. Among the interviewed doctoral students, a clear tendency towards a choice of courses depending on their respective research topics could be noticed. Thus, neither the doctoral students' training through generic courses nor possible positive impact on perspectives on the non-academic labour market are assured.

VI.1.4. Close to the New Public Management Ideal-Type

The analysis of this case study in terms of public management narratives reveals a case which is close to the New Public Management ideal-type. However, the achievement of the absolute ideal-type is impeded by the appearance of one fundamental Network Governance element.

The case study's strong shaping by New Public Management elements begins with the appointment of the professor charged to lead the creation of the doctoral school through the presidency. This scenario largely corresponds to the New Public Management principle "Hands-on professional management" consisting of active, visible, discretionary control of organisations from named persons at the top, "free to manage". Indeed, the charged professor underlined that he got large autonomy in the completion of his task by the presidency. In principle, this delegation principle still applies to the current doctoral school dean to the extent that he is ultimately responsible for controlling varying issues related to doctoral education in particular the related quality. At least from a formal point of view, the vision of a person named at the top and free to manage also applies to the level of the individual PhD programmes, since their heads are the ones deciding about the applicants' admission to the programmes. The creation of the EPFL Doctoral School matches a second New Public Management element, namely the shift to disaggregation of units in the public sector into corporatized units around products, operating on decentralised "one-line" budgets. Varying issues of doctoral education like doctoral students' recruitment, training and follow-up have not only been concentrated within this new structure – the doctoral school and its individual PhD programmes –, but the doctoral school also obtained an own budget. A third New Public Management feature, namely the one of explicit standards and measures of performance, appears throughout the case study. Institutional PhD regulations define a wide range of standards with respect to doctoral recruitment, training and follow-up. In addition they delegate the autonomy to individual PhD programmes to introduce further standards, for instance regarding compulsory core-courses for doctoral students. The two instruments used to realise standards with regard to follow-up, the annual report and the candidate's exam can also be seen as the New Public Management principle of greater discipline and parsimony in resource use. Indeed, in case of (repeated) negative intermediary evaluation through one or both of these instruments, doctoral students can be dismissed in order not to "waste resources" (to say it in a brutal, "business like" way). Then, although the vice-president underlines that his objective to achieve a higher number of doctoral students is not defined in absolute, unalterable numbers, he nevertheless seems to make of it an indicator of success. This condition is definitely fulfilled with regard to the funding formula applied to the EPFL as a whole. The ETH Board allocates part of its funding on the basis of the number of doctorates. Thereby, a further New Public Management principle applies, that is to say the one of greater emphasis on output controls. Finally, also the two last New Public Management features presented on Hood's (1991) list appear in this case study. The grants of excellence introduced in the beginning of the reform as a mean to attract and hold the best applicants, reflect private-sectors styles of management – in particularly the one of greater flexibility in hiring – and also a shift towards greater competition. This latter feature can generally be seen in the whole new recruitment procedure – involving a systematic comparison of applications and a related selection based on certain indicators – and the related objectives formulated as consisting in the attraction of the best doctoral students at the international level.

Thus, the management story of this case study is definitely dominated by New Public Management features. However, as mentioned, it is not completely free from Network Governance characteristics. This concerns in particular the manner the described changes in doctoral education have been decided upon, both at the level of the doctoral school and the PhD programme in Materials Science and Engineering. Considering that all major changes have been voted on by the heads of the varying PhD programmes and the collegial manner those changes have been implemented in the MSE PhD programme, it seems justified to speak rather about lateral than vertical forms of management. This applies even more to the MSE PhD programme to the extent that no standardised training programme with core-courses exists and doctoral students – sometimes together with their supervisors – freely decide about the courses they attend. If the collegial decision-making within the academic profession of materials science and engineering seems to be related to the academic profession's internal culture, the open choice – or non-standardisation of a training programme – appears to be intrinsically related to the interdisciplinary character of materials science and engineering as a scientific field. Finally, the presence of such a Network Governance feature within the management story reveals a certain paradox to the extent that the Network Governance feature of lateral forms of management has been used in order to implement the whole range of New Public Management features!

The observed changes in doctoral education of the PhD programme in Material Sciences and Engineering as well as of the whole EPFL clearly bear the hallmarks of this management story close to the New Public Management ideal-type. The New Public Management traces are even more clearly visible in concrete changes for the following reasons: first, they deal with central aspects of doctoral education like the recruitment, training and follow-up of doctoral students. Thus, they have a comprehensive character. Second, most of the underlying New Public Management governance instruments – both financial and legal ones – are permanent and thereby assure some stability on the way towards the achievement of the defined reform objectives. Third, besides a certain degree of autonomy, those instruments apply in a systematic manner to all scientific disciplines of the given HEI. These comprehensive, permanent and systematic characteristics of the management story strongly support the achievement of the defined reform objectives, that is to say an institution wide cultural change in doctoral education. Indeed, at least to a certain extent, this cultural change has been attained: first, it is not anymore possible for supervisors to individually recruit doctoral students without at least having the agreement of a group of colleagues. Nevertheless, applicants still often contact certain supervisors before applying; second, a compulsory curricular component has been introduced for doctoral students. However, according to the PhD programme, its content is more or less broad and clearly defined. In the case of the MSE PhD programme, the concrete offer is largely determined by the supervisors, partly in an individual, partly in a collective manner. Doctoral students are largely free to choose courses at doctoral but also master level. At least, they have not to attend any compulsory core courses; third, according to the doctoral student, social and scientific networks are broadened thanks to the coursework as well as other activities; fourth, progress control is not anymore exclusively left to the doctoral students and their supervisors but, in addition, carried out by the PhD programmes' heads.

This cultural change has certainly also been supported by the institution's afflux of academic staff who has been socialised in American higher education. In addition, considering the opposition towards such a large cultural change, which nevertheless exists among certain professors, the Network Governance like lateral forms of management certainly were crucial for the hitherto implementation of the profound changes. Simultaneously, identified opposition to an even further "Americanisation" of EPFL's doctoral education into the direction of a veritable Graduate School including the master level, seems having defeated the proponents of such an idea.

VI.1.5. Institutional Managerialism Focussing on Doctoral Education

Among the actors identified in the "Actors' Framework B", those situated at the central (and decentralised) institutional level have been playing the most crucial role in the initiation and implementation of the reform as well as in the current management of doctoral education: the presidency, the doctoral school's dean and his administrative staff but also the heads of the PhD programmes have been strongly shaping the reform process of the whole institution. Thus, this corresponds to what authors like Schimank (2005) describe as hierarchical management, strengthened by New Public Management. From this point of view, the supervisors look like the losers of these developments. However, they still control – partly collectively, partly individually – the most central aspects of doctoral education like the selection of doctoral students and content of the training programme.

Through the annual progress report, supervisors are exposed to additional control. Thus, besides more or less formal evaluation of their performance as researchers and teachers, they also get increasingly evaluated as supervisors of doctoral students. This has an impact on the relationship between the supervisors and doctoral students. At least from a formal point of view, doctoral education does not anymore exclusively happen between the doctoral student and his supervisor but is a potential object of intervention for heads of the given PhD programme or even the doctoral school's dean. Thus, supervisors have to give account to their HEI about their activity as supervisor.

This supplementary evaluation mechanism placed on supervisors should not hide the fact that doctoral students are most strongly exposed to New Public Management elements, in particular the ones of competition and measures of performance. From the beginning until the end of their doctorate, they are evaluated: during the recruitment process, after the first year in the framework of the candidate's exam, regarding their coursework, through the annual reports and finally in the thesis defence.

The application of so many new control mechanisms on supervisors and especially doctoral students at the institutional level are a clear sign: doctoral education has been put at the core of the institutional development. It is not anymore exclusively a personal project of a doctoral student and may be his supervisor. It has been made a central mission of the given HEI as a whole.

VI.2. FUNMAT Research School

This fourth case study deals with the FUNMAT Research School, situated at University of Oslo. FUNMAT stands for a national consortium for research within functional materials and nanotechnology composed of partners from University of Oslo, Norwegian University of Science and Technology (NTNU) in Trondheim, SINTEF in Trondheim and Oslo – Scandinavia's largest independent research organisation –, and the Institute for Energy Technology (IFE) in Kjeller.[83] More particularly at the level of the University of Oslo, FUNMAT has been one of several internally prioritised research areas (*institusjonelle satsninger*) and has existed from 2001 until 2006. FUNMAT Research School reunites doctoral students who work with functional materials and who are essentially situated in two departments of the Faculty of Mathematics and Natural Sciences of University of Oslo, namely the ones of physics and chemistry. Currently, FUNMAT Research School is one out of totally 22 research schools existing at University of Oslo. The latter are distributed on all Faculties except the Faculty of Theology. They strongly vary in terms of size, scope and offer (Universitet i Oslo 2008).

83 Source: www.funmat.no; downloaded in October 2009.

VI.2.1. A Hesitant Reform[84]

The reform story of this case study can be divided into three different episodes. The first one can be named *birth episode*, the second one *hibernation*, and the third one *resuscitation.*

FUNMAT Research School has been founded as one of the first 15 research schools at University of Oslo during the period 2004-2005. With its birth in 2004, three types of changes have been introduced in doctoral education in materials sciences at University of Oslo. The first change has consisted of a seminar where doctoral students met about every other week, without participation of any professor. Within these seminars doctoral students presented and discussed their doctoral research, related experimental techniques and problems they had to deal with. According to interviewed doctoral students, this type of activity was relevant from a scientific and social point of view. Concerning scientific relevancy, they underlined that knowledge exchange – for instance about experimental techniques – took place beyond the boarders of individual research laboratories and even departments (of physics and chemistry). Thereby, they got access to knowledge which otherwise they would not have gotten. Then, thanks to the absence of their supervisors, the presentations as such are seen as a training possibility among junior colleagues, without any fear to blunder in front of supervisors. From a social point of view, doctoral students emphasise the opportunity of contacts, especially in order to integrate foreign doctoral students, but also more generally in case of difficult periods:

> I think it has an impact on the social aspect around things. That you feel that you are connected somewhere. And that you can talk to other people that are in the same position as you are. So if you are extremely frustrated and nothing goes correctly then you can talk to them and they are experienced in the same thing that you are.
>
> (A doctoral student who participated in FUNMAT Research School)

---

84 Unless other sources are indicated, used data originates from interviews with the pro-rector of University of Oslo, a collaborator of University of Oslo's central administration, the dean and an administrator of the Faculty of Mathematics and Natural Sciences, the head of FUNMAT Research School as well as four doctoral students participating in FUNMAT Research School.

The second activity of FUNMAT Research School has consisted of about three yearly workshops. Each of them lasted about two days. In their framework internal and invited lecturers presented particular experimental techniques used in the field of material sciences. The third activity concerns the award of travel grants through FUNMAT Research School. Doctoral students participating in FUNMAT Research School had the possibility to apply for partial funding for stays during their doctoral education lasting up to three months. However, to what extent are those activities something new for doctoral students in materials science? A former doctoral student and administrative coordinator of FUNMAT explained it in the following manner:

> In the natural sciences, a PhD student would usually be part of a larger research group which of course has some activities, has very often seminar series. You have engineers and older students or professors who teach you experimental techniques. I mean there is in practice always in our field some structure in a sense. There is always some sort of structured education, but it's not formalised, it's not part of the PhD education as such. And I guess that's what we tried to do with the research school, to try to create some sort of framework of activities that the PhD student should take part in.
>
> (A doctoral student who participated in FUNMAT Research School)

However, about two years after its start those three FUNMAT Research School activities stopped for about one and a half year. According to our interviewees, this second period, which we name hibernation, is a consequence of the end of FUNMAT as a prioritised research area at University of Oslo.

The hibernation period is followed by what we call resuscitation period. Two factors contribute to this resuscitation. On the one hand, parts of FUNMAT Research School activities, that is to say the workshops, are again taking place since November 2008 (at least two workshops a year). Those activities still run under the label of FUNMAT Research School, but are organised by the Centre for Materials Science and Nanotechnology (*Senter for materialvitenskap og nanoteknologi* – SMN) of the Faculty of Mathematics and Natural Sciences at University of Oslo. SMN acts as the Faculty's strategic unit in terms of coordination of activities within materials science, micro- and nanotechnology.[85] As a

85 Source: www.smn.uio.no; downloaded in October 2008.

second factor contributing to this resuscitation period, another recent initiative, aiming at the creation of a research school in the field of solar cell technology and involving also professors of materials science at University of Oslo, can be cited. In February 2009, the Research Council of Norway allocated one billion (!) Norwegian Krones (~120 million €) to a number of Norwegian research institutions in order to establish and run six research centres for environmentally friendly energy during an eight-year period. University of Oslo is involved in four out of these six centres. One of them, the Norwegian Research Centre for Solar Cell Technology has been granted an annual budget of 40 million Norwegian Krones (~4.8 million €). The University of Oslo has taken the initiative to establish a research school within this field.[86] An involved professor states that, compared to FUNMAT Research School, the offer in terms of training activities will strongly grow. Furthermore, he also underlines that synergies between FUNMAT Research School and the new research school in solar cell technology will be examined.

Those three reform episodes have to be seen within a certain number of contextual elements. Concerning the birth episode, it has first of all to be mentioned that, according to several interviewees at various institutional levels, the national evaluation report of Norwegian doctoral education (Kyvik 2002) and the following recommendations elaborated by a working group of the Norwegian Association of Higher Education Institutions (UHR 2003), played an important role in the research schools' setting on the agenda. Simultaneously, several interviewees of the Faculty of Mathematics and Natural Sciences emphasised that they did not really feel concerned, neither by the problems nor by the solutions identified in those two reports. One interviewee formulated his position in the following way:

> I should be frank and say that when we first got this, we looked at this and said, hey who needs this? Because this, the way we viewed it and still view it to some extent, is that this only institutionalises a lot of the features that were already present in natural sciences' doctoral training. Working in groups, seminars activities, closer following, closer advising. So the way we viewed it, was that, to a large extent, it aimed at the social sciences and humanities where you would typically have the lonely researcher […].

86 Source: http://www.uio.no/for_ansatte/aktuelt/nyhetsbrev/english/news/energy.html; downloaded in October 2008.

As a second factor, related to the first one, it is important to mention that many interviewees underlined the unclear definition of research schools. Apparently, the lack of a clear definition has also been an issue for the Norwegian Association of Higher Education Institutions (UHR), who asked all its member institutions to provide a definition. In its letter addressed at UHR, the University director lists a number of features – disposal of an administrative and a scientific leader, a distinct disciplinary profile, an international network, an offer of courses and meetings for doctoral students, a certain volume, a good balance between the number of doctoral students, post-docs and senior researchers, as well as a dynamic and compulsory scientific and social community – but simultaneously points to the unclear delimitation between PhD programme and research school. It is furthermore underlined that no comparable unit exists abroad (Universitetet i Oslo 2008). At least in the beginning, when the idea of research schools came up, it was not clear for responsible people at the Faculty of Mathematics and Natural Sciences neither what type of content a research school should consist of, nor to what extent this content should help solve identified problems, like the too long duration of doctoral education. As mentioned in the previous quote, they considered that a number of activities already existed. In particular, they pointed to the curricular offer consisting of a number of rather broad courses at doctoral level and the yearly administrative follow-up of doctoral students principally carried out within the Faculty's PhD programme. Hence, rather then reinventing something at the level of a research school, they tried to add something else. This new element especially consists of the doctoral students' seminars but also the workshops, which allow to specifically increase the doctoral students' scientific knowledge and to widen the social contacts between doctoral students from varying research groups and departments.

According to some interviewees, one underlying idea of this additional element is also related to the institutional structure of materials science at University of Oslo. Compared to other higher education institutions, no institutional unit for materials science exists at University of Oslo. Researchers working on materials science are principally distributed on the departments of physics and chemistry. An interviewee states that until some years ago, collaboration between those two departments has not been strongly developed. The prioritised research area FUNMAT aimed at improving this collaboration. A certain number of doctoral positions have been explicitly dedicated to the field of functional materials. As a consequence, and also, more generally, since a large part of research is carried out through doctoral students, professors involved into FUNMAT Research School considered increased interaction among doctoral students also as a mean to generally improve collaboration in the field of materials science.

VI.2.2. Limited Steering Instruments

Again, the three reform episodes have been steered by two types of instruments, namely financial and legal ones. The first financial instrument concerns FUNMAT as a prioritised research area. The area of functional materials is one out of several research areas which have received from the central university level the status of a prioritised area. FUNMAT started when the idea of research schools came up. Possibly as a consequence of this coincidence, the rectorate asked all prioritised areas to create a research school. However, in any case, each prioritised research area engaged in creating and running a research school. Thus, the creation of FUNMAT Research School is the result of this requirement related to the allocation of the status of a prioritised research area and the related funding.

From 2004 to 2005, each initiative aiming at the creation of a research school at University of Oslo has been rewarded by the rectorate by a yearly budget.[87] In the case of Norwegian Centres of Excellence (*Senter for fremragende forskning*) and research schools which are related to other large networks – among which FUNMAT Research School –, this budget corresponds to 50,000 Norwegian Krones (NOK) (~6,000 €). For all other initiatives, the amount is situated between 300,000 and 350,000 NOK (Universitetet i Oslo 2008). However, before obtaining this amount of money each initiative had to be examined. According to the underlying framework conditions (Universitetet i Oslo 2004), this has to be done by an external evaluation committee. However, an administrator of the central university level admitted that

87 For budgetary reasons, four Research Schools created in 2007 have not been getting any financial support.

this initial ambition of external examination has not been implemented, especially because, as a consequence of the vague definition of research schools, the criteria of evaluation were not yet clear… Usually, the recipients of this funding have to write a small yearly activity report for the attention of the rectorate. Finally, the framework conditions for research schools at University of Oslo (2004) set the research schools' duration to four years. A final evaluation has been planned for the year 2008. However, due to the hibernation episode, this evaluation has not been carried out for the FUNMAT Research School. According to interviewees involved in FUNMAT Research School, the obtained amount of money has been used in order to fund the costs related to the workshops and seminars (expenses for invited lecturers, lunch, etc.). FUNMAT Research School has obtained this type of funding until today, hence, beyond the duration of FUNMAT as a prioritised research area and also beyond the initially planned four-year period for the rectorate's funding of research schools.

If this funding coming from the central university level has allowed to fund some of the scientific activities of FUNMAT Research School, it was not sufficient to pay also the research school's administrative costs, essentially consisting of the salary of a part time administrator. The latter has been taken into charge by the FUNMAT project as such. An involved doctoral student got his contract as doctoral student extended. In return he had to accomplish some administrative tasks related to FUNMAT, and in particular, to FUNMAT Research School. However, with the end of FUNMAT as a prioritised research area in 2006, which coincided with the end of the aforementioned doctoral student's contract, no specific source was anymore available to fund this administrative position. As a consequence, nobody was anymore formally in charge of this task. Several interviewees consider the disappearance of this funding source as a reason for the second reform episode, the hibernation. The intermediary solution of the third, resuscitation episode consists in the distribution of administrative tasks on the administrator of the Centre of Material Sciences and Nanotechnology (SMN), one professor as well as a number of post-docs. An interviewee involved in the FUNMAT Research School's running, pointed at the distance between the rectorate's requirement to establish research schools and the weak amount of allocated money:

> I remember that we were discussing that. So there was always the question of, if we had had more money, we could have started more activity, done more things. So we were always saying that it was quite a bit funny that the rectorate was so obsessed with these research schools [...], but they weren't allocating that many resources to them.

Thus, the central university level's allocation is considered rather low. What about possible allocations from the Faculty level? The dean of the Faculty of Mathematics and Natural Sciences states that, in principle, no specific money is allocated from the Faculty level in order to promote research schools. One exception to this principle concerns areas which they consider as particularly important from a strategic point of view. This exception applied to the field of solar energy, where the Faculty invested some specific money. The dean underlined that a research school can be a mean to build an inter-institutional structure for broad research projects going beyond institutional boarders – like it is the case in the funding allocated by the Norwegian Research Council for the field of solar energy. In addition, it can provide visibility to such a research field which does not exist as an own institutional unit. The dean further argues that, increased visibility could also reveal important in order to attract doctoral students. According to an involved professor, it has been agreed that one million NOK (~119,000 €) shall be yearly used for the establishment and running of the new research school in solar cell technology. Thus, at least concerning the materials science area involved in solar energy, the future funding problems seem to be defused.

Although not being part of the training component of FUNMAT Research School, it is worth mentioning the underlying funding mechanism of the so called doctoral courses of the Faculty's PhD programme. With the arrival of the quality reform in 2003, a new funding system has been introduced in Norwegian higher education. Several interviewees explained that, relying on this funding system, the Ministry of Education and Research does only provide funding – per acquired credit points – for courses at bachelor and master levels, but not at doctoral level. The ministerial reward at doctoral level only consists of an allocation per completed doctorate (Kunnskapsdepartementet 2008). Thus, the establishment and running of specific doctoral courses would not be directly indemnified. Or, in other words, the Ministerial allocation related to performances in doctoral education does not directly depend on whether or not doctoral courses are offered by the Faculty. In addition, considering the comparatively lower number of students at doctoral level, the establishment of specific doctoral courses is quite expensive. Hence, direct monetary incentives appear rather low. Indeed, "pure" doctoral courses seem to be rare. Several interviewees underlined that most of doctoral courses figuring in the Faculty's PhD programme are actually "cloned" master courses. Concretely, master and doctoral students follow the same course but under a different label.

The second type of instruments at play, that is to say the legal one, only has a limited steering impact on the FUNMAT Research School. PhD regulations constitute the overall legal framework for doctoral education in materials science. Among others, they define requirements in terms of admission, training, supervision, follow-up and final evaluation (University of Oslo 2007; Faculty of Mathematics and Natural Sciences of University of Oslo 2008). Considering the types of activities carried out in the framework of FUNMAT Research School, only the training component – thus, in the case under consideration the workshops and, at best, the doctoral students seminars – are potentially affected by this legal framework. According to the latter, the training component should correspond to at least 30 ECTS, but ordinarily not exceed 40 ECTS. Furthermore, at least 5 ECTS of the total amount must be collected through courses in research ethics, scientific theory and scientific method. An examination with the result pass/fail forms the framework condition for the credits' acquirement (University of Oslo 2007; Faculty of Mathematics and Natural Sciences 2008). However, participation in workshops and seminars of FUNMAT Research School includes neither exams – and, as a consequence – nor the award of credit points. Thus, from this point of view, FUNMAT Research School activities are not influenced by the given PhD regulations.

Considering the PhD regulations' requirement of at least 30 compulsory ECTS, one may ask the question why the initiators of FUNMAT Research School renounced to organise activities which include the award of credit points. A professor involved into FUNMAT Research School's birth period, argues that this might be related to the question of what a research school should be. He underlines that the initiators' idea was to provide "something useful" which gave an additional value to the already existing structure of the Faculty's PhD programme, consisting among others of regular – though cloned –

doctoral courses. However, his statement on the future research school in solar cell technology also indicates that it might be a question of financial resources at disposal. When referring to this new research school he emphasises that, thanks to the much larger budget, many more and larger courses, eligible for the training component, will be established.

PhD regulations do not affect either the participation of doctoral students in FUNMAT Research School. No article mentions as compulsory to participate in any research school. However, another instrument obliged part of doctoral students in materials science to participate. The employment contract of all doctoral students whose funding was related to the FUNMAT research project included this obligation. All other doctoral students in material sciences, funded through different types of sources were free to participate. With the end of FUNMAT as a prioritised research area, participation became voluntary for all doctoral students.

Finally, alike at University of Bergen, PhD regulations oblige doctoral students and their supervisors to write a yearly progress report. However, this reporting system is not situated at the research school level, but within the Faculty's PhD programme. Once received all reports, the "basic unit" – in the case under consideration the departments of physics and chemistry – writes and sends a summary to the Faculty. Besides the students' progress, supervision is dealt with in this report. Possible divergence to the initial plan has to be specified (University of Oslo 2007; Faculty of Mathematics and Natural Sciences 2008). In case of disagreement between the student and one or several of his supervisors, discussions about possible improvements or other solutions take place at the institute level. In the case of larger conflicts, discussions might take place at Faculty level, in exceptional cases, even at central university level.

VI.2.3. An Unstable Actors' Constellation

Besides the various instruments developed above, actors' constellation provides further insight for the reform story such as taking place in this case study. Regarding the birth period, it is first of all worth emphasising that a vice-rector of University of Oslo was a member of the working group[88] of the Norwegian Association of Higher Education Institutions (UHR) which formulated the recommendation to establish research schools. Several interviewees underlined that, subsequently, this vice-rector actively promoted the idea of research schools within University of Oslo. Second, still with respect to the original input for the creation of the FUNMAT Research School, the dean of the Faculty of Mathematics and Natural Sciences, who at the time also was the chairman of the national FUNMAT consortium, stresses that the national FUNMAT consortium did not play any active role in the creation of the examined research school.

In opposite to the national board of the FUNMAT consortium, the local FUNMAT board at University of Oslo, respectively some of its members, has been involved in the research school's creation. Confronted with the formal requirement to establish a research school – as part of the duties related to the status of a prioritised area –, the head of the FUNMAT board at University of Oslo took the initiative and discussed with about three further people involved in the local FUNMAT prioritised area what type of content a research school could and should include. One of those discussants was the doctoral student charged with related administrative tasks. He characterised those discussions and the resulting decisions as rather informal. Furthermore, with respect to the general running of research schools, a Faculty administrator considers research schools of the Faculty of Mathematics and Natural Science as independently working units. The Faculty only intervenes in order to formally recognise the research schools' activities as being worthy (or not) for the award of credit points. Since FUNMAT Research School activities did not comprise the award of any credit points, it can be assumed that there have been even less interactions between the research school and the Faculty. Thus, FUNMAT Research School has operated in quite an independent manner.

With the end of FUNMAT as a prioritised area and the subsequent dissolution of the FUNMAT Board, nobody was anymore formally in charge of the FUNMAT Research School's running. The doctoral student charged of related administrative tasks finished his contract. Furthermore, the initiator of FUNMAT Research School meanwhile got

88 This working group was composed of one rector, three vice-rectors and one research director representing the five largest Norwegian institutions (UHR 2003).

other tasks and, already quite in the beginning of the school's live, handed the school's lead over to a colleague. All those factors have been put forward by the interviewees in order to explain what led to the hibernation episode of FUNMAT Research School. Internal administrative procedures seem further having been responsible for part of the continuation of this hibernation episode. Concretely, the initiator of the research school stated that once he realised that the research school "was sleeping", he asked the central and Faculty administrations to formally pass on the responsibility of the research school to the Centre of Materials Science and Nanotechnology (SMN). This has finally been accepted by one administrative level after the other, but took some time. Since about autumn 2008, the Centre of Materials Science and Nanotechnology is formally responsible of the research school's running and launched the resuscitation period such as described above.

Parts of the FUNMAT Research School's underlying objectives have already been mentioned. Here, they are systematically itemised. A first objective mentioned by actors involved in FUNMAT Research School's creation and running concerns the improvement of the doctoral training component. They aim at providing doctoral students with knowledge which they would not have acquired through other training activities like the doctoral courses of the Faculty based PhD programme. A second objective relates to the enlargement of doctoral students' scientific network. As mentioned, in particular through seminars, they should have the possibility to meet people from other research groups, departments and even Faculties, who are also working on material sciences. Thereby, they could get to know other scientific methods, techniques and so on. Third, social isolation – and thereby also to a certain extent scientific isolation – should be avoided. The creation of a larger social network should also be facilitated by the aforementioned seminars. Some interviewees consider that such objectives could also be achieved through other, for instance, individual initiatives coming from doctoral students themselves. However, they see in the research school a way to institutionalise such scientific and social networking mechanisms. Finally, one interviewee argues in a symbolic manner. He interprets the creation and running of a research school as an important illustration of their will to progress in doctoral education's reform:

> There was a lot of focus on the research schools. People were very concerned that this was something we need to establish. And we need to show that we are doing something to improve the PhD education.

Besides those declared objectives, it is worth mentioning that some interviewees explicitly denied other objectives. Besides a possible focus on improvements in terms of supervision, several interviewees also specifically denied a potential objective consisting of doctoral students' attraction through the FUNMAT Research School. The further quote may provide some explanations for it:

> I mean in order to be able to have an effect in that sense, the research school would have had to be organised in a very different way than it was, I think. Ok, there was probably, when we announced for PhD positions, there was probably a sentence that there is a research school and that you should participate in this. But I don't think, nobody knew about it before starting I guess. So I don't think it had any role in that sense. It might have had, at some point, if it had continued for a longer time and if it had developed into something more comprehensive. But we didn't get there.

VI.2.4. An Independent Network Surrounded by a Restricting Institutional Environment

The management story of the FUNMAT Research School can be characterised as functioning according to mechanisms of Network Governance and against New Public Management principles. Its institutional environment, however, is determined by a number of New Public Management principles.

Beginning with the institutional environment, one can first of all point to the PhD regulations of the Faculty of Mathematics and Natural Sciences (2008) and of the University of Oslo (2007), which set a number of explicit standards and measures of performance for the Faculty's PhD programme, like the number of ECTS to be acquired during doctoral education and the related conditions as well as the yearly progress reports. The same New Public Management feature applies to the Ministry's allocation per completed doctoral degree. A further New Public Management principle can be recognised in the Faculty's spotty selection of research areas where specific funding is invested in the establishment of research schools. Rather than following a military-style "public service ethic", dealing with all research fields in the same way – meaning investing or not some money for research schools – money is invested where it seems to matter. This might be interpreted as stress on private-sectors style of management practice.

The picture strongly changes when one considers the FUNMAT Research School as such. It does not at all correspond to New Public Management principles especially with respect to three critical points. First, standards and measures of performance are not clearly defined. For instance, this applies to the internal funding instrument of the rectorate for research schools. The criteria of evaluation of the individual applications have not been explicitly defined. The same is true regarding the conditions and evaluation of doctoral students' participation in the research school. On the one hand, one could argue that there is a clear standard condition of participation to the extent that, today, no doctoral student is formally obliged to participate. However, on the other hand, there are no clear measures of performance of their participation. No exams or other types of formal control exist. And even if it seems that the rectorate would probably consider a high rate of participation of doctoral students as such as successful, this assessment is apparently not necessarily shared by other actors who consider research schools as less critical for successful doctoral education in the Faculty of Mathematics and Natural Sciences. A second New Public Management feature, whose opposite appears in this case study, is the idea of a shift to disaggregation of units in the public sector into corporatized units around products. Instead of exclusively being responsible of all types of aspects related to doctoral education, FUNMAT Research School essentially deals with part of the training offer and the scientific and social environment of doctoral students. Regular doctoral courses, administrative follow-up mechanisms of doctoral students as well as admission to doctoral education are principally dealt with at the level of the PhD programme structure within the Faculty and the individual departments. Finally, there can be no question either of a third central New Public Management feature, that is to say of a shift to greater competition. According to the interviewees, the competition for instance for the best doctoral students is no explicit objective of FUNMAT Research School.

If FUNMAT Research School's management story is clearly no case of New Public Management, it comprises a number of Network Governance principles. First, although the range of managing actors is not necessarily greater, the actors' network does not correspond to any institutionally predefined structure. Second, issuing of a structure built on a research project limited in time, a small number of involved people constituted a rather informal self-steering group, which was – and today, in a different form, still is – independent of the Faculty of Mathematics and Natural Sciences. Third, this group has taken some decisions about FUNMAT activities in a lateral form of management. Finally, the yearly activity report of FUNMAT Research School addressed at the central university administration is clearly rather a way of "giving account" to local publics than an ex-post state driven system of checking.

This management story helps to understand the FUNMAT Research School's development and current state. To illustrate the link between the management story and the reform story, it seems to be useful to distinguish the Faculty's PhD programme from the FUNMAT Research School. Thus, there is on the one side the PhD programme which, in line with the New Public Management feature of explicit standards and measures of performance, determines a number of processes in doctoral education: doctoral students complete coursework in order to acquire the required credit points, they write their yearly progress report and the Faculty, respectively the corresponding departments obtain special funding from the Ministry of Education and Research when doctoral students completed their doctoral degree. Hence, those mechanisms seem to be commonly accepted and regularly work as defined. On the other side, there is the research school which is steered in an opposed manner, that is to say without any explicit standards and measures of performance and according to Network Governance features, comprising among others an informal steering group which decides in an independent manner about a number of issues. Theoretically, such a steering constellation smells like great autonomy for the research school. However, this autonomy can only be exercised to a very limited extent. The following two elements restrict this extent: first, the reform field of doctoral education is not anymore virgin but has already been "occupied" by the Faculty's PhD programme. The latter does not only cover a wide range of issues related to doctoral education like admission, training and follow-up of doctoral students, but the related processes are also already quite well established and therefore probably difficult to influence by research schools. Second, the network steering of the research school is unstable and, from a financial point of view, weakly and unstably equipped. Due to the absence of a stable institutional structure behind the research school – like a Faculty or a department – and the limited duration of FUNMAT as a prioritised research area, the temporary disappearance of leading actors and funding was possible. Hence, as a result of those two elements of restriction, the research school's scope and extent of action remained quite modest (and even temporarily disappeared): the training offer has been enlarged through about three annual two-day workshops and doctoral students have been given a structure to develop scientific exchange within a scientific and social network of doctoral students. Currently, only the first of those two elements of reform is still working. However, future developments, like the research network of solar energy – which is again limited in time – will probably temporarily lead to the enlargement of the training offer for, at least, part of doctoral students in materials science at University of Oslo and other Norwegian HEIs.

VI.2.5. A Formal but Non-materialised Reform

The comparison between this case study and the previous one clearly illustrates that a strong national and especially institutional leadership and corresponding impact in terms of internal reforms has its price. Certainly, the political and institutional influence is more strongly visible: admission, training and follow-up are regulated in a legal framework decided upon by those instances. Thus, supervisors and especially doctoral students are again placed under stronger observation. This underlines the increased importance the political and institutional leaders attribute to doctoral education. Yet, besides those legal guidelines, no further input for the concrete reform can be given or even imposed. This is not only due to the vague idea those actors have of a research school but also the missing will or capacity to materialise the reform, i.e. to provide resources for instance to fund specific doctoral courses.

Until now, the studied college could only rely on weak financial and personal resources. As a consequence, the realised reform steps are rather modest. However, this will probably change with the arrival of the millions of the Research Council. Many more activities are expected to be offered. Thus, the resources of the Research Council may reinforce the college's role in the reform process and thereby make it – at least temporarily – a stronger actor in the university governance.

VII. Interdisciplinary Doctoral Schools in Humanities

VII.1. Pro*Doc Aesthetics of Intermediality. Play – Ritual – Performance

Together with six other Pro*Doc projects, the Pro*Doc „Aesthetics of Intermediality. Play – Ritual – Performance“ (Pro*Doc AI) (*Intermediale Ästhetik. Spiel – Ritual – Performanz*) has been chosen by the Swiss National Science Foundation out of totally 30 applications submitted to the first selection round in 2006 (SNF 2007). Its funding period started in 2006 and ends in 2009. Nine doctoral students get their salary directly through this doctoral school and, together with 15 further doctoral students, complete during three years an interdisciplinary training programme which is thematically linked to the topic of their respective doctoral research projects. Pro*Doc AI is run by four professors of University of Basle as well as one professor of University of Bern. The involved professors' disciplinary backgrounds cover media science, German literature, Hellenic studies and theatre studies.

VII.1.1. Systematisation of Doctoral Training and Scientific Exchange[89]

The reform of doctoral education of this case study essentially concerns four issues: the first issue consists of the *traditional apprenticeship-model's systematic enlargement through collective forms of training and scientific exchange.* The second issue relates to the *intensive and regular character* of those training and scientific exchange activities, which take place during the doctoral school's overall duration. The third reform issue consists in the creation of *thematic research projects involving a larger number of doctoral students.* Finally, the forth issue consists in the introduction of an *administrative follow-up* of doctoral students.

The following types of activities, carried out in the framework of the Pro*Doc AI, complement the traditional apprenticeship-model through collective and regular forms of training and scientific exchange: once every other week, doctoral students and the involved five professors meet in a colloquium of research and methods (*Forschungs- und Methodenkolloquium*). The principal focus of this first type of activities is put on the presentation and discussion of doctoral students' research with a particular emphasis on methodological aspects and disambiguation. A second type of activities relates to research seminars (*Forschungsseminare*), which take place once or twice per term. During those two-day events, doctoral students study the current state of art of Pro*Doc AI's framework themes on the basis of a comprehensive number of texts. As a third type of activities, lecture series (*Ringvorlesungen*) – based on doctoral students' research topics – are carried out by external presenters once every other week. The fourth activity, a yearly Pro*Doc conference (*Pro*Doc-Tagung*), is a sort of

89 Unless indicated, data used is stemming from interviews with the vice-rector for research and the encouragement of the next academic generation of University of Basle, the central administrator for research in social sciences and humanities of University of Basle, the central administrator for the encouragement of the next academic generation of University of Basle, the leader of the Pro*Doc AI programme, two further professors involved in the Pro*Doc AI programme (out of which one of University of Bern), four doctoral students completing Pro*Doc AI, two representatives of the Swiss National Science Foundation (SNF) responsible of Pro*Doc, one representative of the SNF responsible of doctoral training in NCCR and the vice-general secretary of the Rectors' Conference of the Swiss Universities (CRUS).

mix between colloquium of research and methods and lecture series. On the one side, doctoral students present their ongoing research and, on the other side, internationally renowned speakers intervene with classical presentations. The conceptual idea rests upon to link both types of presentations in workshop-like discussions. In addition to those four types of activities, some individual doctoral students had the opportunity to participate in further (non-Pro*Doc) conferences and to publish parts of their work in publications, partly edited by Pro*Doc AI professors (Pro*Doc Intermediale Ästhetik 2008). It is important to underline that regular collective training and scientific exchange activities[90] are not necessarily new for all of the involved doctoral students. Several supervisors organise such gatherings for their doctoral students independently of Pro*Doc. However, the novel characteristic consists of the *systematisation* of such activities for a group of doctoral students supervised by various professors. In other words, in terms of doctoral training and scientific exchange, concerned doctoral students are less dependent on their own initiative and the one of their personal supervisor but can benefit from a certain "collective infrastructure or organisation".

As mentioned, the third issue of reform concerns the elaboration of thematic research projects which involve a relatively large number of doctoral students. The change especially concerns the number of involved doctoral students. The traditional Swiss National Science Foundation research project funding for social sciences and humanities (Division I) is not formally limited in terms of maximal numbers of doctoral students which can be funded. However, it seems fair to say that this type of funding does not attain the number of doctoral students which can be funded through Pro*Doc projects. A number of up to ten doctoral students per research project – or even more if one includes associated doctoral students funded through other sources – represents an important step within humanities. Thus, from this point of view, Pro*Doc funding allows the development of specific – in the case under consideration *interdisciplinary* – research fields which otherwise could

90 Considering those different types of activities, it seems difficult to clearly distinguish between training activities on the one hand and scientific exchange on the other hand. However, it also seems that both types of activities take place. Therefore, it is always referred to both of those activities in this case study.

not have been developed in humanities (except through National Centres of Competence in Research – NCCR).

Finally, as part of the conditions related to the receipt of Pro*Doc funding involved professors have to provide to the Swiss National Science Foundation a report. The latter is produced on the basis of individual reports of each doctoral student. The report's content seems to vary with respect to its degree of detail according to the professor. However, doctoral students have essentially to give an account of their present and further research activities, what constitutes a new activity for them.

What was the context of this particular Doctoral School's creation and the related reform? According to the Pro*Doc AI's leader, professors of University Basle's Faculty of humanities (*Philosophisch-historische Fakultät*) have been informed by their dean about the existence of a new funding instrument of the Swiss National Science Foundation, Pro*Doc, and the possibility to submit proposal to the quickly approaching call. The later Pro*Doc AI leader decided to submit an application because he was personally convinced of the necessity to promote the next Swiss academic generation in a more systematic manner, that is to say by providing structures which assure promotion for every doctoral student instead of leaving it up to the individual professors' will. In addition, he and his colleagues were not unprepared to the arrival of this new funding instrument. Although the Pro*Doc model would not exactly correspond to the German *Graduiertenkolleg*, the Pro*Doc AI's leader and other involved professors who were previously working in German higher education recognised some common elements – in particular the idea of promotion within groups of doctoral students – and, therefore, felt familiar with the underlying idea. Moreover, before the Pro*Doc AI's start in 2006, its leader has already organised collective activities for doctoral students during seven years. Financially supported by the University of Basle, he invited experts to teach courses during so called "week-end-seminars".

Interviews with doctoral students show that a certain tension between the doctoral students' own, often disciplinarily shaped interests and Pro*Doc AI related interdisciplinary interests might appear. This tension appears both in the formulation of the research projects and the content of training activities: some doctoral students feel somehow restricted in their research through the overall Pro*Doc AI research thematics and sometimes perceive certain training activities as being too discipline-specific. This difficulty occurred also in an interdisciplinary doctoral programme analysed by Holley (2009). In the present study, several interviewees, doctoral students as well as supervisors, underline the need of time in order to develop interdisciplinary understanding.

VII.1.2. A National Instrument of Governance

Before discussing the main instrument of governance at play in this case study, it is worth mentioning that in the case of the University of Basle, an additional funding instrument focusing on Pro*Doc has been created and used. Considering the short time left until the submission deadline of the first Pro*Doc call, University of Basle's central governing body wanted to provide supplementary support and incentive for potential applicants and quickly decided to offer a total yearly amount of 50'000 CHF (~33,000 €) for activities aiming at the elaboration of Pro*Doc applications. This amount, which has been made at disposal of all applicants during the years 2006 and 2007, could be used quite freely for staff and material.

The main instrument of governance in this case study is Pro*Doc itself. The conceptualisation of this instrument provides information about the types of aspects it aims to steer (or not). First, from a formal point of view, the instrument is not very constraining with respect to the *content of research and training activities*. It distinguishes module of research and module of training. Each Pro*Doc has to be composed of one training module and one or several research modules, comprising individual doctoral research projects. The overall doctoral school has to be coherent. Although not explicitly mentioned, it can be assumed that this means that both research and training modules have to be organised around a common scientific topic or thematic. According to the interviewees of the Rectors' Conference of Swiss Universities (CRUS) and the Swiss National Science Foundation (SNF), this non-constraining character precisely aims at providing enough leeway for diversity in terms of content. Compared to content, prescriptions about *the doctoral schools' size* and *doctoral education's duration* are more clearly defined. SNF and CRUS regulation (2007) ask a minimal number of twelve doctoral students per Pro*Doc, out of which maximally ten are financed through Pro*Doc resources. According to the SNF interviewees, the intention of those two categories of doctoral students (non-/funded through Pro*Doc) is to involve HEIs from a financial point of view, namely by obliging them to bring in institutional or other third resources. Pro*Doc funding for research and training modules is provided for three years. Doctoral students who do not finish within this duration may ask supplementary funding. However, in principle, compared to training modules, research modules as such cannot be extended for entire additional funding periods. The objective related to this funding limited in time consists of shorter doctoral education duration. As fourth aspect, Pro*Doc also seeks to incite cooperative research and training activities between doctoral students and professors (or other academics having the right to supervise doctoral students) of different HEIs. At least two HEIs have to be represented within one Pro*Doc. We read this condition as another federal measure which aims to contribute to clearer *profile building* and thereby a clearer *differentiation between Swiss HEIs*. Another aspect related to institutional structure can be seen in the fact that the central governing bodies of concerned universities have to attest their support of the applications by signing a written declaration. We interpret this measure as a mean to involve HEI governing bodies into the reform and, again, as an incentive to integrate thoughts about institutional profile building (in terms of disciplinary fields of a HEI) at the central level of a HEI. From an administrative point of view, one may notice in particular two aspects: one condition defined by Pro*Doc regulation obliges doctoral students *to be enrolled as doctoral student in their HEI during the whole doctoral period.* We interpret this condition as incentive for the development of uniform practices among HEIs and their institutional sub-units in order to more systematically provide administrative information about doctoral students. An analysis of the Swiss HEIs' PhD regulations (Baschung 2008) showed that currently a large diversity of practice is in place, what is certainly not without any impact on the possibility of administrative follow-up and statistics of doctoral students. As a second administrative measure, successful applicants have to provide *intermediary and final reports* about the evolution and possible changes in research and training modules (SNF/CRUS 2007). In the present case study, each main responsible professor of the three research modules writes those reports on the basis of individual reports produced by each doctoral student. In principle, those reports are handed out to the SNF and not necessarily also to other institutional instances like the involved HEIs' central or Faculty administration.

A third instrument which is currently discussed at University of Basle is a doctoral agreement between doctoral student and the according main supervisor. In case of adoption, such an agreement would deal with intermediate objectives and corresponding deadlines with respect to doctoral research projects. On the basis of such an agreement, doctoral students and supervisors should regularly discuss progress. However, interviewees of the central administration of University of Basle also underline that first, this instrument could not be introduced by force but only by recommendation and, second, the rectorate would not have the necessary practical means to follow up the effective use of this instrument.

VII.1.3. Multilevel Decision Taking

Various circles of actors have been involved from Pro*Doc's conceptualisation until the concrete implementation of the Pro*Doc Aesthetics of Intermediality. As mentioned in chapter IV, a first circle of three actors can be identified with respect to Pro*Doc's conceptualisation. According to a SNF responsible, the SNF has been mandated by the State Secretariat for Education and Research to create a structure which makes possible many flexible forms in terms of concrete content but always with the objective to reduce doctoral education's duration. During Pro*Doc's starting phase, the Rectors' Conference of the Swiss Universities made doctoral education and its standardisation one of its four strategic priorities for the period 2008-2011, what led the Confederation to provide a second funding source – in addition to the SNF-Pro*Doc funding – for special measures aiming at the reform of doctoral education. Considering that it would be regrettable to use different criteria to allocate federal resources aiming at the same subject, CRUS decided to join the initial Pro*Doc project. Thus, since 2008, both funding resources are united in the same budget, allocated in the framework of Pro*Doc and on the basis of the same criteria. According to CRUS, task distribution between SNF and CRUS is carried out in the following manner:

> Swiss National Science Foundation is responsible of the programme's management. It is responsible of launching the call, informing the scientific community, the applications' evaluation and decisions. On its part, CRUS ensures that ProDoc is accompanied by a strategic orientation of universities and compatible with their academic and administrative procedures. To this end, it assigns delegates who are responsible of evaluating institutional aspects when evaluating training modules.[91]

According to CRUS' vice-general secretary, the HEIs' strategic decisions take place at two different levels: first, at the internal level, by accepting or refusing applications of members of the own institution, second, among the united HEIs' delegates who mostly are rectors or other academics, responsible of doctoral education (vice-rectors, deans, etc.). After this double pre-selection, external experts, asked by the SNF, evaluate the applications from a scientific point of view.

With respect to the application phase, the circle of actors obviously concerns in the first place HEIs themselves. In the case of University of Basle, an interviewee of central administration puts forward that, although the rectorate's extra funding for the initiating of Pro*Doc applications has been available for all disciplines, he especially contacted the dean of the Faculty of humanities in order to inform him about this extra funding. This particular information action would be due to humanities' particular needs, both in terms of funding and structured doctoral education. Indeed, Pro*Doc AI's leader has been informed by the dean and, together with other applicants, benefitted from the extra funding. However, as mentioned above, the main reason for the Pro*Doc AI leader to initiate the doctoral school consisted of his previous experience with German doctoral schools and the related conviction of its usefulness. According to interviewed professors, the composition of their group was based on contacts which already existed before the application, also with respect to University of Bern's representative. They underline that the Pro*Doc AI's concrete thematic and the represented scientific disciplines strongly depend on the composition of the group. One involved professor underlined the necessity to let academics organise themselves in a bottom-up process:

---

91 Source: www.crus.ch/die-crus/koordiniert-harmonisiert/projekt-prodoc /prodoc.html?L=2; accessed on December 2009.

> The container is so open. One would have had different possibilities. One could also have designed something in a disciplinary way and initiated for one discipline with for instance all Swiss universities. Our model went into a completely different direction. We quickly found us, simply on the basis of experience and already existing cooperation within the Faculty, simply because they are people you can work with. That's also interesting. I mean, it would probably work badly, if a dean or a rector would say, those three have to initiate that and that. On the contrary, completely spontaneously we said among us, we are the research organisation.
>
> (A professor in humanities)

Once selected by the SNF, professors involved in Pro*Doc AI recruited their doctoral students. Advertisement has been carried out through announcements in Swiss newspapers, different websites and by direct communication to local master and doctoral students. Among others, candidates had to submit a research proposal fitting with the overall research module topic. This fit as well as the candidates' qualification for interdisciplinary research projects would have been the main selection criteria. At least in some cases, interviews with candidates were carried out. Even though applications were examined by several professors, the definitive choice was done by the professors concerned by the respective research module. As mentioned, from a formal point of view, each Pro*Doc also has to associate at least two further doctoral students to the training module who are funded by other types of resources than Pro*Doc. In the case of Pro*Doc AI, 15 such doctoral students are associated to the training module. A large part of them were already involved in the training activities which were carried out by the Pro*Doc AI's leader before Pro*Doc AI.

The activities of the training module developed above as well as the thematic orientation of them and of the research modules have been decided by this group of professors. However, doctoral students are also involved in some decisions of the Pro*Doc AI's day-to-day life: on the one side, in spite of a certain restriction in terms of thematic (and interdisciplinary) orientation – varying according to the doctoral student –, interviewed doctoral students generally feel rather free regarding the development and implementation of their research project. On the other side, in the case of some of the presented training activities, they have the right to suggest inviting scholars they are particularly interested in.

The scientific and administrative working load related to the different training activities is shared by involved professors, invited scholars, doctoral students and an administrative coordinator. Professors mostly act as "animators" but do not directly intervene with own presentations. They distribute the working load as animators among them according to the activity's thematic focus and presenters. In other words, they are in principle present, either if their personal disciplinary focus is concerned, or if a doctoral student they are supervising or a scholar they personally invited is intervening through a personal presentation. The Pro*Doc budget includes funding for the invited scholars' remuneration. However, in spite of multiple written demands to their rectorate, professors of University of Basle do currently not get any compensation in terms of lower teaching load at bachelor and master level.

A series of objectives related to Pro*Doc generally and the Pro*Doc Aethetics of Intermediality in particular have been mentioned by our interviewees. A first objective which is shared by almost all interviewees – from the doctoral student until SNF representatives – consists in a *shorter duration of doctoral education.* In spite of this general consensus about this objective, several critical voices of HEI actors emphasised the ambiguity between the high level of training activities within Pro*Doc and the ambition to simultaneously shorten doctoral education's duration. A similar ambiguity appears concerning another objective mentioned by most actors – among others also in the context of shorter doctoral education –, namely the *"structuring" of doctoral education.* Interviewed actors are unanimous about the necessity to "structure" doctoral education, in particular in humanities. Thus, they all agree on the establishment of some regular activities which should assure that each doctoral student quickly progresses. However, when it comes to discuss concrete instruments which should contribute to doctoral education's structuring, most interviewees are more reluctant. Concerning the structuring effect of training activities, some interviewees again mention the danger of a too high level of activity and a related "scholarisation". Not only this would lengthen doctoral education's duration but, like University of Basle's vice-rector underlines, also withhold doctoral students from becoming independent researchers:

> Then, there have to be some educational elements, but then one has to, I always tell the same thing, I think the very big danger coming from the European structuring

> process is that it goes too far. Then it's again structured studies where they lose freedom. And then the question is asked where those young people learn to take over responsibility for themselves, for their work and so on.
>
> (Vice-rector for research and the encouragement of the next academic generation)

Further instruments aiming at the structuring of doctoral education also meet some resistance in this case study: first, concerning intermediary reports, opinions about its usefulness diverge. Interviewed professors and some doctoral students consider it as an opportunity for doctoral students to account to themselves for their research projects and related progress, whereas other doctoral students see it as a pure administrative measure which justifies the obtained funding towards the SNF. Second, performance control takes place through presentations of doctoral students during the various training activities. However, there are no exams or other types of controls with grades. As a consequence, there are no ECTS points either. University of Basle's vice-rector estimates that at doctoral level, ECTS should not be necessary. Real performance would be rather demonstrated through publications than ECTS points. Nevertheless, administrators at University of Basle's central level report that, although one year ago, ECTS were absolutely no issue in the Faculty of humanities' discussion about doctoral education's reform, they would nowadays already be integrated in the thoughts of the responsible commission in humanities. Third, with respect to presence control of doctoral students, interviewed professors declared that "we are not at school". However, they simultaneously admit that they regularly have to remind doctoral students about their obligation to attend the various training activities.

Besides shorter duration and structuring, a third objective put forward by our interviewees consists in *doctoral students' integration in networks* composed of other doctoral students, professors and invited scholars. The main advantage related to this network issue is seen in improved scientific exchange and supervision for doctoral students. The latter would not anymore depend on the good will of one only person, that is to say the main supervisor and take the risk of complete solitude, but could benefit from inputs coming from several people. Being part of a network would also allow doctoral students to develop social and/or scientific exchange – for instance concerning a particular type of literature – among them or to understand how a scientific community works.

Besides those three more general objectives, a fourth concerns in particular the Pro*Doc Aethetics of Intermediality, that is to say the *development of interdisciplinary research*, which individual scientific disciplines benefit from. According to Pro*Doc AI's leader, an interdisciplinary approach not only brings new inputs into individual disciplines but also makes doctoral students learn to listen to doctoral students from other disciplines and "opens their horizon". Simultaneously, both professors and doctoral students underline how difficult it is to go beyond traditional disciplinary lines of argumentation and to achieve interdisciplinarity.

Finally, a last, somehow overall objective which was strongly emphasised by as good as all interviewees regards a generally *better preparation of the next Swiss generation for the academic labour market*. All interviewees esteem Pro*Doc being a tool which provides doctoral students better changes for an academic career. University of Basle's vice-rector sees it as "a sign of excellence", whereas doctoral students also expect it to be a precious label on the academic job market. Nevertheless, nobody among the interviewed actors deludes oneself about reality on the academic job market. On the contrary, when asked about the type of labour market they educate doctoral students for, interviewed professors answered, in a first step, with a sort of ironic laugh… In a second step, they put forward that acquired competencies like independent working, the organisation of time schedules and knowledge, teamwork, as well as interdisciplinary communication are absolutely valuable and usable on the non-academic job market. Such soft-skills would principally be a side-effect of the scientific activities, without organising many special soft-skills courses.

VII.1.4. An Imperfect Case of the Neo-Weberian-State Narrative

What is the management story of this case study about and what does its concrete impact in terms of reform consist of? Quite a number of features indicate a veritable case of Neo-Weberian-state narrative. However, on the one side, they are combined with some Network Governance and rather weakly pronounced forms of New Public

Management mechanisms. On the other side, since the duration of the instrument, which constitutes all observed Neo-Weberian-state features and which currently mainly steers this reform, is of limited duration, its long term effect – in the sense of the Neo-Weberian-state narrative – has to be questioned.

A first one of those Neo-Weberian-state elements can be seen in the genesis of the Pro*Doc instrument. The initiative came from the State Secretariate for Education and Research, which mandated the Swiss National Science Foundation to design and implement a special instrument focusing on doctoral research and training. As mentioned in chapter IV, SNF interviewees did not identify one single reason for this development, but principally refer to the discussions about doctoral schools and the underlying problems related to doctoral education in humanities and social sciences – like unsatisfactory supervision – which already lasted for years. Thus, the State Secretariate's intervention seems to represent a *reaction* and *adaptation* to those discussions and problems.

Still with respect to Pro*Doc's genesis and the State's role within it, CRUS' participation, which began in 2008, could be a sign for a certain re-appropriation of one reform instrument by HEI governing bodies. However, in a first step it did not look like because instead of trying to change the existing Pro*Doc instrument or to invent a new one, CRUS decided to join Pro*Doc and to allocate supplementary funding to the same conditions as the initial Pro*Doc. Moreover, Pro*Doc is principally managed by the SNF. Thus, it rather seemed that CRUS paradoxically reinforced the State's power (via the SNF), although one also has to notice that HEIs – via their delegates – have formal power to intervene on the actual selection of individual projects. The hypothesis of a re-appropriation seems to apply for the years ahead, since CRUS decided to cease the Pro*Doc programme and to fully assume the responsibility for the doctoral level. Yet, concrete actions have to be awaited in order to confirm this hypothesis.

The third Neo-Weberian-state element, namely to *make new aspects of public activities accessible to outside administrative and political control* clearly applies to this case study. Although some Swiss HEIs explicitly list their training programmes and spotty activities on their respective websites, this is not yet systematically the case for all of them. As a consequence, no general overview exists at the level of the Swiss higher education system. In opposite, all Pro*Doc programmes are explicitly mentioned on the SNF website. In addition, Pro*Doc AI even has an own website which describes research and training activities more in detail. Besides higher transparency concerning the existence of doctoral training offers, the SNF contributes with Pro*Doc programmes also to tighter administrative and political control of doctoral training. This tighter follow-up, carried out through intermediary and final reports, illustrates increased steering power of the state – represented by the SNF – vis-à-vis HEIs by two aspects. On the one side, the SNF, who traditionally is exclusively active in the field of research, entered the field of training. This can certainly be seen as a major change. On the other side, intermediary and final reports are first and foremost addressed to the SNF and thereby escape, at least for the moment, institutional control. A third aspect testifies to the increased administrative and political control, that is to say the obligation for doctoral students who are funded by Pro*Doc to be enrolled in a Swiss HEI as doctoral student during doctoral education's whole duration. The resulting generation of more complete data about doctoral students will be at disposal at institutional but also national levels and, hence, contribute to better administrative and political control at both levels. The possible introduction of doctoral agreements might represent a specifically institutional instrument for University of Basle to follow up doctoral students' progress and thereby to acquire some administrative control by their own.

Concerning the forth Neo-Weberian-state element, namely the *stabilisation of the field's function*, one could certainly argue that Pro*Doc contributes to achieving this end, though it depends on what one more precisely considers as field (e.g. higher education) and especially its function… We here renounce to an extensive interpretation and are content with saying that "well working" doctoral education (we also renounce to give a normative definition of what "well working" means) is certainly of central significance for the field of higher education. However, since the Pro*Doc funding is limited in time, it is questionable to what extent stabilisation may take place.

Currently, the fifth Neo-Weberian-state element, *a more efficient control of the new activities' costs*, seems at least in a first step rather not to apply to this case study. In opposite, supplementary funding is provided in order to fund supplementary doctoral positions and training activities. However, in principle, one could argue that in the medium term, costs related to doctoral research and training could be better controlled because of better cooperation between or concentration in Swiss HEIs. In other words, by obliging Swiss HEIs to cooperate and to build clearer profiles in the field of doctoral research and training, related activities would not be multiplied and scattered over the various Swiss HEIs.

The sixth and last Neo-Weberian-state element, that is to say *a tighter steering of doctoral training and research activities* can be confirmed to some extent. As mentioned, the evaluative and administrative control of doctoral training through the Confederation – via the SNF – is indeed tighter, since this control mechanism did not exist before. In opposite, the same is not necessarily true concerning doctoral research. One among different types of funding sources for doctoral research consists of free research projects funded by the SNF.[92] Underlying conditions like reporting are comparable to those of Pro*Doc. Therefore, there is no significant change in terms of steering from this point of view. At best, there is a change regarding the overall volume of doctoral research monitored by such reports.

Besides those numerous Neo-Weberian-state elements, a number of New Public Management elements can also be identified in this case study. They have two characteristics: in most cases, they do either not exist in a very pronounced form and/or are used as steering instruments by the SNF and not by the HEI governing bodies. Right at the outset, we point to the only exception to this general feature: confronted with the relatively short-dated call for the first round of applications, the HEI governing body of University of Basle provided a proof for *"hands-on professional management"* and created a special internal funding in order to encourage its academic professions – in particular the one of humanities – to apply for Pro*Doc programmes.

A second central New Public Management element, namely *explicit standards and measures of performance* also exist, though to a limited extent: on the one side, by conceptualising Pro*Doc for a three-year duration, the SNF clearly expressed its standard and measure of performance for doctoral education's duration. It also defined a minimal

92 This type of research project is called "investigator-driven research" (in French: projets de recherche libre). As the name says, research topics are not influenced by any political orientations but can freely be chosen by the applicants.

number of doctoral students per Doctoral School and a standardised salary for those who are funded through Pro*Doc. On the other side, explicit standards and measures of performances are less clear with regard to other issues. First, although coherence between research and training modules has to be assured, the actual scientific delimitation per project is not clearly defined. Thus, at least theoretically, it might range between strongly specialised fields to broad interdisciplinary fields. Second, doctoral students are morally obliged to follow training activities but not formally controlled. Third, although their performances are qualitatively evaluated through the respective supervisor, the volume of their performances is not quantitatively measured, for instance through ECTS.

Furthermore, from the SNF's view, there is certainly an emphasis on *output controls* through intermediary and final reports. Presumably, those reports are of importance in the case of new applications by the same applicants. In other words, whatever the effectively applied performance criteria are, reports may be used as performance measure instrument for further resource allocation. Since the same is probably also true for "traditional" free research projects, it is difficult to say, whether and, if yes, to what extent there is a *greater* emphasis on this output control. Independently of this degree question, one can say that for the moment, output controls are rather used by the SNF than by HEI governing bodies, since University of Basle does not (yet?) reward professors involved in Pro*Doc programmes by, for instance, compensating their supplementary work through a reduction of teaching loads at undergraduate level.

A fourth New Public Management characteristic can be seen in the *competitive* feature of the governance instrument Pro*Doc as a whole. The call for Doctoral Schools certainly corresponds to a public tendering procedure. With the support of their HEI governing bodies, academic professions have the possibility to submit applications to the SNF and thereby to enter competition for funding which would allow establishing and running doctoral research projects and training programmes. Considering the number of applications and the number of effectively selected Pro*Doc projects per call, one can say that there is indeed competition between individual applications.

The traditional apprenticeships' supplementation by other forms of supervision and scientific exchange also deserves some interpretation. At first sight, it might be interpreted as a New Public Management element, namely the *disaggregation of units in the public sector*. However, since the traditional apprenticeship has not been abandoned but *complemented* by advising activities through other actors like further internal and external professors and also by exchange among doctoral students, we argue that this change of management should rather be interpreted as an element of Network Governance, namely the one of *emergence of a greater range of actors and interactions*. Finally, considering the genesis of the Pro*Doc Aethetics of Intermediality and the recruitment of doctoral students one may argue that forms of management are rather *lateral* than vertical. The group of professors composed itself and on a voluntary basis, without any strong pressure from other instances like the HEI governing bodies. In addition, each involved professor could finally decide himself which doctoral students to select. From this point of view, we identify a second Network Governance feature which is also visible regarding the Pro*Doc AI's current functioning. This lateral type of management is also visible to the extent that decisions about the training module's detailed composition in terms of invited lecturers are not solely taken by professors, but doctoral students also have their word to say.

What are the consequences of this management story on the reform of doctoral education in this case study? The Swiss National Science Foundation defined a number of New Public Management features like standards and measures of performance, output control, etc. which shape the reform in a first step: first, as a consequence of the standard to submit Pro*Doc applications under the form of coherent research and training projects, a minimal number of doctoral students, benefitting of a Pro*Doc grant, works on more or less related topics. This may engender an accelerated development of certain research fields within certain HEIs. Second, within the given research field, this group of doctoral students is not anymore exclusively depending on advice of their individual supervisors, but – in addition to their supervisor meetings – regularly meets in a group, composed of other doctoral students, supervisors and varying external lecturers. Besides increased scientific exchange, they also get academically trained. An important part of those activities is focused on their respective doctoral research projects. Doctoral students who are benefitting of a Pro*Doc grant normally exclusively concentrate on the mentioned training activities and their own research. After three years they should have finished their PhD and be prepared in a more appropriate way to an academic career than under different conditions. However, if the standard with respect to the overall duration is clearly defined, the one of the training and scientific change activities' volume is not. This provokes fears concerning "the right balance" between research and training activities: an overload of training and supervision activities could engender two unintended effects, namely, that first, doctoral education's duration would rather be extended than shortened, and second that doctoral students are not becoming independent researchers.

The observed Network Governance characteristics are determining with regard to the specific research field and the related training activities. It can be argued that training activities – and possibly to a slightly lesser extent – doctoral research projects have been largely predetermined and shaped by the group of involved professors' research background and interests. The doctoral school's overall scientific thematic as well as its interdisciplinary character are the result of previously existing contacts among professors which led to the composition of this group. Thus, this precise form of Doctoral School, for instance in terms of (inter-)disciplinary character, has been shaped to a wide extent by the involved academic profession. Moreover, in the past already in contact with German *Graduiertenkollegs,* this group of professors was familiar with the idea of collective forms of doctoral education.

Thus, two types of actors – the SNF and the concerned academic profession – have been largely determining the reform in this case. Considering the character and overall mission of those two actors, it does not astonish that this reform is largely oriented towards the maintaining and even reinforcement of doctoral education's traditional *raison d'être*, namely the preparation of doctoral students towards an academic career!

Eventually, although as good as all central Neo-Weberian-state features appear in this case study, it can be contested to what extent they really shape the observed case study and, in particular, more generally Swiss doctoral education in humanities *in the long term*. One reform element which has been engendered in this case study through the Neo-Weberian-state feature of outside political and administrative control is the doctoral students' obligation to give account of their research and training activities twice during their doctoral education and their obligation to enrol as doctoral student. However, due to the limited duration and scope – in terms of numbers of concerned doctoral students – of Pro*Doc, other Neo-Weberian-state features like the stabilisation of the field's function, a more efficient control of the new activities' costs as well as a their tighter steering can be questioned. In other words, even if Pro*Doc AI or any other Pro*Doc project would be provided funding for an extended period of time, none of them can expect eternally living on the SNF's costs. Thus, especially in the case of humanities, who traditionally cannot rely on other external funding other than from the SNF[93] – like from industry – it can be argued that sooner or later it largely depends on HEI governing bodies and to some extent also deans, whether and which elements of reform are any longer going to be sustained, controlled and stabilised. Concretely, it depends on their will to concentrate funding for doctoral grants in certain scientific fields – in order to develop the institution's profile towards a certain direction –, their will to recognise professor's engagement in doctoral training activities as equivalent to teaching activities at bachelor and master levels, on their will to develop an own well working follow-up and support system for doctoral students, etc. Finally, HEI governing bodies may also be of importance when it comes to the question of whether or not and to what extent political demands – coming for instance from the European level – for the development of training activities explicitly preparing doctoral students for non-academic careers shall be taken account of.

VII.1.5. An interdisciplinary College Empowered by the Research Council

This case study illustrates the increased, yet, also reluctant political intervention on doctoral education. With Pro*Doc the largest initiative focusing on doctoral education's reform and funded by federal resources has indeed been created. However, it can be considered as reluctant – though not unusual for the Swiss higher education system – with respect to two factors: first, the Swiss government does not intervene directly, but mandates the Swiss National Science Foundation to act in its place;

93 Rekilä et al. (1999) also put forward the argument according to which not all disciplinary groups have the same possibilities for fundraising.

second, in spite of some framework conditions, decisions about the type of the doctoral school's activities and especially their content is largely ceded to the given college of academics. By this type of intervention, the government, via the Research Council, reinforces the college's role within the reform process, especially *vis-à-vis* its HEI governing body.

Besides the possibility to favour or refuse the application of the given college, the rectorate(s) had no possibility of intervention. Intermediary evaluation reports about the doctoral school – addressed at the SNF – are even not necessarily transferred to the HEI governing body or its administration. Yet, the future will show whether the rectorates can get back some power. Several reasons may favour such a development: first, the college's empowerment is only temporary since the SNF's funding will not last for ever; second, the HEI governing body has the intention to introduce a doctoral agreement which should make possible a better institutional follow-up of doctoral students; third, the Rectors' Conference decided to decouple their funding for the next years from the common pot with the SNF and to launch its own initiative. Depending on what this initiative will consist of, the rectorates might play a stronger role.

Also in this case study the college deserves some special attention. Again, a group of academics has largely acted in a collective manner. However, some changes in terms of the college's composition are noteworthy. First of all, it associates only few supervisors. Thus, further colleagues of the same disciplines within the same institution(s) are not part of it. In addition, it has an inter-institutional, and in particular, interdisciplinary character.

Finally, this case study also illustrates that a doctorate – even in humanities – may get a much more collective character instead of being an as a good as completely lonely enterprise: besides increased exchanges with other doctoral students working on similar topics, doctoral students also get advice and scientific inputs from other experienced academics than only their formal supervisor. Thus, such transformations have a heavy impact on the nature of doctoral education.

VII.2. National Research School "Text, Image, Sound, Space"

The National Research School "Text, Image, Sound and Space" (*Nasjonal forskerskole tekst, bilde, lyd og rom* – TBLR) has been running by a network of academics coming from the humanities Faculties of four Norwegian universities, that is to say the Universities of Agder, Bergen, Tromsø and the Norwegian University of science and technology (*Norges teknisk-naturvitenskapelige universitet* – NTNU[94]). TBLR Research School's main coordinator is situated within this latter institution. Created as a pilot project for the period 2004-2008, TBLR Research School continues to exist in 2009. It focuses on scientific fields related to aesthetics, in particular the concepts of text, image, sound and space. The number of involved doctoral students is varying according to the concrete activity.[95] TBLR Research School can be considered as Norway's first national[96] research school in the field of humanities. Within University of Bergen's Faculty of Humanities, TBLR Research School is currently one out of three research schools.

VII.2.1. Establishment and Decentralisation of a National Research School[97]

The reform story of this case study can be essentially divided into three episodes. The first episode consists of the *establishment of a national research school.* The second episode describes the partial *decentralisation* of the research school's activities towards the individual member institutions. Finally, the third episode consists in the

94 In 1996, University of Trondheim became NTNU.

95 However, TBLR Research School's administration could not provide any precise numbers.

96 Apart University of Oslo, it includes the main humanities Faculties of Norwegian universities.

97 Unless indicated differently, used data originate from interviews with the University of Bergen's vice-rector and administrator responsible of doctoral education, the vice-dean and administrator responsible of doctoral education at the Faculty of Humanities, the national and local heads of TBLR as well as two further professors and three doctoral students involved in TBLR.

renouncement of applying for the status of a national research school and the related funding conferred by the National Research Council.

The interdisciplinary TBLR Research School has been established in 2004. It is addressed at doctoral students in the field of arts and cultural subjects that cover the concepts text, image, sound and space. More precisely, "Text refers to literary criticism and other subjects related to studies of text. Image relates to art history and media studies as well as other subjects with a focus on visual manifestations of culture. Sound refers to musicology and subjects like art history and theatre studies which study auditory aspects of art and culture. Space partly refers to architecture, sculpture, and installation art, partly to interdisciplinary fields like museum studies, landscape studies, and urban studies, and partly to spatial movement within theatre studies, dance studies and other subjects related to theatrical and other bodily expressions of culture."[98] TBLR Research School's activities consist, on the one hand, of methodological seminars – like how to write a doctoral thesis – and, more theoretical seminars and, on the other hand, of larger conferences where doctoral students as well as invited – often foreign – lecturers intervene and mutually discuss their presentations. In addition, on the demand of doctoral students or other involved academics master classes may be organised. Most of those activities take place within one of the involved HEIs. From time to time, an activity is organised abroad, in collaboration with a HEI of the chosen destination, what offers the additional possibility of inviting lecturers of the corresponding HEI.

Several interviewees underline that doctoral students, in principle, could attend such seminars and conferences already before TBLR Research School's establishment. However, they also emphasize important differences between TBLR Research School and other training offers: first, the *diffusion of information about training offers is increasingly organised*. Doctoral students do not anymore have to find information about relevant training activities by themselves or to rely on information of their supervisor, but are automatically informed by TBLR Research School coordinators. Second, *scientific exchange* is organised in the framework of conferences specifically designed for doctoral students. Instead of hoping to get feedbacks from one or another

---

98 Source: http://www.ntnu.no/hf/english/studies/postgraduate/nrtp. Accessed on August 2009.

conference participant, interaction between invited lecturers and doctoral students is planned beforehand. Besides the guarantee for comments, this also assures a more intensive exchange since presented papers are read in advance. Third, TBLR also organises to a certain extent *interdisciplinarity*. The chosen concepts and topics are uniting doctoral students of a large number of scientific disciplines. Through interdisciplinary exchange doctoral students are incited to quit "their own little world" and to discover other perspectives on their own topics. Finally, such a broad thematic basis is also seen as mean to organise the doctoral training offer for as many doctoral students as possible. According to TBLR Research School's main coordinator, this would be necessary because the scientific communities – and accordingly, doctoral training offers – of the concerned doctoral students would often be extremely small.

The second reform episode of the examined case study – *decentralisation* – begins in 2008. As all other Faculties of University of Bergen, the Faculty of Humanities disposes of an own PhD programme and is principally "responsible for providing doctoral students with training at an advanced scientific level" (University of Bergen 2003: §4.2). Since its creation in 2003, the programme's *own* offer in terms of training was essentially limited to activities within institutes and research groups which are part of the Faculty. Available information does not allow to quantify those activities. However, it seems that training activities have been rather poorly developed.[99] Nevertheless, the TBLR Research School coordinator at University of Bergen noticed that the establishment of training activities at the national level has been perceived by certain Faculty members as a loss of power for the local PhD programmes. From 2008 on, an increasing number of TBLR activities are organised within each involved HEI by a local coordination group, but still under the TBLR Research School label. In addition, one yearly conference takes place at the national level. The TBLR Research School coordinator of University of Bergen describes this change as

99 A doctoral student criticises the course offer at Faculty of Humanities by pointing to a NIFU-STEP report (Kyvik and Olsen 2007) which illustrates that doctoral students of Norwegian Faculties of Humanities would be most dissatisfied with the course offer at doctoral level (På Høyden 2008). It has to be specified that the dissatisfaction about the course offer, which is identified within the report, is high with respect to its utility in later working positions.

pendulum, which swings a bit back to the centre in-between the national research school and the local doctoral programme. According to him, this should strengthen the local ownership feeling.

The third reform episode, *renouncement*, stands for the decision not to answer to the National Research Council's call for National Research Schools. Thus, in spite of the opportunity to obtain the status and funding of a National Research School at the end of TBLR Research School's pilot-phase and thereby to secure TBLR Research School's next eight years of existence, no application is submitted.

Those three reform episodes have to be put into a certain number of contextual elements. First of all, with respect to the first reform episode, several interviewees underline the general need for action pointed to in the evaluation report about Norwegian doctoral education (see Kyvik 2002). This report as well as a more detailed report about the University of Bergen (Tvede and Hovdhaugen 2002) identify a pattern of too old PhD candidates, who take too much time to finish and too many who do not finish at all, in particular in humanities. As mentioned, a second contextual element more precisely relates to the curricular component. Doctoral courses, especially in humanities, are perceived by doctoral students as poorly developed. This conclusion results at least from a survey among doctors who graduated in the years 2002 and 2005. The course offer was rather random, not broad enough and of low quality. In Humanities, more than half of answering graduates declared that suggested courses were little relevant and useful for their later work. They asked for more practical courses like research management and project planning (Kyvik and Olsen 2007). The third contextual element concerns the idea of a research school as a necessary reform measure: several interviewees involved into the first reform episode remark that some of their colleagues were sceptical towards the idea of research schools and their involvement:

> They [the supervisors] have doctoral students and they read their papers. That's all they want to do. So it's hard to get people used to the idea that they also have to join the doctoral students, to go to seminars and you know, different kind of courses. So it's very hard work to establish research schools.
>
> (A professor involved in the starting phase of TBLR)

A second series of contextual elements can be developed with respect to the second reform episode, the decentralisation. Scientific, emotional, rational and financial reasons are put forward in order to explain the TBLR Research Schools' reorientation towards the local level. Several interviewees emphasise that TBLR courses did not always attract the same number of doctoral students. Sometimes too many doctoral students were interested, sometimes too few. Involved professors and doctoral students explain this varying interest by the following factors: first, confronted to the activities' high degree of openness and interdisciplinarity, doctoral students feel that the activities' topics are too far away from the doctoral research topics. Second, doctoral students also have preferred other training activities which were closer to their topics because of the increased time pressure. The latter is due to changes in the doctoral degrees occurred during the last decades, that is to say from dr. philos to dr.artium and, finally, to the PhD. With the introduction of the PhD degree, PhD positions' funding is limited to three or – in the case of additional duties – four years. Third, doctoral students have no feeling of ownership regarding the research school. An emotional argument is also put forward concerning supervisors' will to decentralise activities. The TBLR coordinator at University of Bergen emphasises that some supervisors would not like to give things away from the Faculty to the national level. Finally, related or not to this negative attitude towards giving things away to the national level, another interviewee considers financial reasons as a potential driving force for changes in the level of organisation:

> And of course it's also always a discussion of money and resources. So where should they be put? Should they be put into research schools or directly to departments to decide in the most useful way. So there is no big agreement on how to do it.

The third reform episode, the renouncement to apply to the National Research Council's call for National Research Schools, also has to be put into a certain context. The TBLR coordinator at University of Bergen underlines that it has actually always been the intention to apply for money at the level of the Norwegian Research Council. However, once this call has arrived, the TBLR Research School board was not happy about the call's accompanying conditions. Concretely, each university was only allowed to apply as main applicant in four projects, which automatically limits the number of applying disciplines. However, the

TBLR board was not willing to invest time in an application, which would be in competition with other disciplines like physics.

Finally, in spring 2008, that is to say during the same period as the National Research Council launched its call for National Research Schools, the University of Bergen initiated an own broad action aiming at reforming doctoral education at the whole institution. During the consultation phase of the so called "action plan" – the principal reform instrument –, criticism especially came from doctoral students of the Faculty of Humanities. One doctoral student used the term "PhD-Factory" (*PhD fabrikken*) to express his opinion according to which the action plan favours institutional interests shaped by a "logic of production" to the detriment of doctoral students' training. Among others, he underlines that it would be more important for doctoral students to write a doctoral thesis of high quality than to finish it within the standard duration (På Høyden 2008).

VII.2.2. A Series of Institutional Instruments of Management

Two types of instruments of management contribute to shape the reform of the present case study such as described above. The first type of management instrument can be qualified as legal, the second as financial.

Three legal management instruments could be identified. The first one consists of the PhD regulations of University of Bergen, which have been approved and entered into force in 2003, hence just before the establishing of TBLR Research School. Since they concern the whole university, they correspond to what has already been developed in the MCB case study. Thus, among other elements, those PhD regulations more clearly define the doctoral students', the faculties' and the supervisors' responsibilities with respect to doctoral training and follow-up of doctoral students: doctoral students are obliged to complete a training programme of at least 30 credit points, among which the only explicitly defined compulsory training component in theory of science and ethics; the Faculties have either to provide an appropriated training programme or to arrange the candidate's participation in programmes of other Faculties or institutions; in the framework of their application for a scholarship, doctoral students have to define among others their research programme. Then, the regulations state that progress with respect to the doctoral research, such as defined in the application, has to be yearly reported in separate reports, one by the doctoral candidate and another by the principal supervisor. These reports are to be sent to and approved by the faculty or other units to which the Faculty has delegated this function (University of Bergen 2003).

The strength of the link between those regulations and TBLR Research School as such is varying. Concerning the doctoral students' obligation to complete at least 30 credit points through the participation in training activities, one can say that the regulations do not precise that those training activities have to be carried out in a (certain) research school. Thus, no doctoral student is obliged to attend TBLR Research School activities. In other words, if a doctoral student prefers to complete his credit points in a different way, for instance by attending summer schools abroad, he may do that. However, those regulations have an impact on TBLR Research School to the extent that its activities are evaluated in a way or another and, accordingly, deliver credit points to doctoral students. Yet, as we have seen in the case of FUNMAT Research School, the opposite could theoretically be possible. In the case of TBLR Research School, doctoral students who participate are indeed evaluated and awarded in terms of credit points. According to the type of their contribution, for instance the delivery and presentation of a research paper for a TBLR Research School conference or the discussion of another paper, they get a certain number of credits. Like doctoral students, professors and other permanent scientific staff are not obliged to participate in TBLR. PhD regulations of University of Bergen attribute the responsibility for providing a doctoral training programme not to them but to "the Faculty". Several interviewees mention that work related to the running of TBLR and more generally research schools is not yet seen and recognised as regular part of the job. This can be illustrated by the fact that, except the coordinator, no professor involved in TBLR in Bergen is compensated for his additional work, for instance through a lower teaching load at the undergraduate level. Hence, local professors' engagement in TBLR depends on their good will.[100] Finally,

100 A supervisor underlined that other aspects concerning the supervisors' engagement are not clearly regulated either. He mentions the example of the doctoral research project elaboration which has to be done by the potential future doctoral students

the reporting of the doctoral students' progress is not carried out through TBLR but the Faculty's PhD programme. In other words, the training of doctoral students and their follow-up take place in two more or less separate organisational units. They are not necessarily completely separate to the extent that some of their members, like the TBLR coordinator at University of Bergen, may be present in both units. However, in practice they work quite independently one from the other.

Two further instruments with legal character have been introduced since the appearance of the national evaluation report of Norwegian doctoral education in 2002 (see Kyvik 2002). They are both not in direct relation with TBLR Research School as such, but attribute an important role to research schools in the reform of doctoral education. In addition, they suggest a number of reform measures. One of those two instruments, an *action plan for doctoral education* (Humanistisk fakultet Universitet i Bergen 2002) of the Faculty of Humanities of the University of Bergen, has been largely developed on the basis of the national evaluation report. Besides the systematic integration of doctoral students in research schools, it suggests that doctoral students, who began their doctoral education between 2003 and 2005 and who finish not later than three months after their actual funding period, shall receive further funding for an additional six-month period. According to a Faculty administrator, this should on the one side incite doctoral students to finish within the actual funding period and, on the other side, provide them with a salary in order to elaborate further post-doc research projects. However, according to the Faculty administrator, the six-month period had to be reduced to a three-month period for legal reasons. The future of this instrument depends on the Faculty's economic situation, but the interviewed Faculty administrator is quite optimistic with respect to the instrument's impact.

The last legal instrument has the same name as the previous one, namely *action plan for doctoral education* (Universitetet i Bergen 2009). It goes in a very similar direction but concerns the whole University of Bergen. As developed in the first Norwegian case study about the

---

applying for stipends. On the one hand, it would be evident that those applicants would need the help of their potential supervisors in the elaboration of the research project. However, on the other hand, it is not regulated to what extent a potential supervisor is obliged or shall contribute to this elaboration.

Molecular and Computational Biology Research School, this document develops a number of concrete measures of reform. Among others, each doctoral student should have at least two supervisors, have access to a research group and/or research school, and be given the possibility of a sojourn abroad during doctoral education. Furthermore, a new regulation about intermediary evaluation and follow-up of the doctoral students' progress as well as the conditions of the doctoral students' elimination of doctoral programmes shall be established. In addition, information about training opportunities should be collected. This action plan has been decided upon by the university direction (*universitetsstyret*) of University of Bergen. According to the PhD administrator of University of Bergen, it has to be implemented by the faculties until 2015.

Concerning the second type of instrument of management, that is to say the financial instrument, four such instruments could be identified in this case study. The first one can be qualified as internal to the Faculty. According to their respective numbers of involved doctoral students, each of the four universities participating in TBLR has to contribute a certain amount of money. According to a Faculty administrator in Bergen, about 160'000 NOK (~20,000 €) have been paid for TBLR Research School activities in 2008. In addition, the Faculty of Humanities also invests money in order to exempt the TBLR Research School coordinator of University of Bergen from other tasks. A professor involved in TBLR Research School's establishment emphasises that the mobilisation of this money has not been simple at University of Bergen. At the time, responsible people at Faculty would not have understood what TBLR was about and why it had to be funded. Furthermore, TBLR had to be thematically broad in order to present a critical mass of potentially concerned doctoral students and, thereby, to get the funding. Thus, interdisciplinarity was somehow an implicit funding condition.

Although not directly related to TBLR Research School, a further internal funding instrument of the Faculty of Humanities is worth being mentioned. Institutes receive a certain sum of money for every completed doctoral degree within their unit from the Faculty. The exact sum depends on two factors, first on whether the degree has been completed within the standard duration of three, respectively four years, and second, on gender. According to a Faculty administrator, 45,000 NOK (~5,400 €) or 30,000 NOK (~3,600 €) are allocated for women and men who completed the degree within the standard duration. The respective amounts are reduced to 15,000 NOK (~1,800 €) and 10,000 NOK (~1,200 €) if the degree has been completed after the three or four-year deadline.

The third financial instrument can be considered as an external one, to the extent that it comes from outside of the University of Bergen, namely from the Norwegian Research Council. Funding of this type can be asked in order to finance national doctoral courses. However, also in this case, a critical mass of doctoral students represents a funding condition. At least ten doctoral students have to participate. According to the main coordinator of TBLR, this condition may cause a problem to the extent that one never knows in advance how many doctoral students finally will attend such a course.

The fourth and last identified financial management instrument is also an external one and has been introduced with the quality reform in Norwegian higher education in 2003. According to a funding system defined by the Ministry for Education and Research (*Kunnskaps-departementet*) – the result-based reallocation (*resultatbasert omfordeling*) – universities get a certain amount of money, among others, according to the number of completed doctorates. As mentioned in the previous case study situated at University of Bergen – MCB Research School – the total amount per completed degree received by the university from the Ministry depends on the year.[101] In 2009 it was 370,000 NOK (~44,000 €). The university then allocates this amount to the Faculties. 75% of the allocated sum is determined by a stable basis, 25% is based on effective results in terms of completed doctoral degrees. The Faculty of Humanities then keeps the allocated amount since most doctoral research and training is funded at the Faculty level.

VII.2.3. A Bottom-Up Movement

The previous section shows that quite a number of instruments of management focusing on doctoral education have been introduced

101 The annual variation is due to the fact that the total amount allocated by the Ministry for completed doctoral degrees is stable from year to year. Thus, the allocated amount *per doctoral degree* depends on the total number of completed doctoral degrees.

during the last seven years. Though to varying extents, TBLR Research School, is steered by those instruments. However, the latter do not suffice to explain the reform of doctoral education, such as carried out through TBLR Research School. The fact that the described instruments come from different levels of governance – Faculty, university and ministry – also launches the question of the driving actors behind the described reform episodes. Thus, this section pays particular attention to those driving actors and their objectives.

According to our interviewees, the initiative for the establishment of TBLR Research School came from its current main coordinator at NTNU in Trondheim. Confronted to the national evaluation of Norwegian doctoral education, this coordinator felt the necessity to act. He contacted people of the Faculties of humanities of the other Norwegian universities in order to put into place a national research school. The contact person of the University of Bergen was pleased about the invitation to participate since he considered that there was a need to become active and "it [the idea of research schools] was in the air". Except the University of Oslo, who itself already had quite a number of doctoral students in the field, representatives from all other universities accepted to be involved. Thus, a national steering committee, called TBLR Board, with a representative of each involved institution has been composed. In addition, this TBLR Board has been accompanied by a Danish professor who already had important experience in the running of research schools. At the time, the latter was employed by NTNU in Trondheim. Today he is the head of the Copenhagen Doctoral School in Cultural Studies at University of Copenhagen which encompasses the same scientific disciplines as TBLR Research School. Simultaneously, he is still member of the TBLR Board. All interviewees underlined that TBLR is the result of a bottom-up initiative. An administrator at central university level remarked that TBLR indeed corresponded to what the university board and the central research board were wishing to happen. However, he also emphasises that those bodies would never have imposed the establishment of research schools in one or another scientific field.

Central decisions about TBLR Research School activities are taken within the TBLR Board. During their annual meeting, they discuss issues like the non-application to the Norwegian Research Council's call for National Research Schools. According to our interviewees, this decision has been taken autonomously by the TBLR Board and accepted by the Faculty of Humanities of the University of Bergen. Besides such particular issues, the TBLR Board also decides about issues like the number of yearly arrangements. However, the TBLR Board does not go as far as deciding for instance about key note speakers. This kind of decision is rather left to the local TBLR Research School coordinators and, where applicable, further involved people at the local level. In the case of a national TBLR Research School conference organised in Bergen, the local TBLR coordinator asked several people of different scientific disciplines whether they would help him in the organisation and implementation of the conference. Thus, another, local, committee composed of academics willing to contribute to the research school' activities, has been established. Last but not least, it is also worth mentioning that the Faculty of Humanities of the University of Bergen created a steering group for doctoral education at the Faculty level (*styringsgruppe for forskerutdanning*). This steering group comprises a Faculty administrator, the research dean, a representative of the centre for science and ethics as well as the coordinators of the three existing research schools the Faculty is involved in. Among others, the objective of the steering group consists in a certain coordination of the diverse doctoral training activities existing at the Faculty.

With respect to TBLR Research School (and other research schools in humanities), our interviewees share a common number of objectives. According to the interviewee, the emphasis slightly changes. Some underline TBLR Research school's actual activities as such as objectives, whereas others pay more attention to the output of those activities. The offer of a network within which exchange between scholars and doctoral students can take place is the central objective for most of the interviewees. Exchange is usually understood as presentation and discussion of research results both by lecturers and doctoral students. Besides a general quality improvement of doctoral students' dissertations, this type of exchange also includes a second important objective, namely to avoid isolation of doctoral students. Furthermore, interdisciplinarity is simultaneously seen as an objective in itself but also as a mean, which contributes to beneficial exchange. Among the more output oriented objectives, one may cite a higher completion rate as well as a shorter duration of doctoral education, an issue which is omnipresent in the interviewees' answers.

VII.2.4. A Case of Network Governance

If we translate the observed instruments, actors and objectives of governance into the language of our three public management narratives, the management story of this case study essentially consists of a research school which is strongly shaped by elements of Network Governance and surrounded by an national and institutional environment managed according to New Public Management mechanisms.

With respect to New Public Management, we notice first of all several elements which may be ranged in the category of explicit standards and measures of performance: with the introduction of the PhD degree (instead of the older doctoral degrees), the funding period has been standardised to three or four years, within which doctoral students are ought to finish their research and training component of at least 30 credit points. The achievement of this goal is monitored by the yearly progress reports at the Faculty level.

A second New Public Management element, greater emphasis on output controls, appears in the Faculty's allocation per completed doctoral degree and the introduction of the result-based reallocation which the Ministry uses to award supplementary money to universities and their units according to the output of the PhD system.

A third New Public Management element could be seen in the creation of TBLR Research School as a disaggregation of units in the public sector. However, considering TBLR Research School as a unit that provides supervision and training, we interpret TLBR Research School rather as complementary to the previously existing units in this field, namely the apprenticeship model and the Faculty's PhD programme, than the latter's disaggregation. Then, the Norwegian Research Council's incentive instrument of National Research Schools could have induced another New Public Management element, namely competition. However, since the TBLR Board renounced to an application, TBLR Research School is not really concerned by such a New Public Management element until today. Finally, in the case of the Humanities Faculty of the University of Bergen, the underlying condition of critical mass, might be interpreted as a last New Public Management element, namely as stress on greater discipline and parsimony in resource use.

With respect to Network Governance, one can first of all point to the existence of new networks which do not correspond to usual institutional units. Such a network can be seen in the national TBLR Board, within which inter-institutional interactions take place. Especially concerning the first management episode, but also the second one, those interactions clearly go beyond the actual institutional boarders of HEIs. In addition, the presence of a Danish colleague within the TBLR Board and the collaboration with foreign institutions show that inter-institutional interactions even go beyond national frontiers. Besides this inter-institutional network, a second, internal network can be identified. Also this internal or local network, which decides upon local TBLR activities, is different from other Faculty structures like the Faculty's steering group for doctoral education.

As a second Network Governance characteristic, one can cite both networks' quite high self-organising and self-steering capacity. Apart from the underlying condition of interdisciplinarity, the TLBR Board and, to a certain extent also the local TBLR Research School network, autonomously decide upon very central issues of the research school: first, what kind of interdisciplinarity in terms of disciplines and thematic; second, what kind of activities; third, how many activities, etc.

A third Network Governance characteristic consists in the lateral forms of management within TBLR Research School. First of all, this can be illustrated by the manner the local and national networks are constituted. People are asked by the coordinators, but nobody is obliged to participate. Furthermore, lateral forms of management are also visible in the decisions upon TBLR Research School activities, which are taken within the national and local TBLR Boards or – with respect to the organisation of master classes and to a certain extent also the local activities – even by doctoral students themselves.

Fourth, the existence of a steering board at national and local levels displays that power on TBLR Research School is coordinated at multiple levels of governance.

Last but not least, the two action plans instruments at Faculty and university levels can be considered somehow in between the Network Governance and the New Public Management narratives. On the one hand, they look like a mean to diffuse good practices. On the other hand, the one at central institutional level has a constraining character. In the case of TBLR Research School, most of the new standards defined by the action plan will remain without any effect, except for instance the obligation to introduce multiple supervision arrangements.

After this description of the management story in the language of our public management narratives, attention is paid to the link between this management story and the concrete reform. When contemplating New Public Management and Network Governance instruments more attentively, one notices two characteristics: first, New Public Management instruments all come from outside of TBLR Research School itself, that is to say either from the Ministry or from the central university level. Second, TBLR Research School's core activities as such, i.e. collective training and supervision of doctoral students, are almost not shaped by those instruments. In the case of New Public Management instruments, rather framework conditions of doctoral education like the overall duration, training volume and follow-up mechanisms of doctoral students are concerned. Three exceptions can be noticed to this non-shaping impact of governance instruments: on the one hand, as a consequence of the standardised training volume, the doctoral students' performances in the framework of TBLR Research School activities are measured and rewarded through credit points. On the other hand, the Humanities Faculty's funding of TBLR Research School implied the underlying condition of critical mass. *De facto* this has an impact on the general character of TBLR Research School, namely its interdisciplinarity. Finally, the action plan at central institutional level may force the academic profession to formally introduce multiple supervision arrangements.

Thus, quite some elements of TBLR Research School's activities are not influenced by New Public Management or Network Governance instruments. This does, however, not mean that they would not deserve any attention in this analysis, to the contrary. For instance, no supervisor at the Faculty of Humanities of the University of Bergen is obliged to be involved into research schools. Hence, their participation depends on their perception of research schools' relevance. It has been noticed that, in spite of a context broadly shaped by the claim for the establishment of research schools, no unanimity prevails with respect to this issue among supervisors of humanities. Therefore, by far not all Humanities scholars are involved in TBLR activities. In addition, no clear definition of research schools is related to existing instruments of management. Thus, those two open issues leave some room for manoeuvre to effectively involved actors and their reform objectives. In the case of TBLR Research School, two types of networks, operating at the national and local levels, could be identified. With respect to the actual reform, the first important, though trivial, point to be mentioned consists in the fact that a group of people sharing the same goal, namely to introduce collective forms of training and supervision in a certain (interdisciplinary) scientific field has been constituted. One single person or a group of people with opposed objectives would probably not have achieved this goal. Furthermore, according to an interviewee involved into TBLR Research School's establishment, the presence of a Danish professor with previous experience regarding research schools in his country has also been shaping TBLR Research School. If one compares the Doctoral School, which is led by this Danish professor and TBLR Research School, one indeed notices very similar forms of activities and involved scientific disciplines. Thus, it seems that knowledge transfer from Denmark to Norway has been carried out to a certain extent.

This relatively large room for manoeuvre is also expressed in TBLR Research School's quite strong self-steering capacity. The latter also became visible in the second and third reform episodes. With respect to the second reform episode, it was the local TBLR Board, which decided to introduce some more local activities. On demand of doctoral students, who wished more activities based on their interests, and perhaps also as a reaction to the occasional mismatch between activities and numbers of participants, the local TBLR Board decided to do so, again on a voluntary basis. It is difficult to say, to what extent emotional reflections and those related to funding – spent by the local Humanities Faculty – might also have contributed to this decision. Considering certain supervisors' reluctance of "giving something away", the underlying idea could have been to spend money rather "at home" than at a national level where its spending is not under direct control. Finally, the TBLR Board's self-steering capacity looked also quite strong in its decision to not apply to the Norwegian Research Council's call for National Research Schools. However, it must also be underlined that the Faculty's steering group for doctoral education agreed on this issue. Thus, it would be interesting to know if the local TBLR Board could also have imposed its decision in case of disagreement with the Faculty's steering group for doctoral education.

Last but not least, it is worth underlining that interviewed supervisors mentioned the fact that not every doctoral student will find an academic or non-academic research position after completion. Several interviewees, especially at administrative and higher levels of institutional governance, mentioned the necessity to think about ways to prepare doctoral students for jobs outside of academia. The idea of transferable skills has come up in this context. In the case of TBLR Research School, this idea has been implemented to the extent that transferable skills are taught in academic writing courses. However, first and foremost those activities are still connected to academic purposes. From this point of view, one could argue that supervisors' minds are increasingly open towards the idea of preparing doctoral students also for non-academic positions, without, however, changing the academic core of doctoral education.

VII.2.5. A Specialised National College of Academics

Like in the first case study situated in the University of Bergen (V.2.), the increased national and institutional focus on doctoral education is clearly visible. However, besides the central PhD regulations and the institutional action plan, a further action plan of the Faculty of Humanities expresses the will of reform also at the Faculty level. Again, this increased importance attributed to doctoral education has a concrete impact on doctoral students, and to a minor degree, on supervisors: doctoral students regularly have to give account towards the Faculty of their progress, whereas supervisors have to give their own view on the doctoral students' reports. Thus, through this management instrument, especially doctoral students are under greater pressure, in particular regarding time of completion.

Almost aside from those institutional measures, the TBLR Research School developed its own reform measures like the organisation of doctoral conferences and lectures specialised in the given interdisciplinary field. Like in the previous case studies, those measures are the result of a collective action of a number of voluntary academics. The composition of this college again takes another form than the one which is based on all colleagues of a given discipline within a given HEI. In the present case study, the college is inter-institutional, interdisciplinary and acts at the national (and, in parallel, local) level. Simultaneously, it is specialised and does by far not integrate all potential academics of the concerned scientific disciplines.

Although the number of activities organised by the TBLR Research School is inferior to the one of the previous case study, the type of impact on the nature of the doctorate in humanities is the same: thanks to collective activities like doctoral conferences, the enterprise "doctorate" is not anymore lonely.

VIII. Doctoral Schools in Finance

VIII.1. Swiss Finance Institute PhD Programme

The Swiss Finance Institute (SFI) PhD Programme is an inter-institutional PhD programme run by three regional centres which are constituted of finance professors of six Swiss HEIs. The Léman Centre is composed of faculties from University of Geneva (UNIGE), University of Lausanne (UNIL) and the Federal Institute of Technology Lausanne (EPFL). The Zurich Centre includes researchers from University of Zurich and the Federal Institute of Technology Zurich (ETHZ), whereas the Lugano Centre affiliates faculties of the University of Lugano (*Università della Svizzera italiana* – USI). In 2009, the SFI PhD programme assembles altogether 75 doctoral students, out of which 24 belong to the Léman Centre, 28 to the Zurich Centre and, finally, 23 to the Lugano Centre.[102] According to a programme coordinator, twenty doctoral students a year are normally selected for the whole SFI PhD programme. Respective shares of doctoral students of the three centres would approximately correspond to the formula "8 Léman – 8 Zurich – 4 Lugano".

102 Source: www.sfi.ch, accessed on May 2009.

VIII.1.1. Building a Network Doctoral School in Finance[103]

The SFI PhD programme is the result of two main episodes of reform. The first episode can be called *individual approach*, the second one *collective approach.* The individual approach episode, lasting from 1997 until 2003, consists in the gradual creation of several PhD programmes in finance which resemble to Anglo-Saxon PhD programmes in this field. Concretely, those newly created PhD programmes correspond to the "Anglo-Saxon model" (a) from a structural point of view – that is to say being structured in a first phase devoted to a specialised training programme and, in case of successful completion, a second phase focusing on doctoral research –, (b) with respect to the type of thematic fields covered in the courses, (c) to the extent that English is the teaching language and (d) by their deliberate recruitment of doctoral students from abroad. Finally, though not necessarily being a specific Anglo-Saxon practice, it is also worth mentioning that at least part of those newly created PhD programmes also include more or less regular gatherings of all doctoral students and professors involved in the respective programme, during which each doctoral student presents his research progress.

The second reform episode, *collective approach*, consists in the creation of a network doctoral school within which a varying number of HEIs collaborate. Currently, cooperation principally takes place in advertisement within the international academic area through the label "Swiss Finance Institute PhD Program", the offer of a range of specialised courses to doctoral students who are in the research phase, in supervision and final evaluation of doctoral students as well as in placement efforts taking place for instance by the doctoral graduates'

103 Unless other sources are indicated, data originates from interviews with a Swiss National Science Foundation responsible for National Centre of Competence in Research (NCCR), vice-rectors for education at University of Lausanne (UNIL) and University of Geneva (UNIGE), the central administrators in charge of the doctorate at UNIL, UNIGE, University of Lugano (USI) and University of Zurich (UNIZH), the UNIZH administrator in charge of the Bologna process' implementation, the Swiss Finance Institute (SFI) doctoral programme leaders at UNIL, UNIZH and USI, the administrative coordinator of the SFI doctoral programme at UNIZH, three further professors teaching in the doctoral programme and supervising doctoral students and three doctoral students.

presentation on the common web-site.[104] However, in spite of this partial cooperation, each of the three centres has its own training programme for doctoral students in the first phase. This programme covers subjects including Economics, Financial Economics, Corporate Finance, Mathematical Finance and Econometrics. According to the centre, the number of first year courses varies between ten and twelve[105]. A number of topics is taught within all three centres, whereas a few others are exclusively offered in one or two of the centres. Besides a small number of courses taught by invited professors, the core of first year courses is provided by own professors. According to a PhD programme coordinator, the respective professors' specialisations explain this partial diversity in terms of course offer.

The first step of reform, that is to say the gradual creation of individual Anglo-Saxon like PhD programmes in finance, took place within different kinds of context. The first such PhD programme was created in 1997, under the label FAME, at the Universities of Lausanne and Geneva. According to the head of the SFI PhD Léman programme, no PhD programme in finance comparable to those in the USA and England existed in Swiss HEIs until the second part of the 1990s. Confronted with the lack of such PhD programmes in Switzerland, an individual professor of University of Lausanne created a PhD programme of this type. A particularity of this PhD programme consists in a type of grant which allows doctoral students concentrating on a training programme during the first year without having any other duty like teaching. The funding of this costly type of PhD programme was assured by a private banker, himself a fervent supporter of academic research and doctoral education. The context of the second PhD programme's creation – in 1999 – was very similar. The initiator of this programme arrived as professor in the recently created University of Lugano and identified the establishment of a doctoral programme in Finance as a way to respond to a missing offer. On the one side, based on his experience at a Canadian HEI, he was conscious of the potential of

---

104 Although not necessarily being a collective action, it is also worth mentioning that some doctoral students are given the possibility of a research sojourn within a highly renowned foreign HEI, among others as a further promotion for the students' on the academic labour market.

105 Source: www.sfi.ch, downloaded the 30.10.2009.

doctoral students from neighbouring Italy. On the other side, he saw it as an opportunity to educate young people who could be of help in a possible later establishment of a master of finance at USI. As his colleague from Lausanne, he was supported by banks, that is to say the regional banking association. He underlines that this financial support made possible a quicker start of the PhD programme than if he would have asked money from the Swiss National Science Foundation. Finally, the third doctoral programme was created in 2002 at University of Zurich in the framework of the National Centre of Competence in Research (NCCR) Finrisk. The offer of doctoral training is one among several requirements related to the establishment of each NCCR. According to several SFI PhD programme coordinators, the promotion of academic research and doctoral education in the field of finance through NCCR Finrisk can be seen as the result of converging interests of a number of actors: Swiss universities wanted to become more competitive in the field of finance research, whereas the banking industry and the government were worried about the lack of expertise in one of the key sectors of Swiss economy.

The creation of this third PhD programme in finance was simultaneously the start of the second step of reform. University of Zurich is the "leading house" of the NCCR Finrisk, however, all Swiss universities doing research in the field of finance[106] are partners within this NCCR. Collaboration between NCCR Finrisk HEIs is not only limited to research but also concerns doctoral training. Specialised courses are commonly organised and particularly offered to second phase doctoral students of the respective HEIs. Anticipating the end of the NCCR Finrisk and arguing that a critical mass of professors and doctoral students would be necessary in order to obtain visibility on the worldwide "research map" in finance, several professors prepared the creation of a permanent inter-institutional organisation. With the support of the Swiss Banking Association the private foundation "Swiss Finance Institute" emerges in 2006. SFI is active in the production of basic research in finance as well as in the offering of executive education and doctoral training. According to our interviewees, HEIs and with them the individual professors willing to be part of SFI have to fulfil a certain

106 Besides Zurich, the universities of Lugano, Lausanne, Geneva, Basel, Neuchâtel and St.Gallen are also part of the NCCR Finrisk.

number of (non-formalised) requirements: for instance, a HEI needs, first, a minimal number of finance professors, who, second, are carrying out basic research of a certain quality in finance. According to the three programme directors of Lausanne/Geneva, Lugano and Zurich, this explains why, besides the two Federal Institutes of Technology, only four HEIs (out of seven participating in NCCR Finrisk) are part of the SFI. This also influences the organisation of structured doctoral education in Finance. The doctoral programmes of the SFI HEIs are institutionalised into a PhD programme presenting itself as one only programme, the Swiss Finance Institute PhD programme. Thus, HEIs which are not part of the SFI do not participate in SFI PhD programme either.

VIII.1.2. Institutionally Varying Instruments of Governance

A number of concrete instruments of governance have contributed to the implementation of the two reform episodes described above. We identified five such instruments: first, a financial one, second, a formal change in professors' employment contract, third new recruitment procedures of doctoral students, fourth, performance controls related to the training programme, and fifth, changes in the institutional PhD regulations. Generally speaking, one can say that those instruments are shaped and used in partly varying manners according to the HEI. Since, this may have an impact on the concrete result of reform, we also emphasise these differences in the following presentation of those instruments.

As mentioned, doctoral training is also one central component of NCCRs and thereby a condition for the attribution of related funding. As mentioned, this condition is described as consisting in „the promotion of talented young researchers at doctoral and post-doctoral levels and the advancement of women in research careers (FNS 1999: 5)". Another important condition related to NCCR funding consists in collaboration between several HEIs. Hence, from this point of view, it *may* also have an impact on the manner doctoral education is organised, that is to say, also in a collaborative way between several HEIs. However, NCCR regulation does not give any precise information about the structural form doctoral training should be carried out within NCCRs. Doctoral schools[107] are mentioned as possible special measure for training (FNS 1999), but from a formal point of view, there is no obligation to organise doctoral training in an inter-institutional way. Yet, in the case of the NCCR Finrisk, it led, at least to a certain extent, to the creation of inter-institutional structures with respect to doctoral training. Nevertheless – and in this respect this instrument has been used in varying manners – concrete doctoral courses of the first year are not identical.

A second instrument, namely a change within *professors' employment contract which integrates teaching duties at doctoral level,* is only very rarely used. If it could be used in all SFI HEIs, teaching at doctoral level is at least not yet automatically part of professors' contract. Thus, SFI professors' involvement in terms of teaching at doctoral level is often depending on other factors than formalisation in their employment contract, like their degree of seniority and experience, teaching load at bachelor and master level, research interests, etc.

All SFI HEIs share a number of aspects related to the third instrument, that is to say *new recruitment procedures* of doctoral students: first, they advertise together with the SFI label in order to attract doctoral students. Second, on their common web-site, they indicate the requirements related to the application procedure. Each candidate has to send a CV, a copy of grade transcripts and the university master degree (in finance, economics or equivalent), a letter of motivation, at least two sealed letters of reference (respecting a predefined scheme) and an indication testifying to the capability to follow courses in English (e.g. TOEFL[108]). GMAT (Graduate Management Admission Test) or GRE (Graduate Record Exam) are not formally required but highly recommended. Two yearly application deadlines at the end of January and March exist. In opposite to these commonly shared aspects, the evaluation of candidates is separately carried out within each of the three centres. Each candidate has to send the application directly to his preferred centre. Then, an individual committee composed of several professors evaluates the applications. At the moment of the present study's realisation, SFI Zurich was the only centre that carried out interviews (in Zurich or by phone) as a supplementary evaluation measure.

---

107 In the case of this document the German term “Graduiertenkolleg” has been used.
108 TOEFL: Test Of English as a Foreign Language.

The fourth instrument introduced in all SFI HEIs consists of an *intermediate performance control* in the framework of the PhD training programme. Concretely, doctoral students have not only to follow a training programme but – depending on the course and teaching professor – also to pass for instance written, oral or "take home" exams. In addition to the evaluation of individual courses through those exams, doctoral students also have either to write a "summer paper" (Zurich and Léman centres) or to complete a "comprehensive exam" (Lugano centre), in order to begin the second phase, that is to say, the research phase. In case of failure, doctoral students have the opportunity to retake exams once or to improve the summer paper. If they do not succeed in the second try and within clearly defined time slots, they are obliged to quit the PhD programme.

If the evaluation of applicants and candidates is carried out separately by each centre, the *legal anchorage* of the described reforms is an even more "local" matter. Concretely, each participating HEI, or more precisely, the corresponding institutional unit (e.g. department of finance) has its own PhD regulation. Those different regulations take into account the reforms in varying manners. Two main differences can be noticed: the first one concerns the degree of explicitness and detail with which the SFI PhD programme is taken into account, the second difference regards the im/possibility to carry out a "free" doctorate in the field of finance. Concerning the first difference, PhD regulation of University of Lugano (Università della Svizzera italiana 2006) allows most leeway by prescribing that a training programme of at least 30 credits has to be defined in collaboration with the supervisor, whereas the regulation at University of Lausanne (Université de Lausanne 2006) defines the completion of the whole SFI training programme of the first year as compulsory. Visibly, changes related to the FAME PhD programme have been taken into account in the corresponding regulation at University of Geneva (Université de Genève 2001). Yet, SFI did not provoke any further legal change in the recently elaborated new regulations (Université de Genève 2009). The opposite is true for the University of Zürich, where even the individual courses figure within the regulations (Universität Zürich 2008; 2009). Yet, the SFI PhD programme does only appear under this name within the corresponding regulation at University of Lausanne. With regard to the second difference, it is again the Finance PhD regulation of University of

Lausanne that is most explicit: the completing of the SFI PhD programme is the only possibility to carry out doctoral studies at University of Lausanne in the field of finance (Université de Lausanne 2006). In opposite, the corresponding regulation at University of Zurich explicitly mentions three varying possibilities to carry out a doctorate: first, a relatively "free" doctorate limited to the production of a doctoral dissertation and the participation in six doctoral seminars (equivalent to at least 18 credits), as second type a "structured PhD programme", comprising course work corresponding to 36 credits, a research proposal equivalent to 15 credits and a doctoral dissertation and, finally, the third type, a "structured Fast Track PhD programme", requiring 60 credits at the master level, 36 credits at doctoral level and a research proposal equivalent to 30 credits (instead of a master thesis) (Universität Zürich 2008; 2009). The regulations of University of Lugano do not precise whether a free doctorate is possible. However, the leader of SFI Lugano underlines that this is indeed the case.

VIII.1.3. A Strong Academic Profession Sustained by the Banking Industry

The reforms out of which the SFI PhD programme results do not only concern Swiss doctoral education in finance as such but have to be considered in a broader perspective including the development of finance as an academic discipline in Swiss HEIs. In each initiative, that is to say the early doctoral training programmes FAME in Lausanne/Geneva as well as the one in Lugano, the NCCR Finrisk and the SFI, doctoral education has been seen as one component of reform – though a very central one. Due to this strong nesting between the development of doctoral education and the one of the scientific field of finance as such, actors of governance are partly but not always identical for those two elements. Generally, the most crucial role has been played by the *academic profession*. During the whole reform process until today, the latter has benefited from the financial support of private actors, i.e. the Swiss banking sector, and, during the NCCR's duration, the federal authorities. Yet, it is striking that HEI governing bodies have played a very marginal role within this whole reform process (with respect to doctoral education)!

According to our interviewees, all three individual initiatives in Lugano, Lausanne/Geneva and Zurich have been triggered by individual professors. As good as all of them having been directly exposed to the Anglo-Saxon academic community during their previous career, they initiated the creation and development of PhD programmes including among others an intensive one-year training programme. Besides the structure, involved professors also indicate that they copied to a large extent Anglo-Saxon PhD training programmes from the point of view of the content. However, those extensive training programmes also require resources in terms of teaching staff. In some cases, especially in the beginning, the limited number of professors in finance made it necessary to cover teaching activities by invited professors from abroad. Since the number of faculties in finance in Swiss HEIs has been increasing since the beginning of those individual initiatives, almost all first year courses are nowadays taught by SFI professors who, per centre, decide upon the training programme content. In addition, each professor teaching a doctoral course individually decides upon the evaluation form. As mentioned, professors also take charge of the selection of doctoral students. Each centre has its own committee composed of several professors who evaluate the applications and select the candidates. Finally, professors are naturally also responsible of doctoral students' supervision. In principle, each doctoral student has one main supervisor. In some cases, they also get advice from other faculties who may be affiliated to the same HEI or to another SFI HEI or from invited professors.

The Swiss banking sector has played an important role within this reform process: according to our interviewees, it contributed, on the one side, to a quick and unbureaucratic start of the individual initiatives in Lugano and Lausanne/Geneva. On the other side, the Swiss Banking Association nowadays yearly allocates 7 million CHF (~4,52 million €) to the SFI and thereby also to doctoral education. More concretely, this funding is used to fund the salary of all first year students, some courses, a specific secretary and the promotion of the PhD programme (e.g. on specialised web-sites like the Social Science Research Network). All in all, SFI expenses in relation with doctoral education was of almost 875,000 CHF (~565,000 €) in 2007 (SFI 2009). A number of Swiss banks which financially support the SFI are represented within the so called "SFI Foundation Board". However, the main SFI PhD programme coordinator underlines that this foundation board does not take any decisions with respect to doctoral education by its own initiative. Yet, in case of measures aiming at changing the PhD programme's nature and having financial consequences for the SFI, those measures have to be approved by this board. For instance, the academic profession suggested the introduction of research sojourns in prestigious American HEIs for the best SFI doctoral students. After the positive evaluation of this suggestion by the "SFI Scientific Council", composed of currently five foreign professors, the SFI Foundation Board formally approved it. Thus, another SFI programme coordinator summarises the situation in the following way:

> Yes, for the scientific decisions there are scientists from outside of Switzerland to do the assessment. It's needed to have an outside assessment but clearly not from people from the financial services industry. At least not for the research and doctoral education. Executive education is closer related to the need of industry. Here they may say the topics that are missing, but clearly not at the research or PhD level.
>
> (A SFI programme coordinator)

Besides representatives from the Swiss banking sector, one rector per SFI centre is member of the SFI Foundation Board. An interviewed vice-rector estimates that those three rectors play a role of control rather than of impulse. He mentions that there were some reservations within his HEI towards the financial engagement of private actors. The presence of HEIs rectors in this board should assure that there would be no scientific intrusion coming from the banking sector. Except their presence within the SFI Foundation Board, HEI governing bodies have remained very discrete during the described reform process. In one case, a HEI governing body has been involved in the PhD regulation's amendment as a consequence of the SFI PhD programme's establishment. Yet, this amendment was carried out on demand of the academic profession and not of the HEI governing body as a reaction to ongoing reforms. This tendency of a rather passive attitude of the HEI governing bodies towards reforms in doctoral education also seems to prevail in the other SFI HEIs because PhD regulations have not been amended since SFI's creation. It is true that, for instance in the case of regulations of University of Geneva (2001), certain central aspects, like the two-phases-structure with related exams, have already been taken into account in the framework of the anterior PhD programmes like the FAME PhD programme. However, PhD regulations do not handle and formalise in a systematic manner other aspects like the selection procedure of doctoral students. Each regulation only deals with partial elements like for instance the constitution of the selecting committee or the possibility to ask credentials for sufficient language knowledge. One element which is formalised in none of the regulations concerns the requirement of letters of recommendation. Generally, disciplinary communities are quite autonomous, from a legal and practical point of view. SFI HEIs governing bodies are conscious of the large disciplinary diversity and the related varying research and education traditions within their institutions. During the interviews they put forward that, to some extent, it would not be desirable, and, due the traditionally strong departments, not be possible either to impose those different scientific communities a common framework with respect to doctoral education expressed in a unique PhD regulation. As a consequence, decisions related to the reform of doctoral education, such as taken by the academic profession in finance, are not strongly conditioned and constrained by HEI or Faculty wide (PhD or other) regulations. Furthermore, vice-rectors and administrators at central HEI level did not only underline that reforms which led to the SFI PhD programme have been carried out in a bottom-up manner but that, in addition, they have less control of ongoing activities. For instance, interviewees at University of Geneva emphasised that, in opposite to other PhD training programmes, the HEI governing body and administration have no institutionalised access to the programme's evaluation. The vice-rector explains this difference by the PhD programmes' varying funding base: in the case of other PhD programmes University of Geneva funds at least part of activities, whereas SFI PhD programme's costs are essentially taken into account by SFI and its external funding partners. Finally, it is worth mentioning that in spite of the HEI governing bodies' quite marginal role in the described reform process, it is still the HEIs as such who awards the title of doctor and not SFI. According to the SFI PhD programme leader, the SFI label is even not mentioned on the doctoral diploma.

Last but not least, the Confederation played an important role in the development of research and doctoral training in the field of finance. Its role was less important from a technical point of view, that is to say regarding concrete elements of reform like the PhD programme's structure in two phases. Yet, it was crucial with regard to the general agreement to promote the development of the scientific domain of finance through a NCCR. In order to be selected, NCCR projects have to be positively evaluated by reviewers from the National Science Foundation and then selected by the Swiss federal government, the Federal Council. Thus, NCCRs are not only selected on the basis of scientific but also political criteria. Indeed, some interviewees underline that federal authorities had the explicit will to promote the field of finance because finance is an economic key sector of Switzerland. According to one SFI PhD programme coordinator,

> the banking industry and the government were worried about the lack of expertise which is costing very dearly to Switzerland, as you may have seen in the newspapers recently. So to spend a few millions is some sort of insurance policy. I mean if it does not work, nothing is lost, if it works it may save a few billions.[109]
>
> (A PhD programme coordinator)

Furthermore, another SFI PhD programme coordinator underlined that the secretary of state for education and research incumbent at the time, Charles Kleiber, wanted a durable establishment of the academic field of finance through the SFI. We also interpret Kleiber's presence in the SFI Foundation Board during SFI's initiating phase as a commitment for the stable development of finance within Swiss higher education. In the case of the NCCR Finrisk, the generally strong support coming from the Confederation also has a material impact on doctoral education. During its whole duration (2001-2009), the NCCR Finrisk allows, besides the financial support of certain training activities, also the funding of a large number of assistant positions assuring the doctoral students' salaries after their first year within the PhD programme.

With respect to defined objectives, our interviews showed that there is a large homogeneity of opinion among interrogated professors: the SFI PhD programme shall attract the best doctoral students from all over the world, give them the best possible education, make them attain the highest possible quality in research production and place them in

109 The interviewee alluded to events which occurred *before* the big crisis (the interview was carried out in February 2008). Hence, the insurance policy did apparently not work very well…

prestigious, if possible, American HEIs. By working in those institutions of reference, former doctoral students improve the SFI's reputation and help to attract further promising doctoral students and professors. Thus, those mechanisms can be called "virtuous circle". This type of relationship between highly renowned doctoral programme and the attraction of quality doctoral students and professors has also been pointed to by Gumport (1993) and Kwiram (2006) for the American higher education system. Although interviewed SFI professors are absolutely conscious of the fact that not all doctoral students will find a place within a HEI or that some of them decide to do a non-academic career, they nevertheless define the future placement of their current doctoral students in HEIs as first goal. This competitive attitude is reflected in the ambition which appeared throughout the interviews and can be represented in the following quotation coming from a SFI PhD programme coordinator:

> It [the SFI PhD programme] is supposed to become one of the best in the world, certainly. There is the ambition to become the best in Europe.

Involved professors do not only agree on the overall objective but also on the concrete measures this "virtual circle" shall be promoted by. No major opposition to the students' selection through committees, the concrete content of the training programmes or any other implementation measure appeared in our interviews. In addition, as good as all finance professors of SFI HEIs teach in the framework of the SFI PhD programme or are at least figuring on the list of SFI professors, what confirms the general view resulting from the interviews. The SFI PhD programme's concrete components have been largely inspired by or even copied from American HEIs. This can be illustrated by the following quotation stemming from the SFI PhD programme leader:

> The objective was to have a model which would work but which could also be recognised by foreign institutions as valid model because they created it themselves. And thus, this allowed us to better place our students. [...] To make sure that that our students follow a curriculum which is similar to the one of American universities so that, when American professors read the student's CV, they think that is a normal curriculum. That makes sense for me.
>
> (SFI PhD programme leader)

The objectives defined by the academic profession are not in competition with those of other interviewed actors. HEI vice-rectors generally emphasise the importance to let academic professions themselves create PhD programmes according to their disciplinary needs and some of them explicitly acclaim the SFI's ambition to achieve high scientific quality. As mentioned above, financial industry and the federal government also appreciate the production of academic expertise in this particular field without formulating any further requirements with respect to concrete implementation measures.

VIII.1.4. An Actively Managing Network Profession

What is the management story of this reform? With respect to the three public management narratives we notice that elements of each of them can be identified within this case study. However, the Network Governance narrative clearly predominates compared to the New Public Management and, in particular, the Neo-Weberian-state narratives.

A first striking Network Governance feature of the SFI PhD programme consists of its *diverse composition in terms of steering actors*: on the one hand, professors and rectors from varying Swiss (and in the case of teaching professors also foreign) HEIs are present. On the other hand, a non-academic type of actor can also be identified with the Swiss banking industry. Although HEI governing bodies and the banking industry are formally part of the SFI, that is to say through their representation in the SFI Foundation Board, most concrete decisions with respect to doctoral education have been taken by the SFI academic profession. Thus, we can identify a second network within the network, namely what we call the SFI PhD programme network – composed of finance professors of SFI HEIs – within the SFI network. The SFI PhD programme network has a *high self-steering capacity*: members of this network have been taking decisions upon recruitment procedures and, partly, admission conditions of doctoral students, the training programme's content and performance evaluation of doctoral students. However in the framework of those decisions, individual SFI centres have been given some autonomy for individual solutions (e.g. concerning part of training programme's content, etc.). This partial autonomy can be interpreted as a sign for *lateral forms of management*, thus, decisions through negotiation rather than in a top-down mode, what corresponds to another Network Governance element. Finally, as professors' employment contracts do not necessarily include the obligation to teach doctoral courses, this question is also regulated by the academic profession itself.

Besides these strong Network Governance elements a number of New Public Management elements appear in this case study. They essentially have two characteristics: first, they all focus on doctoral students. The typical New Public Management element of *greater competition* applies to the recruitment of the doctoral students. SFI HEIs try to compete with other HEIs to get the best doctoral students. Only the best applicants are chosen for the SFI PhD programme. Then, once in the PhD programme, doctoral students have to complete a standardised training programme within a clearly defined duration. If they do not achieve those performance criteria, they have to quit the PhD programme. Thus, in addition to competition, there is another central New Public Management feature, that is to say *explicit standards and measures of performance*. The second characteristic of observed New Public Management elements is that almost all of them have been initiated and are currently managed or controlled by the academic profession and not by the HEI governing bodies or the state! One exception of a New Public Management element initiated by the state consists in the NCCR as public tendering procedure. Yet, since, with respect to doctoral education, this instrument is not very constraining, one can say that the state assumes a typical Network Governance state role, namely the role of a relationship facilitator. With respect to the Neo-Weberian-state element of state interventions aiming at a more cost effective organisation of public activities, one can argue that in the case of Finrisk and the resulting SFI PhD programme, this effect has indeed been achieved to a certain extent: collaboration between HEIs as it takes place within the SFI PhD programme, that is to say common advertisement, common activities in the field of course offer (though only in second phase of PhD programme), supervision and evaluation of doctoral students. However, it would go too far to speak about administrative and political control of activities related to doctoral education (except to a certain extent regarding the funding of PhD positions) through the state.

What are the consequences of those changes in management on Swiss doctoral education in finance as such? The network(s) of actors behind this case study strongly shape many reform aspects. Financially strongly supported by the Swiss banking industry and the Confederation, the network of Swiss professors in finance – which has been concentrated on a reduced number of HEIs after a sort of internal selection process – is equipped with great power, especially vis-à-vis their respective HEI governing bodies. It has been argued that since HEI governing bodies do not play a predominant role from the financial point of view, they have no tangible argument in order to ask the academic profession to give account of their (reform) activities. The resulting self-steering capacity allows them to organise doctoral education according to a model which they all recognise as valid. Since, in the case of finance this is the Anglo-Saxon model, Swiss doctoral education in finance is largely reformed and standardised according to this model. The network's strong self-steering capacity goes so far that they are able to introduce their own standards and measures of performance, which, with respect to certain elements, vary a lot compared to other disciplines present at their home universities: a two-phase structure comprising a one-year extensive course programme – taught in English and containing "standard PhD courses" – and a research phase is introduced. In addition, the first phase is sanctioned by exams and other performance controls. The academic profession's culture shaped by the New Public Management feature of greater competition has an impact on the advertising and recruitment procedures for doctoral positions, but also on the possible elimination of doctoral students who do not fulfil the standards of performance. Besides this severe measure of performance, such a competitive model also opens the way towards increased internationalisation.

However, a further Network Governance characteristic, namely lateral forms of management, also have a strong impact on the observed case study: in spite of the general consensus about the introduction of such a PhD programme model, individual groups of professors leave themselves some autonomy in the concrete implementation. This can be seen for instance in the differences among course programmes and the manner doctoral students are selected (with/-out interviews). More importantly, this autonomy appears in the fact that at University of Lausanne, the SFI PhD programme is the only way to be awarded a doctorate in finance, whereas HEIs like Zurich and Lugano still maintain the possibility to award doctorates to people who do not follow any training activities or at least not as many as in the SFI PhD programme. Thus, a more or less "free" doctorate is still possible in Lugano and Zurich which is particularly important with respect to doctoral students working in the finance industry and doing their PhD part-time. What does that mean regarding doctoral education's *raison d'être*? One can definitely say that in the case of finance, Swiss doctoral education is not re-oriented towards a non-academic direction. It is true that some HEIs maintain the possibility of a "free" and thereby possibly also more professionally oriented doctorate. Yet, the general tendency is rather to reinforce doctoral education's academic character!

VIII.1.5. An Empowered College Boosts its Scientific Field

In terms of governance and the doctorate's role, the following central observations can be made: as mentioned, through the funding coming from the national government and private companies, the involved college of academics' situation has been empowered vis-à-vis their rectorates. Compared to other case studies, the college's composition is rather "traditional": as good as all professors of the given discipline within the involved HEIs actively or passively participate in this doctoral school. Its partly inter-institutional character – applying to some decisions – is the only element which may be considered as deviating of a "traditional" composition.

The fact that doctoral students are exposed to a number of managerial elements like the competitive recruitment procedure and the intermediary performance control emphasises the role doctoral education plays for this scientific field and community, namely the role of an accelerator in terms of quantity and quality.

VIII.2. PhD programme in Finance at NHH[110]

The analysed PhD programme belongs to a HEI called the Norwegian School of Economics and Business Administration (*Norges Handelshøyskole* – NHH), which has been awarding doctorates since 1957 (NHH Brochure 2005). According to its current rector, the NHH PhD programme exists in a "modern" form – with course work and supervisor committees – since the early 1980s. Today, the PhD programme contains five different specialisations, namely in Accounting, Economics, Finance, Management science, as well as Strategy and Management. In 2007, the whole PhD programme was composed of 101 PhD students (NHH 2007). During the 2003-2007 period, 21 doctoral students have been enrolled in finance.[111] For the same period, the annual number of recruited PhD students in finance varied between 3 and 5.

VIII.2.1. Internationalisation and Integration[112]

The 2000s have brought two important kinds of change into this PhD programme in Finance. The first kind, starting in 2002, can be qualified as *internationalisation*. Concretely, the content of the existing course programme has been compared to the PhD training programmes of famous American Business Schools. According to our interviewees, the training offer has subsequently been enlarged and standardised according to the "US model", consisting of a structured training programme with a

110 This case study has been published in Baschung (2010).

111 Source: NHH Department of Finance and Management Science.

112 Unless other sources are indicated, data used originates from interviews with the NHH rector, the dean of the NHH PhD programme, the office manager at the Department of Finance and Management Science, the leader of the PhD programme's specialisation in finance, two further professors involved in the PhD training programme in finance, four doctoral students and one person of the Norwegian Research Council. All those interviews took place in June 2008, except the ones with the Dean of the PhD programme and the interviewee of the Norwegian Research Council (February 2009).

certain number of "standard courses".[113] Internationalisation also took place from a linguistic point of view: all courses are taught in English. Finally, nowadays advertising for the PhD programme is carried out at a broad international level. Indeed, the number of applicants has more than sextupled[114] between 2004 and 2007.[115] A central aim of those three measures consists in the development of a competitive PhD programme, attracting Norwegian and foreign doctoral students of high quality.

The second kind of change, which can be qualified as *integration*, started in 2008. As mentioned earlier, the Norwegian Research Council launched a call for National Research Schools. The latter were conceptualised as networks including a number of Norwegian HEIs collaborating in doctoral education, particularly in the offer of PhD training activities. NHH submitted an application for a National Research School for Business and Administration and was selected by the Research Council to establish one of totally five National Research Schools. NHH is the leader of this National Research School "Business Economics and Administration", which associates 13 other Norwegian HEIs – among which several small university colleges – and started operating in August 2009.

Numerous circumstances help to explain those two changes. Concerning *internationalisation*, three major reasons are put forward by the interviewees. The first one is clearly related to the arrival of new faculty in the Finance and Management science department over these past years. All those faculty members had some exposure to American higher education before arriving at NHH. As a reaction to the institution's internal requirement to cut costs in PhD courses, two of them elaborated a strategic document suggesting either to close down the PhD programme or to follow the example of good American PhD programmes and to increase the number of courses. Given the institution-wide internationalisation tendency, the second option was

113 Mandatory courses: scientific methods, advanced microeconomic theory, advanced econometrics, asset pricing I, empirical finance; Elective courses: topics in corporate finance, dynamic asset pricing theory, capital structure and credit risk, economics of insurance. Source: www.nhh.no. Accessed on August 2009.

114 Source: NHH Department of Finance and Management Science.

115 No precise numbers of foreign applicants were available. However, it can be assumed that the increase of the total number of applications is largely due to applications from abroad.

chosen. Secondly, the reform of the training programme has also been helped by changes at the lower degree levels provoked by the Bologna process. Before the latter's implementation at NHH, the degree structure consisted of a four-year degree, a two-year post-graduate degree – comprising specialised courses aiming at the preparation of a doctorate and the elaboration of a doctoral research project – and, finally, the doctorate. In the framework of the Bologna reform, specialised courses of the post-graduate programme were not integrated into the master degree but replaced by general courses, which are more relevant for professions in business. As a consequence of those structural changes, doctoral students would lack specific knowledge, which they now have to make up for during the doctorate. Furthermore, they also have to prepare their doctoral research project during the PhD programme. Thus, doctoral students are confronted with an even more demanding schedule. A third contextual element consists in the competition coming from the national non-academic labour market. Although the salary of Norwegian doctoral students is very high[116] – if not the highest – in international comparison, it is not competitive enough compared to the earnings a master graduate in finance can get in Norway's finance industry. As a consequence, like other scientific disciplines (see Enders and De Weert 2004), NHH has difficulties to attract native students for a doctorate. Hence, in order to get sufficient (good) candidates, NHH has to advertise and recruit doctoral students outside Norway.

According to our interviewees, the developments which led to what has been called *integration* have their origin in an evaluation report of Norwegian doctoral education published in 2002. As mentioned earlier, this report points to a certain number of problems related to doctoral education in Norway: there are too few candidates, who are too old and who take too much time to finish their doctorate. A series of improvement measures are suggested in this report, among which the establishment of so-called research schools (*forskerskoler*) (Kyvik 2002). The Norwegian government took up the idea of research schools and mandated the Norwegian Council of Higher Education Institutions (*Universitets- og Høgskolerådet* – UHR) together with the Research Council of Norway (*Norges Forskningsråd*) to elaborate a scheme for

116 Annual salary: 353,000 NOK (ca. 40,000 €). Source: www.nhh.no. Downloaded: March 2009.

National Research Schools (Utdannings- og forskningsdepartement 2005). Simultaneously, the government announced the granting of financial resources for the founding of National Research Schools. In 2008, a call for applications was sent out to all Norwegian HEIs.

VIII.2.2. Reinforcing and Novel Instruments

The presented changes have been carried out through a number of concrete instruments. This section provides a detailed picture of the four newly identified instruments: *a new recruitment procedure* of doctoral students, a *contract* to be signed by new doctoral students, the introduction of an incentive *policy instrument* and the ministry's *result-based reallocation.*

The new recruitment procedure first consists of increased efforts in the recruitment of doctoral students, particularly, although not exclusively, at the international level. First of all, broader channels of advertisement are used: the PhD programme is announced in "The Economist", on specialised web portals and HEI networks, and finally, through direct emails to students who took the GMAT (Graduate Management Admission Test) or GRE (Graduate Record Exam test) and declared being interested in doing a PhD. As a second measure, the application process has been increasingly formalised. Besides a statement of purpose, a research proposal, transcripts and diplomas, curriculum vitae and letters of recommendation, applications must also include – since 2007 – GMAT/GRE and English language certificates. Two application deadlines exist (1st of November and March each year). Also since 2007, interviews are part of the selection process which is mainly carried out by a group of Faculty members but has to be approved by three different institutional bodies: the departmental board, the academic programme committee for doctoral education (*programutvalget for doktorgradsutdanning*) and the academic appointment committee (*tilsettingsutvalget*).

The second new management instrument, implemented since 2007, consists in a *contract* which has to be signed by doctoral students (NHH 2007a), their principal supervisor, the head of the department and the dean of the PhD programme. Also inspired by American business schools, this contract concerns four issues related to doctoral education.

The doctoral training programme represents the first issue: the contract simultaneously defines a minimal number of 45 credits to be acquired and a range of precise courses ("core and mandatory courses", courses in philosophy of science/ethics, teaching). All courses are sanctioned by an exam, which, in case of failure, can be retaken once. Core courses must be passed within two years from the beginning in the PhD programme. A second issue dealt with in the contract concerns doctoral research: students are required to complete a "short research paper" by the end of the first summer, a "research paper of working paper quality" by the end of the second summer and to present an additional paper in the fall term of the 4th year. If the evaluation is negative, students are given respectively two or three additional months in order to improve the first and second research papers or to write new ones. Altogether, the dissertation should normally consist of a collection of three research papers. A third issue tackled by the contract concerns supervision. However, this issue is dealt with in a much vaguer manner, that is to say without any precise information about the frequency of supervision meetings for instance. In addition, final "responsibility for completing the PhD programme lies with the student" (NHH 2008: 3-4). As for the fourth issue, the contract also clearly defines a time when doctoral students are obliged to present their ongoing research. Finally, by signing this contract, students commit themselves to promptly reporting to the department any failure to meet the requirements or expectations in this contract. In any case, doctoral students have to submit annual progress reports (NHH Finance 2008). Among all five disciplinary specialisations within the NHH PhD programme, the contract in finance is the one which goes into most details and defines the strictest requirements. For instance, the number of credits to be gained within the course programme is the highest of all. These different degrees of rigour are the results of the departments' decision to "agree to disagree".

This contract can be seen as a reinforcement of previously existing follow-up mechanisms. In its "standard regulations for the degree of Philosophiae Doctor (PhD)", the Norwegian Council of Higher Education Institutions *recommends*, since 2004, the writing of a yearly report, which ought to "reveal insufficient progress in doctoral work and inadequacies in academic supervision" (Norwegian Council of Higher Education Institutions 2004: section 12). Indeed, such reports have also been used at NHH. Yet, considering the limited resources for doctoral positions and – in international comparison – the decent doctoral salaries, some interviewed professors judge those previously existing follow-up instruments of doctoral students as not being efficient enough and requirements towards doctoral students as having lacked a clear legal basis for sanctions against doctoral students who did not fulfil requirements. With the new contract, it is possible to eliminate doctoral students from the PhD programme, if they do not fulfil the requirements formalised by contract. According to an interviewee, this emergency brake is even more necessary because the scientific background of an increasing number of recruited doctoral students with non-Scandinavian education, who are therefore not as well-known at NHH, may sometimes be misjudged. Finally, interviewees also put forward that the deadlines defined in the contract should contribute to fulfil the requirements which are increased as a direct consequence of the Bologna reform at the bachelor's and master's degree levels.

As mentioned, the third management instrument consists in the introduction of an incentive policy instrument, initiated by the government and aiming at the establishment of National Research Schools. In September 2008, the Research Council of Norway revealed the results of the selection process: five out of 27 applications had been chosen. 115 million NOK (~13.65 million €) are distributed among National Research Schools which cover the scientific fields of "Business Economics and Administration", "Climate Dynamics", "Educational Research", "Medisinsk bildedannelse" and "Structural Biology". Funding shall be distributed over eight years (2009-2016) and cover expenses for courses, internationalisation measures (travelling costs of invited lecturers, etc.), measures to develop supervision practices and board meetings. No expenses are earmarked for doctoral salaries. One National Research School must include at least 20 doctoral students and 4 to 8 supervisors coming from a network regrouping several HEIs. On the basis of those characteristics one can say that National Research Schools are no comprehensive policy instrument addressed at the whole national higher education and research system, with respect to doctoral education. More precisely, this policy instrument has three important limitations: first, in addition to some potentially new possibilities regarding supervision and scientific exchange, it essentially applies to the training offer (as well as its organisation and coordination). Hence, it does not concern the allocation of doctoral positions to the various HEIs or the recruitment of doctoral students in particular. Second, in this first and, according to a representative of the Norwegian Council of Higher Education Institutions, possibly sole application round, only five National Research Schools were selected. This means that, at least at the moment, a majority of scientific fields and doctoral students are not concerned by this initiative.[117] Third, National Research Schools are only funded for a limited period of time. In a first stage they are funded for the 2009-2013 period. In case of positive intermediate evaluation, their funding is to be pursued until 2016.

Finally, the result-based reallocation (*resultatbasert omforderling*) of the Ministry of Education and Research of course also concerns NHH. As mentioned, in 2009 the allocated amount per completed doctoral degree was of 370,000 NOK (~44,000 €).[118]

VIII.2.3. A Bottom-Up and Top-Down Initiative

This section examines the types of actors behind those changes and the types of objectives motivating their actions. The changes that have occurred have not been promoted and implemented by one single actor. Nevertheless, in the case of internationalisation of the PhD programme in finance, one type of actor particularly stands out: a group of young Faculty members who, prior to their recruitment at NHH, have been exposed to American doctoral education programmes in finance. Strongly shaped and convinced by the latter's superiority, they launched the idea of recruiting doctoral students on a broader international basis, to adapt the previously existing training curriculum to the programmes of successful American Business Schools and to introduce a contract. Their motivation rests on the will to actively participate, contribute to and, as much as possible, stand out within the international – mostly American – academic finance community. This can be illustrated by statements of those faculties about overall objectives:

---

117 In 2008, a total number of 7,776 doctoral students were enrolled in Norwegian HEIs; Source: Norwegian Social Science Data Services, www.nsd.uib.no. Downloaded: March 2009.

118 Unfortunately, no further information about the amount's distribution within NHH could be received.

> So our goal is to make sure we produce researchers that will be productive and make important contributions to the field and the way we will see whether we have succeeded or not is to what extent we are able to place them at good universities or research departments.
> I train them for the AFA, the American Finance Association. So [...] the ideal student will go there.
>
> (Two professors involved in the PhD programme)

Their ultimate objective consists in improving the school's reputation on the international market, which should help to attract new outstanding doctoral students and faculty. Hence, like in the SFI PhD programme, those objectives build a sort of *"virtuous circle"*.

If the initiative for internationalisation and the related management instrument can be largely qualified as a *bottom-up initiative*, it also benefited from the support of other actors, partly situated at higher levels within the institutional hierarchy. According to a professor who was strongly involved in initiating this change, it was particularly the PhD programme dean who supported the ideas from the very beginning. Compared to young finance Faculty members, the objective the dean relates to the change induced by the contract varies to a certain extent in its emphasis: doctoral students must complete a high quality dissertation within four years, and as few as possible should drop out. Besides the dean's support of the PhD programme, finance Faculty members also benefited from the support of faculty from the economic department. They shared their ideas to a large extent. Faculty members from other, "softer" disciplines, however, were more reluctant to the introduction of such a detailed contract, among other things because of a different type of doctoral research output (one monograph rather than several articles). Since changes like the introduction of the contract have to be accepted by the academic programme committee for doctoral education composed of several disciplines[119], finance Faculty members could not introduce the contract within their field without the agreement of the representatives for the other specialisations. As mentioned above, the compromise consisted in "the agreement to disagree", that is to say the contract was introduced for all specialisations but adapted to respective

119 The academic programme committee for doctoral education is composed of the PhD programme dean, one representative of each of the five departments and one doctoral student representative.

specificities. Thus, all in all, one can say that from an institutional-organisational point of view, decisions about changes related to doctoral education are the responsibility of specialised bodies (PhD programme dean and academic programme committee for doctoral education) and not the central school board. However, the rector indicates that, in spite of this formal competence of the academic programme committee for doctoral education, the PhD programme dean discusses such important strategic issues with him and the departments' directors. If the rector agrees on the objectives formulated by faculty in finance and the PhD programme dean, he also emphasises the institution's responsibility to attract and educate PhD candidates for the Norwegian higher education system and business.

The actors who initiated internationalisation are almost identical to those who have implemented it. As mentioned, in each disciplinary speciality a group of Faculty members selects doctoral candidates. Yet, this selection has to be confirmed by the departmental board, the academic programme committee for doctoral education and the academic appointment committee. Also concerning the training programme's content, the academic profession in finance is not completely autonomous in its decisions: the interdisciplinary academic programme committee for doctoral education has to formally accept the suggested specialised courses. Considering the strong influence of American PhD training programmes, one can say that the omnipresent "US model" heavily intervenes from a cognitive point of view. Decisions about who is taking in charge the teaching of PhD courses are taken within the academic profession itself. Criteria are respective competences and teaching charges at the bachelor and master's levels.

If internationalisation has been exclusively initiated and implemented by internal institutional actors, the initiative and implementation of the National Research Schools are largely driven by actors from outside of the institution. As mentioned, National Research Schools can be considered as the result of the national evaluation report of 2002 and the subsequent suggestions elaborated by the Norwegian Council of Higher Education Institutions and the Research Council of Norway. Hence, in the case of integration, the range of involved actors is enlarged with governmental and intermediary actors of the national higher education system. The Research Council has been given the operational lead for this government-funded initiative. According to the responsible administrator objectives related to those National Research Schools are the following: to set standards for other research schools and institutions regarding the doctoral education's duration, the quality of the courses and the doctoral dissertations, as well as to make smaller institutions with weakly-developed PhD training programmes benefit from larger institutions, which should altogether improve the overall quality of Norwegian doctoral education within the concerned scientific fields.[120]

According to the PhD programme dean, NHH submitted an application because they were encouraged to do so by the National Council of Business Administration Education (*Nasjonalt råd for økonomisk-administrativ utdanning*)[121] and, as leading Norwegian institution within the field of business and administration, they felt a responsibility to apply. Hence, the idea for this application did not come from within NHH. However, this does not mean that, in addition to national interest, NHH would not also find its own interests in the National Research School. This can be recognised in the definition of objectives as made by the NHH PhD programme dean and current director of this National Research School "Business Economics and Administration": the overall objective consists in the improvement of Norwegian doctoral education in the corresponding disciplinary fields, starting from recruitment to job application, which should attract and produce more doctoral students for Norway. Simultaneously, the National Research School purports to increase the number of doctoral students attending NHH courses, which is currently very low (sometimes courses are attended by only 2 or 3 doctoral students). Concerning the decision-making process within this National Research School the dean underlines its non-constraining character. It is going to be a network of 14 actors without any decision power. Hence, the introduction of common standards like a contract, such as defined by the NHH PhD programme in finance for instance, could not be imposed by this network to all its participants but only through voluntary adoption.

---

120 Sources: see also www.forskningsraadet.no, accessed on March 2009.

121 This body is a disciplinary section of the Norwegian Association of Higher Education Institutions and is principally constituted of representatives from all 27 Norwegian HEIs active in education within the field of business administration. In addition, student representatives, external representatives and observers complete the 40 members body.

VIII.2.4. New Public Management dominating Neo-Weberian-State

So, what is the story of change in the management of this PhD programme in finance about? And how is it linked to the concrete reform? If the developments observed above in terms of instruments, actors and objectives are translated into the language of our three public management narratives, a combination of all can be noticed.

The two instruments of governance leading to the PhD programme's "internationalisation" episode, namely the new recruitment procedure and the new contract, contain a large number of constraining New Public Management elements: private styles of management in the form of increased use of PR techniques as well as explicit standards and performance measures are visible in the new recruitment procedure. Explicit standards and performance measures as well as greater emphasis on output control are translated in the new contract. In addition, greater emphasis on output control also appears in the Ministry for Education and Research's reallocation based on the number of completed doctoral degrees.

Besides those instruments, the assemblage of actors and the objectives at play also have an important impact on the concrete reform: first of all, it is crucial to underline that the initiative for internationalisation came from a group of professors in finance who were previously exposed to successful American PhD programmes (which according to them share a similar model in terms of structure and content). Those professors have faith in the New Public Management-shaped objective of "competition", expressed by the above-mentioned "virtuous circle". As another, subsidiary objective, they also emphasise the importance of parsimony in the use of resources funding doctoral students' salaries. Their common "American experience" and outlook explain why they quickly agreed on the type of PhD programme to be developed: a PhD programme structured into two more or less separate phases, the first phase consisting of a training programme composed of what they consider as standard doctoral courses, the second phase principally dedicated to research activities.

However, it must be emphasised that the academic profession in finance could not make a decision upon their reform plans in a completely autonomous manner. They needed the support of their colleagues from the other specialisations because decisions about such kind of issues are formally taken within the interdisciplinary academic programme committee for doctoral education. The latter is reminiscent of another New Public Management element, namely the disaggregation of monolithic units in the public sector in favour of corporatized units around products – the "doctorate" product. However, the introduction of the contract was not carried out by the PhD programme dean and the academic programme committee for doctoral education without consulting the rector and the department directors. Hence, decentralisation and the delegation of tasks to a specialised unit is not complete or – to formulate it in Network Governance language – the "academic programme committee for doctoral education" network has no strongly developed self-steering capacity. In practical terms this means that the academic profession in finance also needed the support of the rector and the heads of department. With respect to formal support expressed by the academic programme committee for doctoral education, the "agreement to disagree", which can be considered as Network Governance-like lateral forms of management, was crucial for the implementation of a reform respectful of the wishes of the academic profession in finance, namely a more severely regulated PhD programme, than for the other specialisations. The rector's agreement, ensured by his principled sharing of the high quality doctoral education objective, was equally important. Last but not least, it is also essential to underline the context of those reforms: reform efforts have been made both during a reform-friendly period and within a reform-friendly institutional environment, shaped by profound changes in curricula and a move towards internationalisation.

Through the incentive policy instrument "National Research Schools", the state entered the scene and started the second episode, which somehow recalls the Neo-Weberian-state narrative: the state adapts to new activities within a field of the public sector – the (uncoordinated) development of new PhD training offers within Norwegian higher education institutions – and adapts by formalising new aspects of those activities through a new policy instrument. Indeed, the National Research Schools could be seen as a means to rationalise the constantly developing offer of PhD courses in Norway but also to promote new ones in certain disciplinary fields. However, for three reasons, the Neo-Weberian-state story is not completely accurate: one has to notice that first, the state's intervention only concerns some scientific disciplines and HEIs; secondly, it is limited in time and finally, it does not formalise all new activities taking place in the field of doctoral education, like the recruitment of an increasing number of foreign doctoral students. These features reject the idea of the Neo-Weberian-state objective according to which the administrative and political control of all new activities is at play for the state. They rather confirm the official objective, namely to build networks of HEIs within which smaller institutions with weakly-developed PhD training programmes would benefit from larger institutions and to set standards in terms of quality and duration. With respect to the instrument's impact on the reform of the analysed case study, it is important to underline that this instrument, besides defining the overall dimensions of National Research Schools in terms of the number of participating doctoral students and supervisors, does not require any precise features concerning for instance the content or the structure of National Research Schools. Hence, this policy instrument is not very constraining and has a limited scope on doctoral education. Therefore – and even if National Research Schools are not yet completely implemented – the assumption may be made that the current course offer of our case study will be complemented and made accessible to a broader range of doctoral students from other HEIs, but not fundamentally reformed. With respect to formal decision-making, one can expect that this national network will be (even) less self-steering than the internal "academic programme committee for doctoral education" network identified above. Thus, decisions upon the recruitment of doctoral students as well as other issues hitherto managed by the academic profession will still remain in the hands of the NHH academic profession in finance. However, this does by no means hinder the spreading of "good practices". It will be particularly interesting to observe whether and to what extent stricter contracts will also be diffused within affiliated HEIs.

What is the link between this management story and the effective reformed elements? This link can be summarised in the following way: in the examined case study, the first episode consists of an academic profession in finance which – thanks to a common competitive objective, lateral forms of institutional management and a favourable reform context – succeeds in implementing a PhD programme that is strongly influenced by American business schools standards, as well as regulated and shaped by a high number of measurable and controllable indicators of performance. The second episode consists of the Norwegian state, which, via the Research Council of Norway – and with a new policy instrument primarily aiming at the improvement of doctoral education's quality through the integration of smaller institutions into networks led by bigger institutions – contents itself with providing funding for improved doctoral course offers and, possibly, supervision activities. Thus, one can say that those two episodes are shaped by varying actors using instruments which have a differing management or steering power and pursue different aspects of reform in the field of doctoral education. To simplify, compared to the state, the academic profession's management instruments are much more constraining and comprehensive in their scope. Furthermore, they presumably also share a more unified objective of reform. Accordingly, the concrete reform is currently much more strongly shaped by the first management story episode and it will probably remain so in the future.

As a result, the studied PhD programme's reform essentially consists in what has been called internationalisation: compared to the situation existing before this reform process, doctoral students are increasingly sought abroad, the training programme's content resembles the top American Business Schools and is exclusively taught in English, and, finally, the academic profession in finance increasingly makes efforts to place their doctoral students on the international academic labour market after the completion of their PhD. With respect to the doctoral programme's *raison d'être*, one can again say that the observed changes in the management of doctoral education do *not* challenge doctoral education's *raison d'être* as a degree which is principally – though not necessarily exclusively – preparing for an academic career. On the contrary, through the described changes, this mission has been rather reinforced.

VIII.2.5. Doctoral students in the Eye of the Multi-level Management Storm

In the present case study, doctoral education – and thereby doctoral students – became the object of a series of management elements. From the national government until the college of finance supervisors within the given HEI, the intensity with which management instruments are exercised on doctoral students steadily increases: the funding instruments applied by the national government principally aim at the HEIs as such, but they nevertheless can have an impact on doctoral students, in particular in the form of stronger institutional pressure to complete doctorates within time. Indeed, this time pressure has been transformed into a new contract between the institution and the doctoral students which allows doctoral students' expulsion in case of non-respect of the defined deadlines. The latter as well as other requirements in terms of course work have been defined in an even more precise manner through the finance college of academics. Hence, an actual chain of managerial pressure – concerning all HEI actors – can be identified. However, the main and final part of this pressure is rested on the doctoral students' shoulders.

Part 3:
Transversal Analysis

IX. Comparing Public Management Stories and Reforms

This first transversal chapter has a double function: it provides an overview of general trends within and comparison of the observed public management stories and reforms of doctoral education. In the framework of these comparisons, the four identified variables are discussed regarding their explicative power for identified management stories and doctoral education's reform. Simultaneously, wider lessons about university governance are drawn on this basis. Thereby, all four research questions formulated in this study's introduction can be answered. Previously, triggers and obstacles of the doctoral school movement in Switzerland and Norway are developed in an amalgamated manner, what also contributes to the general understanding of the doctoral school movement and the related doctoral education's reform in Switzerland and Norway.

IX.1. Triggers and Obstacles of the Swiss and Norwegian Doctoral School Movement

The eight examined case studies allowed the discovery of a series of contextual elements which can be seen as triggers and promoters but also obstacles of the doctoral school movement – and the related reform of doctoral education – in Switzerland and Norway. This section summarises and analyses those varying contextual elements.

A first major result of this analysis consists of the finding according to which broader issues related to the nature and development of the national (and international) landscapes of higher education served as triggers for the doctoral school movement. It is particularly the *profile and stratification issue*, pointed at in chapter IV, to which the doctoral school movement is tightly related. In several case studies –

"Biomolecular structure and mechanism", "FUNMAT" and "Swiss Finance Institute" – the concerned scientific fields within the respective HEIs benefited from what can be called national and/or institutional research priority setting policies. In the latter's frameworks, the creation of doctoral schools or similar arrangements for doctoral students' training was an underlying condition in order to get funding. If in the case of FUNMAT research school, this incitation did not lead to a strong and stable organisational unit, the two other doctoral schools developed further into visible structures which reinforce the position of those disciplinary fields, already favoured through political priority setting. Through investments in terms of doctoral students' attraction and selection as well as improvements in their training offer, these disciplinary fields continue their quantitative and qualitative growth and thereby secure, stabilise and improve their position within changing national and international higher education landscapes. Hence, doctoral schools may be exploited by scientific disciplines and HEIs in order to hold their ground within an increasingly stratified higher education landscape. From this point of view, doctoral schools may fulfil a similar competitive function as American graduate schools do (see Clark 1995).

Besides such strategic triggers, more *research based reflections* – which are however also related to the profile issue – are at stake and served as impetus for the creation of research schools. MCB research school and FUNMAT research school have been triggered, among others, by the will to foster interdisciplinary research and/or to overcome institutional-structural barriers to research cooperation. Regarding the latter point, it can be reminded that in the case of Bergen, the interdisciplinary field of molecular and computational sciences reunites researchers from five different institutional units, distributed on four different Faculties and research organisations. Concerning materials science in Oslo, one has to keep in mind that the University of Oslo does not dispose of an institutional unit of materials science. Researchers of this field are distributed on the institutes of physics and chemistry. Thus, an underlying idea of those two research schools consists of bringing together doctoral students with varying disciplinary and/or institutional backgrounds and thereby making them exchange respective knowledge. Hence, in both cases, doctoral students' central role in research production has been recognised and is seen as an instrument to achieve objectives in terms of interdisciplinary and inter-institutional research cooperation.

Economic reflections seem to be identifiable in the "Swiss Finance Institute" case study. The fact that banks contribute with important amounts of money to the running of the doctoral school can be interpreted as wish to promote the production of scientific expertise and/or of highly competent work force for the banking sector, what finally may result in economic success.

Furthermore, varying types of *international influences* have also been mentioned as sources for the doctoral schools' development. First, the arrival of an increasing number of academic staff who gained experience in American higher education has strongly contributed to the development of doctoral schools. This has notably been the case for the doctoral schools "materials science and engineering" and "biomolecular structure and mechanisms" as well as both doctoral schools in finance. It is worth mentioning that, without being the actual source of origin, doctoral schools in other countries like Germany and Denmark also served as examples. Second, if the Bologna process and the related recommendations were not directly at the origin of the examined doctoral schools' creation, it nevertheless influenced the reform movement as such. On the one side, broader developments at institutional level – in particular at University of Bergen and the University of Zurich – are certainly also due to "Bologna". Thereby, the reform issue "doctoral education" has been maintained on the agenda and put on agendas of disciplines which were inactive in terms of reform. On the other side, the restructuration at lower levels, that is to say at bachelor and master level, also led to changes at the doctoral level, as it has been demonstrated in the case of finance at the Norwegian School of Economics and Business Administration.

Finally, although quite trivial, one further trigger, which is more specifically related to *qualitative improvements of doctoral education*, is worth being mentioned in the Norwegian context. On the one hand, the national evaluation of Norwegian doctoral education (Kyvik 2002) and the related recommendations elaborated by a working group of the Norwegian Association of Higher Education Institutions were omnipresent in interviewees' contextual descriptions. As mentioned, the main issues of this evaluation report consisted in the too low number of completed doctorates, too long overall duration and too old graduates.

On the other hand, some interviewees also pointed at the underdeveloped and inappropriate course offer at doctoral level. Thus, research schools have been seen as a mean to solve these problems.

Besides those triggers, a number of obstacles, responsible of unequal developments in doctoral education's reform, could be identified. A first major obstacle consists in the mostly rather *limited funding base* for the development of doctoral schools and their activities. Especially in the Norwegian case studies, no or only little additional funding has been allocated to initiators of research schools by national or central institutional authorities (with the exception of the national research school initiative which, however, concerns only a fraction of the existing research schools). Thus, new tasks carried out by research schools often had to be financed by existing budgets at Faculty or department levels. In the case of American graduate schools, Clark (1995) argued that graduate education's costs would be many times higher than undergraduate education's and that the success of the former depends on cross-subsidization through the latter. Considering that doctoral research as such is funded through varying channels and structures, it would be interesting to separately compare the costs of the other activities – like in terms of recruitment, training, etc. – and administrative infrastructure between American graduate schools and Norwegian and also Swiss doctoral schools in order to know more about necessary funding for their running. For the moment, it seems that the amplification of the doctoral schools' movement in Switzerland and Norway and the existing doctoral schools' further development – for instance in terms of the course offers' volume – is limited by the rather low amount of available resources.

Besides limited funding, *existing traditions* built an important obstacle in doctoral schools' development. Active or passive resistance to reform could be identified in case studies from almost all examined disciplines (except finance). Considering that their previous practices were sufficient, a part of professors did not engage in doctoral schools' running or had to be strongly convinced. Resistance not only came from professors' side, but also from doctoral students. Some of the latter assumed that they were not anymore students, who had to attend courses and complete exams. Thus, they insisted on their status of young researcher.

Finally, confusion about the term "Graduate School" combined with arguments related to the *master degrees' value on the labour market* have inhibited the doctoral school movement's amplification on an institution-wide level at the federal institute of technology in Zurich. A graduate level, including the master and doctoral degrees, has been seen as a possible devaluation of the master degree. The same arguments have also prevented its sister institution in Lausanne from developing further the existing doctoral schools into graduate schools which include both the master and doctoral degrees.

IX.2. University Governance: General Trends and Patterns

After having summarised and analysed triggers and obstacles of the doctoral school movement such as observed in Switzerland and Norway, attention is turned to the identified management stories of the individual case studies. Thereby, the first two research questions, formulated in this study's introduction, can be answered. A first section provides an overview of general trends in terms of dislocations in university governance on the basis of the observed management stories. A second section discusses the identified differences in terms of management stories on the basis of the national, institutional, size's and disciplinary variables. General patterns of university governance are developed and discussed by means of this analysis.

IX.2.1. Dislocation of Power Towards Partly Redefined Colleges

As a reminder, the first, general research question has been formulated in the following manner: can one observe any changes in the Swiss and Norwegian university governance (polity and politics) on the example of doctoral education's reform taking place during the first decade of the 21st century, and, if yes, how can those changes be characterised?

The first part of the question can be answered in a clearly affirmative manner. First of all, a change concerning the intervening actors can be noticed. If one considers the actors figuring in our "Actors'

Framework B" (Chapter III.4.), one sees that all of them intervene in a manner or another on doctoral education. Thus, as a first statement, one can say, that doctoral education is definitely not anymore an issue dealt with exclusively between the doctoral student and his supervisor. On the contrary, it has been attracting a large number of actors outside HEIs – like national and partly regional governments and bureaucracies, intermediary agencies and companies – and inside HEIs – like central institutional and Faculty leaders and bureaucracies as well as individual professors and supervisors.

Does the intervention of this increasing number of actors mean that supervisors have lost their power on doctoral education in favour of the other actors? Of course, the degree of intervention of those "new" actors varies from case to case (see next section). Nevertheless, the general answer – and second statement – can be formulated in the following manner: supervisors have lost some of their power as individuals, yet, they keep or even have increased their power as college! Concretely, decisions concerning for instance types and, even to a greater extent, contents of activities of the examined doctoral schools are largely taken by the supervisors' colleges in a collective manner. This applies in particular to the volume and nature of the curricular component, but also to supervision and scientific exchange activities. It applies to a lesser extent to doctoral students' recruitment and – in Norway – follow-up, which are also (formally) controlled by Faculty and central institutional administrative units, in addition to the supervisors' college. In other words, doctoral education's heart in terms of training is still largely in the hands of the academic profession! Thus, this means, in opposite to what has been put forward by Gingras and Gemme (2006), the academic profession's monopole on doctoral education's core is not basically challenged! Power remains "at the bottom".

What about the other actors' role and position? Generally speaking, the state, the public research funding agencies and companies seem not to have the ambition to intervene directly and in an operative manner on doctoral education. Yet, through their manner of intervention – that is to say mostly by attributing funding to colleges of supervisors to rather moderately defined conditions – they endow the colleges with considerable power *vis-à-vis* their rectorates and presidencies. Thus, instead of putting themselves in a strong position – for instance by defining very constraining funding conditions –, they enforce colleges towards the HEIs' central governing bodies. In other words – and as a third statement – they rebalance the power within HEIs in favour of the colleges of academics!

A fourth, important statement must be made concerning the colleges as such. The case studies have shown that the enforced power of the colleges does not correspond to a general comeback to university governance based on "academic self-governance" (Boer et al. 2008). Firstly, because the other actors nevertheless have some power, and, secondly and most importantly, because the composition of the college which holds power may strongly vary. The college may have a "traditional" composition, consisting of all chair-holders of a given discipline within a given HEI. Yet, it may also consist of a part of these chair-holders, of an interdisciplinary or even inter-institutional group of supervisors. Hence, colleges are partly redefined. Such interdisciplinary and especially inter-institutional colleges often go beyond existing institutional structures' boundaries. Thus, this leads to the conclusion that existing governance structures of HEIs are put into question! This finding of power in the hands of varyingly composed colleges differs compared to what Prewitt (2006) recently noticed concerning American graduate education:

> One of the themes in the history of graduate education, and in attempts to change it, is the increasing power of the disciplines and the departments that house them on university campuses. Though the need for work that crosses disciplinary boundaries is increasingly on the institutional agenda, and many universities are creating new incentives to encourage such work, doctoral education remains a locally controlled process: admissions, curriculum, and quality standards are all controlled by the department's graduate faculty. As any graduate dean will testify, disciplines and departments rule the day when it comes to shaping the experience of doctoral candidates. In short, departments have tremendous power and are deeply resistant to external pressures for change; they are, if you will, part of the stasis side of the story.
>
> (Prewitt 2006: 32-33)

However, if one considers Henkel's report about shifting boundaries between British HEIs and their political, economic and social environment, the finding of strong, redefined colleges in Swiss and Norwegian doctoral education is actually not very surprising. Henkel (2007) argues that – mainly as a consequence of policies favouring science-technology-innovation relationships – existing boundaries between HEIs and their environment are much less clear-cut than before the 1970s. In addition, boundaries between scientific disciplines have also been blurred since interdisciplinarity has been given a lot of political and thereby financial importance. In this context, Henkel distinguishes those academics who lost their power from those academics who increased their power:

> Academics no longer have a monopoly of influence on organisational goals, strategies, structures and cultures. For some this has meant loss of control of their academic academic [sic] agendas, loss of disciplinary location, loss of self esteem and loss of identity. Others have succeeded in accommodating and exploiting new demands and connections without deviating from their main agenda, even if the contexts in which it is pursued have multiplied. Moreover, their disciplinary identity may remain central in that process. Others, again, have exploited the breaking down of boundaries between the academy, business and government and, in particular the opportunities for shared space, exchanges of research personnel and facilities to increase their power and significantly enlarge their arenas of knowledge production. Multiplying commercial and inter-institutional relationships have enabled them to exert greater leverage on multiple funding sources than was conceivable in the past.
>
> (Henkel 2007: 198-199)

Thus, the identification of such redefined groups of academics or colleges in Swiss and Norwegian doctoral education – "interacting" with actors beyond the institutional boundary – seems only to reflect broader observations about dislocation of power in higher education and research. They distinguish themselves from other academics who could not or did not want to adapt to the new environment.

Nevertheless, the colleges' enforced position is interesting if one considers some other assumptions existing in scientific literature. In terms of dominating actor(s), the New Public Management narrative is often considered as attributing an important role to actors at central institutional level, thus, for instance rectors, presidents or deans (see e.g. Schimank 2005). However, the case studies have shown that New Public Management elements like standards and measures of performance and shift to greater competition have been introduced and are being largely used as a steering instrument by the colleges. This finding is striking because literature about managerialism and New Public Management in higher education often qualifies the introduction of such mechanisms as loss of power for the academic profession (Deem et al. 2007; Amaral et al. 2003; Schimank 2005). However, the opposite applies to some case studies: thanks to the introduction of such New Public Management elements the colleges have a tighter control on doctoral education! This finding confirms what has been underlined by Meek (2003), namely that inputs for managerial reforms can also come from the academic profession.

A sixth statement concerns the durability of this power dislocation in favour of the colleges. As mentioned, by providing funding to colleges of supervisors for the creation and running of doctoral schools, governments, research funding agencies and companies enforced the position of the supervisors' colleges. However, since – in most of our case studies – funding is not durable, the colleges' gained power may also be subjected to variation! Thus, the pendulum might move to the HEI governing bodies if colleges do not succeed in finding stable funding sources.

Finally, besides those findings about the at least temporarily stronger role of the colleges, one must not forget the object of the increased managerial power, namely doctoral students. Whether more or less increased managerial power is exercised through the state, institutional leaders and/or the colleges themselves, final pressure is transmitted on this last actor in the chain!

After having presented those seven major observations in terms of power dislocations, some more nuances have to be developed on the basis of the individual case studies. This more subtle analysis is carried out in the next section.

IX.2.2. Types of University Governance: A Matter of National Political Systems, Institutional Profiles and Disciplines

When discussing the implementation of managerialism in higher education, de Boer (2003) underlines – by using a colour metaphor – the importance of "path dependency", varying reactions and the stress with which managerial reforms are implemented:

> Suppose that red, yellow and blue university structures are exposed to the very same black [managerial] reform. What will be the action of black on the three other colours? The first conclusion is that each university's colour will change. The

> second conclusion is that they will change in the same direction: all universities developing darker colours. The third conclusion to be drawn, however, is that the universities continue to have different colours! Red and black do not yield the same colour as the yellow and black mixture. The ultimate colour of a university depends, of course, on the precise composition of the mixture of colours. If you were to add enough black, the other colours would disappear.
>
> (De Boer 2003: 105)

As table 7 summarises, different colours – that is to say management stories – indeed appear according to the case study. This is not astonishing, even less because – as shown in chapter IV and the case studies – not all of them were exposed to the same dark colour. However, this does not completely resolve the question of the underlying reasons for those different results. Therefore, this section answers the second research question which has been formulated in the following terms: *to what extent do observed changes in university governance vary according to the national governance patterns (centralised vs. federal state), institutional types, the size of HEIs and their disciplinary communities and scientific disciplines?*

Doctoral/Research School	**Episode**	**Dominating narrative**	**Complementary narrative(s)**
Biology CH (1)	*Pioneer*	Network Governance	New Public Management
	Corporatisation	Network Governance	New Public Management
	Institutionalisation	Neo-Weberian-state	Network Governance and New Public Management
Biology NO (2)	*Local Networking*	Network Governance	New Public Management
	Continuity	Network Governance	New Public Management
Materials science CH (3)	*School wide cultural change*	New Public Management	Network Governance
	Stagnation and adaptation	New Public Management	Network Governance

Materials science NO (4)	*Birth*	Network Governance	New Public Management
	Hibernation	Network Governance	New Public Management
	Resuscitation	Network Governance	New Public Management
Humanities CH (5)	*Systematisation*	Neo-Weberian-state	New Public Management and Network Governance
Humanities NO (6)	*National Research School*	Network Governance	New Public Management
	Decentralisation	Network Governance	New Public Management
	Renouncement	Network Governance	New Public Management
Finance CH (7)	*Individual approach*	Network Governance	New Public Management and Neo-Weberian-state
	Network approach	Network Governance	New Public Management and Neo-Weberian-state
Finance NO (8)	*Internationalisation*	New Public Management	Network Governance
	Integration	New Public Management	Neo-Weberian-state

In grey: close to the narrative's ideal-type

Table 7: Case studies and their dominating narratives

Regarding the first variable – the national one – the following observations can be made: table 7 shows that the Network Governance and New Public Management narratives are most present in both countries. However, Norwegian research schools are more often dominated by the Network Governance narrative than Swiss doctoral schools, although the opposite assumption could be made if one refers to broader tendencies in Swiss and Norwegian higher education (see Baschung et al. 2009; Bleiklie 2009). This unexpected difference can be explained by the varying reform stories of doctoral education in Switzerland and Norway and the resulting varying nature of doctoral schools. Unlike in Switzerland, most elements of reform which are shaped by New Public Management – that is to say standards and measures of performance regarding curricular components and follow-up of doctoral students – have been tackled in Norway in the framework of the Faculty based PhD programmes. Thus, this reform step has been carried out before the creation of research schools and in a different structural framework (Faculty instead of e.g. inter-institutional network), whereas it has mostly been part of the examined Swiss doctoral schools. In other words, if one adds to the general assessment of Norwegian case studies all New Public Management elements developed within Faculty based PhD programmes, the overall management story of doctoral education's reform in Norway tends again more towards a greater importance of New Public Management elements than in the Swiss reform story. Thus, managerial reforms applied to the whole higher education system seem indeed to be rather accepted in the centralised state Norway than in the federal state Switzerland. However, is it really the variable "centralised vs. federal state" which makes the difference regarding the stronger acceptance of the one or the other public management narrative? Comparative studies have been carried out especially regarding the appearance of New Public Management. Hood (1995) refuses the hypothesis of the "English disease", arguing that New Public Management also shows up in non-English speaking countries. Pollitt and Bouckaert (2004) consider that countries can be classified according to certain patterns. They distinguish between conservative reformers – like federal Germany –, modernizers – like northern and central European countries – and marketizers or minimal states essentially consisting of Anglo-Saxon countries. Hence, at least in this study, the "centralised vs. federal state" variable seems not to shine out as a generally determining variable. However, in the present analysis, one can argue that this variable nevertheless matters to the extent that a system-wide introduction of New Public Management principles – like standards and measures of performance regarding curricular components and follow-up of doctoral students – has better chances to be realised in centralised Norway than in federal Switzerland.

In both countries, the Neo-Weberian-state narrative is only relatively weakly present. This confirms the view according to which the national governments have been relatively reluctant in their intervention on doctoral education's reform during the very recent past. Governmental initiatives for doctoral schools have started only after several years of debate and in a non-comprehensive manner. Reasons for the national governments' relatively weak intervention might consist in scarce financial resources and the lower priority on the political agenda compared to other issues like undergraduate students' supervision or politically oriented research. Since interventions of national governments do not fundamentally differ in terms of degree of engagement and, in addition, share a very similar nature – that is to say are both incentive policy instruments – the variable "federal vs. centralised state" seems not to be particularly relevant.

In contrast, the variable "federal state vs. centralised state" might again take a stronger effect concerning the (non-)engagement of cantonal authorities in doctoral education's reform. The cantonal government of Zurich decided to financially contribute to doctoral education's reform within "its" university, whereas all other cantonal governments of the examined case studies renounced to such supplementary financial contributions. An interviewed vice-rector considers the non-engagement of cantonal authorities as an indicator for the future division of tasks between the federal and the cantonal governments in the field of higher education:

> One gets the feeling, but I'm going to be caricatural, the task of research, innovation, economic development, a certain standardisation of norms, one sees well that, at the level of tertiary education, it increasingly rests on the Confederation. And this seems rather logic. One sees with the new law on universities that the Confederation progressively gets more weight and I believe that everything which relates to research, the next academic generation also, may achieve a certain sensibility at the level of the Confederation. I have the impression that at the level of the cantonal authorities, one deals much more with basic education. One wants to have well educated people, but who enter the job market, perhaps quite quickly with good masters because this is a bit what has been decreed as being the end of basic studies.
>
> (A vice-rector)

The next variable which can be examined regarding its effect on identified management stories consists of the *type of higher education institutions*. In both countries, two types of HEIs are present within the chosen case studies. In Switzerland, cantonal universities and federal institutes of technology are represented, whereas universities and one specialised university institution are taken into consideration in Norway. Cantonal universities and Norwegian universities mostly amalgamate a broad range of disciplinary fields. In contrast, federal institutes of technology as well as specialised university institutions concentrate on a more limited spectrum of scientific disciplines. According to the typology of Lepori et al. (2010), the first group of HEIs belongs to generalist institutions, whereas the second group belongs to specialist institutions. The two case studies which are close or almost correspond to a New Public Management's ideal-type are situated within specialist HEIs. One of those HEIs is specialised in Economics, the other in engineering and natural sciences. Contextual elements of our case studies showed that resistance to broad, standardised reforms especially appeared in case studies situated within generalist institutions. Thus, one can make the hypothesis that the New Public Management narrative – one central element of which consists of standards and measures of performance – meets fewer difficulties in specialist institutions than in generalist HEIs. This hypothesis is supported by an observation made by Mora (2001: 107):

> Academics tend to identify more strongly with their discipline, than with their university. As a result, fragmentation within universities is inevitable, thus making it difficult to implement actions that are used in business.

In other words, the bigger the disciplinary fragmentation of a HEI is, the more difficult is it to impose New Public Management on an institutional-wide basis.

Considering that the variable "type of HEI" seems to apply, one may ask the question why another also rather specialist HEI, namely the federal institute of technology of Zurich, is not dominated by New Public Management features with respect to doctoral education's reform. Indications for possible explanations come from interviewees of other HEIs. An interviewee of the University of Zurich judged it impossible to impose a standardised reform of doctoral education in a top-down manner within his HEIs, because the Faculties would be too powerful. Meek (2003) noticed a positive relationship between *size* of higher education systems and institutions and the complexity of the management task. The bigger a higher education system or institution, the more difficult they are to be managed. Thus, if Faculties of the University of Zurich are considered powerful and the doctoral education's reform is not steered in a straight New Public Management mode but in a more negotiated Network Governance mode, this might also be related to the HEI's size. After the University of Zurich, which unites almost 26,000 students in autumn 2010, the federal institute of technology of Zurich is the second largest Swiss HEI and, with 15,000 students,[122] amalgamates the double number of students compared to the federal institute of technology of Lausanne (~7,400 students). With its 2,824 students (in 2010),[123] the second HEI which is close to the New Public Management ideal-type, NHH, is even smaller than EPFL. Thus, if, in addition, one considers that all case studies situated in rather large HEIs (cases 1, 2, 4, 5, 6 and 7) are at least equally determined by New Public Management and Network Governance or even dominated by the Network Governance narrative (see Table 8), one may make the assumption that the *variable size* also applies with respect to the public management narratives. Hence, the smaller a HEI is, the higher the probability that New Public Management mechanisms may be imposed on an institutional wide-basis. In opposite, the larger a HEI is, the higher the probability to meet Network Governance mechanisms.

The last variable, that is to say, the *disciplinary one*, also seems to play a certain role with respect to the type of public management narrative. It is striking that New Public Management elements like competition, explicit standards and measures of performance as well as private-stiles management are especially present in the finance case studies, whereas such elements are largely absent in the case studies of humanities. In contrast, the Norwegian case study in humanities is strongly shaped by the Network Governance narrative. The Swiss counterpart's Neo-Weberian-state and New Public Management elements can be considered as a consequence of the Pro*Doc programme rather than of intrinsic disciplinary features. Case studies in biology and

122 Source: www.bfs.admin.ch; accessed on January 2011.

123 Source: http://dbh.nsd.uib.no ; accessed on January 2011.

materials science, which have been to a wide extent unconcerned by state interventions, are situated in between New Public Management and Network Governance narratives. Thus, it seems that besides some individual "interference" through the Neo-Weberian-state narrative, the four disciplines can be placed on a continuum between New Public Management and Network Governance narratives. Soft pure sciences tend to be close to the Network Governance narrative. The more disciplines become hard or applied, the closer they are to the New Public Management narrative.

The general dominance of New Public Management and Network Governance in the examined case studies as well as their relative importance according to the main issues (see next section) is illustrated in a more detailed manner in table 8, which reinforces the discussion carried out above.

Doctoral School	**Issue**	**NPM Elements**	**NG Elements**
Biology CH (1)	Recruitment	Private-sectors styles of management Greater competition Stress on discipline in resource use	A greater range of actors and interactions
	Curricular training	Explicit standards and measures of performance	A greater range of actors and interactions Coordinating power shared by actors operating at multiple levels Lateral forms of management State as relationship facilitator
	Supervision		A greater range of actors and interactions
	Scientific exchanges		A greater range of actors and interactions Self-organising and self-steering capacity

Biology NO (2)	Curricular training	Disaggregation of units in the public sector Explicit standards and measures of performance	State as relationship facilitator A greater range of actors and interactions Lateral forms of management
	Supervision	Explicit standards and measures of performance	A greater range of actors and interactions
	Scientific exchanges		Lateral forms of management
	Follow-up	Explicit standards and measures of performance Greater emphasis on output control	
Materials science CH (3)	Recruitment	Hands-on professional management Disaggregation of units in the public sector Explicit standards and measures of performance Greater competition Private-sectors styles of management	
	Curricular training	Explicit standards and measures of performance	Lateral forms of management
	Follow-up	Disaggregation of units in the public sector Explicit standards and measures of performance Stress on discipline in resource use Greater emphasis on output control	
Materials science NO (4)	Curricular training	Explicit standards and measures of performance Private-sectors styles of management	
	Scientific exchanges		A greater range of interactions Self-organising and self-steering capacity Lateral forms of management
	Follow-up	Explicit standards and measures of performance Greater emphasis on output control	Give account rather than ex-post state-driven system of checking

Humanities CH (5)	Recruitment		Lateral forms of management A greater range of actors and interactions
	Curricular training		Lateral forms of management
	Supervision		A greater range of actors and interactions
	Follow-up	Explicit standards and measures of performance Greater emphasis on output control	
Humanities NO (6)	Curricular training		A greater range of actors and interactions Self-organising and self-steering capacity Lateral forms of management Coordinating power shared by actors operating at multiple levels
	Scientific exchanges		A greater range of actors and interactions Self-organising and self-steering capacity Lateral forms of management Coordinating power shared by actors operating at multiple levels
	Follow-up	Explicit standards and measures of performance Greater emphasis on output control	
Finance CH (7)	Recruitment	Greater competition	Self-organising and self-steering capacity
	Curricular training	Explicit standards and measures of performance	A greater range of actors and interactions Self-organising and self-steering capacity Lateral forms of management State as relationship facilitator

Finance NO (8)	Recruitment	Private-sectors styles of management Greater competition Explicit standards and measures of performance	
	Curricular training	Explicit standards and measures of performance	
	Follow-up	Explicit standards and measures of performance Stress on discipline in resource use Greater emphasis on output control	

Table 8: Presence of NPM and NG elements per reform issue and case study

On the basis of the presence of the three narratives' features within the eight case studies some general patterns in terms of relations between combinations of variables and management stories shine out. The following formulations reflect them in an ideal-type manner:

- Ideal-type one: elements of New Public Management have the biggest chance to impose on a broad basis in case of hard and applied sciences situated in small, specialist HEIs within centralised countries.
- Ideal-type two: in soft pure sciences, situated in larger, generalist HEIs of federal countries, it is the Network Governance narrative which is likely to impose.

Correspondingly, mixed forms of those two combinations of variables lead to situations in between New Public Management and Network Governance. The following Simplified Governance Patterns Scheme illustrates those patterns. The closer a combination of variables is to one of the ideal-type combinations, the closer a case can be situated to one of the two poles.

This scheme is called "simplified" because it does not necessarily adequately take into account the degree of potential influence of each of the four variables. For instance, the country variable appears as most determining variable, whereas the disciplinary variable seems to have the weakest impact. In spite of this too static illustration, this scheme should allow to indicate the general idea developed above. However, it is important to underline that the patterns presented in this scheme have been built on the basis of a rather limited sample. Hence, this scheme has to be considered as a hypothesis which has to be further tested!

Simplified Governance Patterns Scheme:

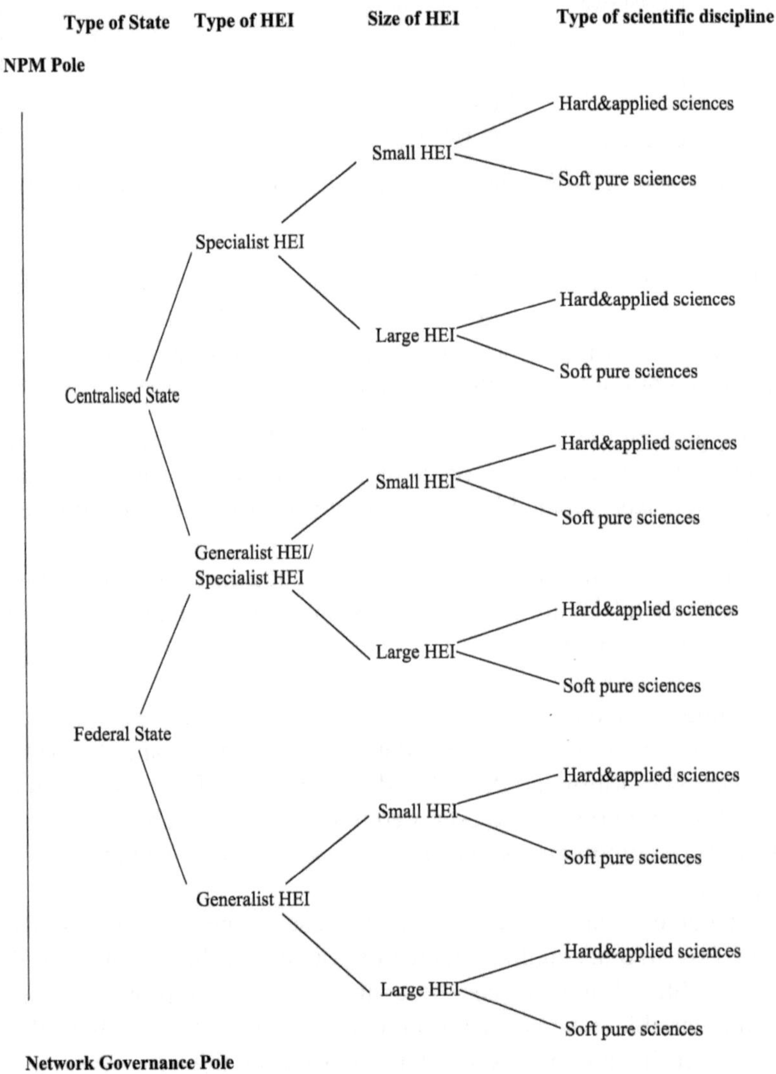

IX.3. Issues of Reforms in a Comparative Perspective

By analysing triggers and obstacles as well as underlying governance patters, the two previous sections of this chapter developed among others an explicative framework for the reform of doctoral education such as occurred in Switzerland and Norway. This third section analyses the content of the doctoral school movement and the related elements of reform. These findings are discussed and interpreted in the light of the reform issues identified at the European political level. Then, it summarises and compares all reform issues which have been observed in the framework of the eight case studies. The analysis points at relevant variables. Thereby, this study's third and fourth research questions are handled.

IX.3.1. Reform Issues and Comparison with Political Debates at European Level

This section has two functions. On the one side, it answers the third research question, namely what the doctoral education's reform in terms of practices consist of. On the other side, those reform elements are considered in the context of the political debates at European level.

Concerning the third research question, the reform issues observed in the eight case studies can be summarised in six distinctive categories, namely,

- Recruitment
- Curricular component
- Supervision
- Scientific exchange
- Follow-up
- Career

What types of new practices are parts of those six categories? Within the category "recruitment" are ranged *efforts in terms of attraction and selection of doctoral students* which go beyond traditional practices consisting of advertisement within local or national newspapers and direct recruitments of local graduates through individual supervisors. Thus, such additional efforts go from broad advertisement at international level in the name of a PhD programme label, over intensified selection procedures including interviews *in situ* and oral presentations through applicants until the selection through committees composed of a group of professors. Chapter X will deal more in detail with those efforts in terms of doctoral students' recruitment.

The category "curricular component" stands for *courses attended by doctoral students*. In all case studies, those varying course offers have been either created from scratch or strongly differ compared to the previously existing ones. Often, but not always, they are exclusively dedicated to doctoral students. Three categories of courses can be distinguished. First, courses focused on a mono-disciplinary scientific field, second, courses concentrated on an interdisciplinary scientific field and third, transferable skills courses focused on academic work.

Thesis committees composed of at least two supervisors from inside and sometimes outside the doctoral students' laboratory or HEI constitute the reform element of the category "supervision". Thus, instead of one only supervisor, doctoral students get more or less regularly feedbacks from several supervisors.

The category "scientific exchange" includes new practices of interaction focussing on doctoral students' research and training which go beyond usual exchange between doctoral student and his supervisor(s) or, in the case of laboratory based sciences, the research group. In the case of the examined case studies, this includes *interactions within a group of doctoral students, mostly enlarged by local and external invited scholars*. Such interactions may take place in the framework of seminars, conferences and retreats specifically organised for doctoral students.

Regular reporting about doctoral students' progress in research and training essentially constitutes the category "follow-up". The underlying idea consists of an initial definition of a research and training project, sometimes containing deadlines, and its regular examination. In mostly yearly cadences, doctoral students and/or their supervisor(s) write reports about doctoral students' progress. Delays have to be justified. In addition, the quality of doctoral students' supervision may also be a topic which is dealt with in such reports. Recipients and control instances of those reports vary between doctoral schools, Faculties and research funding agencies. Final decision-making in case of disagreement between doctoral student and supervisor(s) – revealed in reports – devolves on the doctoral schools' or Faculties' scientific and administrative leaders.

Finally, reform efforts in terms of "career" which could be identified in the case studies include *courses on career planning* and concrete actions promoting the doctoral students' *placement* on the academic labour market. The latter consist of visiting sojourns in highly renowned HEIs and participation in central international conferences of the corresponding field, where doctoral students present their "job market paper".

In the case of the categories "curricular component" and "scientific exchange", the border in between may be blurred. On the one hand, scientific exchange between doctoral students and other scholars may take place during courses. This seems to be the case in particular in the examined doctoral schools in humanities. On the other hand, specific "scientific exchange" activities like retreats may also include courses. Thus, there may be some mixed forms. Furthermore, an important issue which explicitly appeared in some case studies, but which is probably present in all of them, consists of *social exchange*. Since the latter is difficult to identify, it does not build an own category of reform. However, it is nevertheless worth being mentioned because it may be determinant in order to avoid doctoral students' social – in particular for people coming from outside of the given HEI – and scientific isolation as well as to promote doctoral students' socialisation within the academic environment.

To what extent do those six identified categories of reform issues correspond to the reform issues debated at European political level?[124] In other words, do reforms which have been implemented during those last years aim at the same issues or are underlying objectives completely different? In the case of political debates at European level, it seems to be most appropriate to use the European University Association's report of 2007 as a point of reference, because it was EUA who has been

124 We renounce to a specific comparison with reform requirements at national level, since the latter (in Switzerland and Norway) are much less explicit than at European level and – concerning for instance overall doctoral education's duration, scientific environment, etc. – are widely included in those formulated at European level.

mandated by the Ministers to elaborate recommendations on the reform of doctoral education (see I.1.1.).

When comparing the six categories as such to the six general recommendations developed by the EUA report (EUA 2007), the degree of match seems to be relatively high. EUA's first recommendation, that is to say to maintain flexibility in admission and to assure equality in access seems to be more or less followed. An indicator for flexibility can be seen in the increasing recruitment of doctoral students from foreign higher education systems (see chapter X.). The observed efforts in terms of attraction and selection of doctoral students also include clearer definitions and a certain standardisation of criteria of selection. Thus, the latter may inhibit unequal treatments of applications. The general process of selection of Norwegian HEIs which comprises examinations of applicants through collective committees also aims at avoiding unequal treatment. However, besides one exception,[125] no other special measures promoting equality, for instance concerning gender, could be noticed.

The second recommendation, concerning supervision, is only partly present in the case studies. Transparent contractual frameworks between doctoral students, supervisors and the institution as well as multiple supervision frameworks indeed exist. Yet, continuous professional skills development of academic staff (as supervisors) and performance reviews of supervisors are as good as absent! At best, supervisors' performance is examined through doctoral students' yearly reports, provided that the latter dare criticising their supervisors' performance… The recommendation to properly recognise supervision activities as a task of academic staff through its inclusion in their workload and task description is widely realised in the case studies. However, tasks descriptions do mostly not include any quantitative or qualitative indicators and do mostly not consider either additional workload related to the running of doctoral schools.

125 For instance, University of Bergen has the so-called "Quota Scheme", which is "a funding scheme offered by the Norwegian government to [master and PhD] students from developing countries and countries in Central and Eastern Europe and central Asia. The objective of the Quota Scheme is to provide relevant education that will benefit the students' home countries when they return." Source: http://www.uib.no/education/collaboration/the-quota-scheme; accessed on December 2009.

Third, could efforts to develop transferable skills through interdisciplinary dialogue among doctoral students as well as various forms of courses taught by academics and external consultants be identified? The least that can be said is that almost all analysed case studies contain curricular components of more or less pronounced interdisciplinary character, which might promote interdisciplinary dialogue among doctoral students. With respect to courses, it is striking that almost all courses which do not explicitly focus on the state of the art of the given fields in terms of theory and research – thus more applied courses like academic writing, specific techniques, etc. – focus on academic work, whereas the underlying political idea consists of developing skills usable on the non-academic labour market. Thus, this either means that actors deciding upon those courses are not willing to go into this direction and want to concentrate efforts on the development of academic skills or that those actors think that such academic skills may also be useful on the non-academic labour market. In any case, it seems fair to say that the curricular component does not change doctoral education's academic character.

Fourth, on the basis of the studied doctoral schools' activities, it can be said that the recommendation to monitor the development of time to degree for doctoral candidates is realised through the reporting process. Fifth, concerning the recommendation for universities and authorities to promote attractive research careers and career perspectives inside and outside of academia, it can be said that some efforts have been made. Again, most of implemented measures focus on academic careers. No particular measures with partners outside academia have been initiated.

Finally, as a last EUA recommendation, HEIs are encouraged to include doctoral programmes in their strategies for internationalisation for instance by offering funding for doctoral students' mobility. Indeed, such funding instruments exist in the examined case studies. It can further be argued that internationalisation of doctoral programmes also takes place through the recruitment of an increasing number of foreign doctoral students.

IX.3.2. Comparing Identified Reform Issues Between Case Studies

Hence, if one considers the categories of reform issues identified in all case studies together, one may conclude that all broad reform issues dealt with at European political level are indeed present. Concrete recommendations are also implemented, though to varying extent. Variance can be noted in particular regarding the examination and training of supervisors as well as doctoral education's character, which seems to be shaped first and foremost by academic objectives. Besides those general findings, it is important to note that the presence of the six identified reform issues strongly varies according to the case study. This section aims at indicating identified variations and discussing them on the basis of the national, institutional, size's, disciplinary as well as other variables. Therewith the fourth and last research question is handled. Table 9 summarises the presence of those six reform issues within the eight examined case studies.

	Recruitment	Curricular component	Supervision	Scientific exchange	Follow-up	Career
Biology CH	■	■	■	■		■
Biology NO		■	■	■		
Materials science CH	■	■		■	■	
Materials science NO		■		■		
Humanities CH		■		■	■	
Humanities NO		■		■		
Finance CH	■	■		■		■
Finance NO	■	■			■	

Table 9: Case studies and presence of reform issues

Several variables have to be mobilised in order to discuss the varying presence of reform efforts in terms of doctoral students' *recruitment*. First of all, it seems to be a question of disciplinary and also institutional cultures. The will to become more competitive on the international scientific scene by recruiting the "best doctoral students" is especially visible in the case of finance but also life sciences and clearly less present in discourses among interviewed scholars in humanities. Institutional policy may explain new forms of doctoral students' selection in the case study of materials science in Switzerland, where the discourse about "recruiting the best doctoral students" was less present among interviewed professors. However, new selection procedures have nevertheless been implemented as part of a comprehensive institutional policy. Besides the factor of disciplinary culture and institutional policy, the factor size may further explain variation. Chapter X will show that measures aiming at the attraction of strong doctoral students also have a cost and that different types of resources – among others a high number of doctoral positions – are necessary for such reinforced efforts in terms of doctoral students' attraction and recruitment. For instance, in the case of a relatively low number of doctoral positions per domain, some actors argue that high investments are not worth and do not implement particular measures in order to attract doctoral students, like in the Norwegian case study of biology. Finally, those variables can be complemented by further arguments for varying recruitment practices and preferences in terms of candidates. Such arguments, among which the "brain-drain issue", will be developed in chapter X.

A *curricular component* is present in all of the chosen case studies, though with strongly varying volumes and conditions of evaluation. Thus, in addition to traditional forms of learning like "learning by doing" or learning in the framework of the "apprentice-ship model", other forms of learning complement the overall research training. It is crucial to underline that the curricular component is *not a replacement* of older forms of learning but a *complementary form*. The same can be said concerning scientific exchanges which do not replace but complement one-to-one supervision through the principal supervisor(s).

Multiple supervision can also be seen as an enrichment of the one-to-one supervision model. It is difficult to explain why multiple supervision only exists in the biology case studies. First, it may be a question of disciplinary and institutional size. The larger a community of a given scientific field in a particular HEI is, the higher the number of potential sources for scientific advice. In the Swiss biology case study, the following quote of a doctoral student underlines this idea:

> I mean, our institute is quite consistent from the topic's point of view. Of course, there are different techniques, but it is structural biology. And most of contacts which were useful for me, are those which are close [from a geographical point of view]. That means, you go up one floor, you have any detail question about a technical problem and you know that this person has already done it. Then you walk around in the building and then you actually find all knowledge you need.
>
> (A doctoral student in biology)

Some doctoral students in other disciplines stated that it was difficult to find further professors in the same institution who were competent in the doctoral students' research field, a condition in order to get an added scientific value. Of course, multiple supervision does not necessarily need to be limited to supervisors of the same HEI. However, the quote also indicates the practical aspect of such additional advice through other people than the principal supervisor. In other words, spontaneous contacts seem to be easier within the same institution or building than if the corresponding person is geographically far away. Besides the size's variable, a second observation may further explain the absence of formal multiple supervision in the other case studies: many doctoral students – especially in experimental sciences – emphasised that, despite the lack of formal multiple supervision arrangements, they got additional advice from other scholars in an *informal way*.

Practices in terms of knowledge transmission varying between disciplines may explain to some extent the differences regarding *scientific exchange* between, on the one side, the finance case study in Norway and parts of the Swiss finance case study and, on the other side, all other disciplines. It is striking that the training programmes in finance are the largest ones in terms of volume and regarding its overall importance in the whole doctoral education process. In both case studies, course work occupies as good as the whole first year of doctoral education and may even take some time in the following years, whereas it is rather seen as a complementary element in the other disciplines. The training programmes in finance also have the strongest "school-like" character. Specific courses have to be attended and are evaluated by different types of exams. Interviewees seemed to attribute much less importance to other types of knowledge transmission – like what has been defined as scientific exchange – than to course work.

Differences regarding the presence of *follow-up mechanisms* can be largely explained by the national and institutional variables. Although not visible on table 8, all Norwegian PhD students have to write – as a consequence of national regulation – yearly progress reports and send them to their respective institutional units, like their institute or Faculty. However, except the case study in finance, those institutional structures differ from those of the research schools. Therefore, they do not figure on table 8. Again, it is the comprehensive institutional policy of the Swiss case study in materials science which explains the presence of follow-up mechanisms. In the Swiss case study in humanities, reporting is principally an obligation related to the funding obtained by the Swiss National Science Foundation. However, since this reporting is directly addressed to the funding agency and passes by institutional instances, it seems rather to be a way of giving account on the obtained funding than a weighty instrument in terms of progress control. Finally, it is also important to mention that some doctoral students have to regularly write small reports about their progress for their supervisors, independently of institutional regulation. This reporting, which in some cases is carried out weekly (!), could be identified in particular in the Swiss case studies of biology and material sciences. Thus, in some cases, informally regulated reporting processes already exist at the research group level for instance, independently of doctoral schools.

The spotty presence of actions in terms of academic and non-academic careers' promotion within doctoral schools illustrates the currently low importance attributed to this issue. This low priority position may be due to varying ambitions and views on responsibilities. As mentioned in chapter IV, Swiss and Norwegian doctoral graduates have relatively little problems to find relevant and satisfactory jobs. Hence, the national variable – in terms of a favourable (non-academic) job market – may apply to a certain extent. Academics might consider that the job is done and that no further measures in terms of career promotion are necessary, whereas others have the ambition to deliberately place their doctoral graduates in renowned HEIs. However, some interviews, especially in finance, showed that further measures in terms of academic career promotion will follow in a later stage of the reform process.

Hence, the different variables' effect can be summarised in the following manner: first, one can say that the disciplinary variable has a particular impact on recruitment practices, the curricular component's content, volume and mode of evaluations as well as scientific exchange activities. Even if it was not possible to interrogate underlying disciplinary characteristics in the framework of this study, it seems plausible to explain varying practices – or in-/existing reform(s) – regarding those three issues by following the basic argument put forward by Trowler and Becher (2002), that is to say that academic cultures – and related practices – are closely connected to fields of enquiry. Second, the variable "size" certainly has an impact on varying practices – or in-/existing reforms – in terms of recruitment and supervision. Third, the national variable, in terms of centralised vs. federal state but also in terms of a favourable (non-academic) labour market, has an impact on follow-up mechanisms and promotion activities for academic careers. Finally, the institutional variable – in terms of uniform institutional practices – may also have an impact on recruitment of doctoral students.

IX.4. Relating Governance Patterns and Reforms

The case studies' chapters developed in detail the link between governance patterns and reform outputs. This section aims at demonstrating this link with regard to broadly observed reform tendencies. It is argued that the latter consist of a certain *structuring, standardising and opening of doctoral education*, whereas maintaining its *academic character*. Simultaneously, it is underlined that those tendencies vary according to the case studies.

Taking the New Public Management as example, it can be argued that certain of the narrative's main elements like explicit standards and measures of performance have a *structuring and standardising effect on doctoral education*. The Norwegian case study in finance, which is mostly shaped by this New Public Management element, indeed represents the case of strongly structured and standardised doctoral education. It is strongly structured to the extent that applicants for doctoral positions have to apply to clearly defined points in time, doctoral students have to complete a training programme and to produce research papers within a given time schedule and to report about their progress in defined periods of time. Moreover, it is standardised to the extent that applicants have to respect the same large number of precise conditions, doctoral students have to attend the same basic course programme, to complete the same type of exams with certain minimal grades and to achieve the same number of credits without which it is impossible to receive the PhD degree in the field of finance within the given HEI. Another example illustrates the case of less strongly structured and standardised doctoral education. The Norwegian case study in humanities showed that doctoral students also have to provide yearly reports about their progress and to attend courses as well as other activities, which correspond to a standardised number of credits. Yet, doctoral education is much less structured to the extent that there are no explicitly imposed intermediate deadlines for the completion of the course component, the related evaluations and the production of doctoral research. It is also less standardised to the extent that, besides one only course in theory and ethics of science, doctoral students can freely choose their course programme and sometimes even the mode of evaluation. In other words, doctoral students can also get their PhD degree by attending activities in another framework than the research school which exists in their HEI. Hence, those two examples clearly demonstrate that differentiation between situations has to be made when reporting about structured and standardised doctoral education. This becomes even clearer when one has a look at the Swiss situation. Considering that doctoral regulations differ to a larger degree in Swiss than in Norwegian higher education, that, from a formal point of view, individual issues of doctoral education are much less structured than in Norway, and that only a small part of Swiss doctoral students attend doctoral schools, it can be stated that Swiss doctoral education globally is less structured and standardised. Thus, in spite of the evident identification of an increasing number of structured and standardised elements of doctoral education in certain cases, it would be too premature, at least for the moment, to speak about a general movement towards structured and standardised doctoral education, especially in Switzerland.

Similarly to the New Public Management narrative, it can be argued that elements of the Network Governance narrative also shape doctoral education. For instance, as a consequence of the inter-institutional and/or even interdisciplinary networks of actors managing the organisation of common training activities for doctoral students an *increased opening of doctoral education* can be observed. Doctoral education's opening may take place regarding several issues: doctoral students have easier access to a larger choice of organised training activities, they enlarge their scientific environment and exchange beyond their usual institutional and/or even disciplinary boundaries, the way towards increased multiple supervision arrangements is simplified and additional information and possibilities in terms of careers become visible. Again, the type and degree of this opening depends on the individual cases. In the Swiss case studies in finance and biology, the opening has particularly happened in terms of institutional boundaries, whereas it especially applies to the disciplinary boundary in both case studies in humanities and the Norwegian case study in biology. Concerning the degree of opening, one may quote the Swiss case study in finance as a case of partial opening in terms of training programme, since all courses of the first year are provided by the individual local programmes and doctoral students only commonly attend courses from the second year on. On the contrary, all training activities of the Swiss case study in biology are in principal attended by doctoral students from both involved HEIs.

It has been revealed that central components of doctoral education – like the content, structure and often also the volume of doctoral education's curricular component and supervision of doctoral students – are still and, in some cases, even increasingly steered by the supervisors' colleges. We argue that *existing forms of doctoral education therefore still are strongly dominated by an academic character*. This seems at least to be confirmed by the elements of reform which have been identified for the examined doctoral schools. Especially observed changes in terms of additional training activities, rather seem to focus on the academic character of doctoral education. Besides the main part of the curricular component, which consists of theoretical and partly methodological courses focussing on specific scientific disciplines or a particular interdisciplinary field, courses like academic writing and ethics in science also build a (rather small) part of doctoral education's reform. However, only very few transferable skills courses explicitly focusing on the non-academic labour market could be identified. Again, this statement about doctoral education's academic character has to be differentiated to a certain extent because some individual doctoral research projects, of course, are carried out with a more applied or professional perspective. This is particularly the case in disciplines like materials science which can be situated between engineering and natural sciences. Yet, a further study would be necessary to examine whether and to what extent more applied doctoral research like industry-based research is carried out. Concerning the academic character of doctoral education, Probst Schilter (2009) showed for the field of communication sciences in Switzerland that different realities are hidden behind the same label. For instance, certain doctoral students clearly exercise scientific activities within the international scientific community, whereas others carry out rather local activities like teaching, administration and mandated research.

IX.5. Implications for Academic Work

Besides this general relationship between changes in doctoral education's governance and reform of doctoral education developed in the previous section, more concrete implications on academic work are also worth being mentioned. Again, implications vary according to the case study. Yet, the most "radical" examples are taken in order to illustrate observed and – if applied on a broader basis – future potential changes in academic work. Three actors or units – doctoral students, supervisors and doctoral schools – are taken as point of reference in order to demonstrate changes in academic work.

As a consequence of the described reform elements, doctoral students' work is more diversified, intensified and increasingly formalised in terms of tasks. It is diversified to the extent that, in addition to their tasks in the field of research and – may be – teaching and administration, they also got the new "old" task of a student, namely to attend courses. Meetings with their supervisor and scientific exchange with other senior academics or doctoral students may always have taken place. However, through the introduction of thesis committees and regular seminars, conferences and retreats, those activities are intensified. Finally, the writing of progress reports are a (supplementary) activity which formalise doctoral students' work. They are definitely not anymore their own master of their research, but increasingly controlled and thereby lose some freedom.

Supervisors' work is more formalised, intensified, increasingly specialised and collective. Formalisation of doctoral education through formal follow-up procedures like annual reporting also has an impact on the supervisors' work as an advisor. It is not anymore enough to informally advise doctoral students in more or less regular meetings. Moreover, supervisors have to regularly judge in a written way their doctoral students' work and, may be, to give account of their own work as supervisors. Furthermore, supervisors who engage in the described reform movement are confronted with an intensified working load regarding their teaching and supervision activities. In addition to their mostly usual teaching task at bachelor and master level, they also have to prepare demanding courses for the doctoral level. Participation in thesis committees, doctoral seminars, conferences and retreats also increases their activities as advisers. By engaging for such activities and others related to doctoral schools – for instance administrative ones – some supervisors are disburdened from tasks like teaching at bachelor level. Thus, it can be argued that a certain specialisation like in teaching at graduate level may take place. Yet, specialisation also takes place concerning the new tasks related to doctoral schools. For example, some supervisors do not teach at doctoral level. However, they participate in the committee that selects a first series of applicants for doctoral positions. The latter activity is also a good example for the increasingly collective character of supervisors' work. Thus, instead of selecting doctoral students individually, at least part of the selection process is carried out in a collective way. Besides the recruitment activity, supervision and scientific exchange also becomes more and more collective. Doctoral seminars, conferences and retreats are often not anymore organised and led by one only supervisor but by several of them in common. Increasingly collective forms of academic work have already been noticed by Zinman (1994). Thus, this working form has also attained doctoral education.

Finally, the unit "Doctoral School" is also a place, where changes in academic work can be observed. Some specialisation and professionalisation takes place. Specialisation can be seen in the creation of particular dean positions for doctoral education. Deans of Graduate

Schools exist since a long time in American higher education, whereas deans of doctoral schools are a recent invention in Swiss and Norwegian higher education. Professionalisation is visible at the administrative level of doctoral schools (or the central institutional or Faculty level). Administrative aspects of recruitment procedures, diffusion of information about doctoral conferences and seminars as well as the administrative follow-up of doctoral students are not anymore casual activities exclusively taken charge of by motivated supervisors. In opposite, they are sometimes outsourced to new administrative units who make of them their core business. Thereby, another aspect of higher education at least partly becomes the object of what Bleiklie (1998: 308) – in the Norwegian context – calls Entzauberung of academic affairs:

> Academic work can be administered as any work in any service-providing agency. We are faced with an ideal that clearly indicates professionalisation and differentiation of the leadership roles and administrative functions. It emphasises the separation of previously pervasive and interwoven functions of scholar, administrator and leader. It also emphasises a more comprehensive administrative responsibility and leadership which embraces planning, resource management, personnel policy, productivity measures, as well as public relations.

X. Recruiting on the International Doctoral Students' Market: Unequal Attitudes and Resources

As developed in individual case studies and chapter IX, the recruitment of doctoral students constitutes a central issue in doctoral education's reform. An increasing number of efforts are carried out in order to attract and recruit the internationally "best" doctoral students. Thus, a perspective shaped by "competition" and "market logics" is adopted. However, as pointed out in chapter IX, this perspective is not shared by everybody. The present chapter aims at shedding light on the diverging place of doctoral students' recruitment on the reform agenda. This is done by developing two main arguments: first, different attitudes exist among supervisors concerning the recruitment of international doctoral students; second, the latter require several types of resources.

X.1. The International Doctoral Students' Market under Development

Different types of markets exist within higher education: for staff, students, grants, etc. (Jongbloed 2003). The types of market doctoral students belong to are varying and ambiguous. In certain countries, like Japan, doctoral students pay tuition fees and are considered as students, whereas in others, like Norway, they receive a regular salary and are – from this point of view – considered as young researchers. Whatever the precise situation, the European doctoral students' market is under quantitative and qualitative development: in the context of the knowledge-based economy, the conference of European ministers responsible for higher education underlines the need to increase the production of PhDs (Ministers responsible for Higher Education 2005). Indeed, the number of doctoral students and thereby doctors increases in Europe (Kehm 2006). Qualitative developments happen with regard to doctoral students' nationality. HEIs do not anymore exclusively recruit their doctoral students locally or nationally, but increasingly at international level. Two main reasons are behind this qualitative development: on the one side, a declining interest of native students to do a doctorate in certain disciplines is noticed. On the other hand, this is also due to the expanded global competition for the bright minds (Enders and de Weert 2004).

Studies on the academic labour market show that the degree of internationalisation varies according to countries and scientific disciplines (Welch 1997). Also in the case of *doctoral students' markets*, we notice varying degrees of internationality between countries, disciplines and, correspondingly, HEIs. How can one explain those differences in degrees of internationality? Different types of arguments can be put forward: first, the above mentioned declining interest of native graduates to do a doctorate is often related to the higher economic attractiveness of the non-academic job market. However, those salary disparities concern certain disciplines more than others. For instance, graduates in finance find much higher salaries in the financial industry than in academia (Baschung 2010), whereas this does not necessarily apply to graduates for instance in humanities (Bundesamt für Statistik 2008). A second reason is related to graduates' im-/mobility. On the one hand, Musselin (2004) showed – concerning academic labour markets – that a number of formal and informal requirements towards candidates, varying according to the national context and scientific disciplines, hinder researchers' mobility on the European academic job market. On the other hand, im-/mobility may also be related to the graduates' preference to "stay at home" (Kiley and Austin 2008). Based on the examination of recruitment processes and related rationales, this chapter argues that the doctoral student bodies' varying degrees of internationality can be explained by one further factor: the *availability of different types of resources for recruitments on the international doctoral students' market*, that is to say financial, organisational, administrative, evaluative and legal resources.

This argument is developed on the basis of empirical data stemming from the eight case studies, developed above. Before developing this main argument, this chapter conducts two additional elements: the first one consists in reminding that the quest of the "best" doctoral students on the *international* market is not necessarily a generally shared recipe.

Based on testimonies stemming from the case studies, two types of arguments favouring recruitments of "local" or national candidates can be identified (X.2.). Those arguments are based on reflections upon research production and the production of highly qualified employees for the national labour market. The second element consists in the identification of differences between Switzerland and Norway in terms of doctoral students' recruitment procedures and in the examination of their impact on the degree of the doctoral student body's internationality (X.3.). After this preliminary discussion, the different types of resources in the recruitment of doctoral students on the international market are developed and exemplified (X.4.) and, finally, examined by the case of natural sciences in Swiss higher education (X.5.). A general conclusion (X.6.) will build the end of this chapter.

X.2. Arguments for "Local" and National Recruitments

Though the idea of looking for – possibly the "best" – doctoral students on the international market is widespread, it does not completely dominate discourses and practices of recruitment. Other arguments related to the provision of highly educated employees for the "own", local or national labour market as well as reflections related to research production which favour the recruitment of "local" or national candidates could also be identified within our case studies.

The first type of argument *related to the labour market* can be situated within the *brain-drain* issue. The following quotation shows that native doctoral students are expected staying within the country after the PhD's end rather than foreign doctoral students:

> [...] we should have a lot of focus on making PhD programmes attractive for Norwegian students as well. Simply because there is this big need for people with PhDs in economics and business in Norway. And we are probably the biggest supplier for PhDs for Norwegian candidates in business in particular. So that's a national responsibility that we have to produce good people with high PhD education in Norway.
>
> (A Norwegian HEI rector)

The next quotation also underlines the national dimension but can be distinguished compared to the previous one to the extent that doctoral education is considered as the first step in a career and that a native doctor moving to another country is not necessarily lost forever. In addition, it puts forward the importance to *promote the own youth*:

> *Thus you said that the point is not only to attract the best doctoral students worldwide, but also to think about the next Swiss academic generation:* [person A] Yes, of course. *What is the background? Is it the thought that if we attract only foreigners, they will go abroad after the doctorate?* [person B] [...] I mean in the sense that we have to better use our potential we have in Switzerland. Otherwise, we have nothing. We have our youth and this potential should be used in a better way. That's my point. Hence, it's rather an economical idea. And afterwards, if the Swiss leave [go abroad], all the better, they can come back, that is not the problem.
>
> (Two administrators of a Swiss HEI)

If the two previous quotations underline the national dimension, but are open towards the type of labour market – in terms of academic or non-academic labour market – the next quotation clearly relates the national dimension to the needs on the local or national *non-academic labour market*. It thereby accentuates an issue the two previous quotations already hinted at and which, since a certain number of years is also increasingly underlined at European political level – for instance in the framework of the "European Research Area" (European Commission 2003) –, namely that doctoral education also may and should open the way towards careers outside of academia:

> To have the best researchers as such is laudable. But the question is what for! Is it to improve the schools' reputation or is it also to provide extremely competent people to our industrialists? I think it is possible to have good doctoral students without this permanent elitist view by which our engineers are not taken care of. [...] Of course, we want to attract the best from outside, but one has to pay attention at having a clear discourse with respect to our industrials. I discussed with enterprises like [X] and others who say that research at [HEI Y] is very good and that they are happy about that, but that they see us first and foremost as providers of very good engineers and very good doctors, let's say in brackets at local level, without having to look after them I don't know where.
>
> (A Professor in materials science and engineering in a Swiss HEI)

With respect to doctoral students' nationality, another type of arguments related to *research production*, appears in our case studies. Those arguments also seem to favour rather local recruitments. A first argument consists in the *familiarity* of a local student with certain research topics:

> The ideal thing would be to [...] bring in the own young academics [meaning students who already participated at certain activities at doctoral level during their undergraduate studies] for the next stipends. Those scholarship holders [...] would already have grown during four, five years within those topics. If I have to recruit somebody from outside, I would partly need one year until they actually become familiar with those topics, with what we are doing in particular here.
>
> (A professor in humanities of a Swiss HEI)

A second argument put forward consists in the match between the doctoral student and the *type of research*, in the case under consideration research which is carried out in collaboration with industry. In the case of Australian higher education, Neumann (2007) observed that especially in natural sciences and engineering, risk minimisation – that is to say a preference for local or at least native English-speaking candidates – is applied in the selection of doctoral students. The following quote indicates similar reflections and confirms what has been underlined by Salminen-Karlsson and Wallgren (2008), that is to say that not each doctoral student can handle collaboration with industry:

> It's the professor, the laboratory that has projects and with the projects he has the money. [...] With respect to know-how, I have very specific needs what concerns doctoral students. We do not always have the right candidates within this pool [where all applying candidates are put into] for those projects. Sometimes we have good candidates, but we cannot take them. And sometimes we have the funding but not the right candidates. So we look for them elsewhere [...]. Perhaps half of our projects are related to industry, this is typical for material sciences. Doctoral students who do their doctorate within industry are between scientific and economic thinking. Thus, they have to integrate both. Not everybody can do that. That is why the selection of doctoral students is important. You need the contact with the doctoral student [meaning candidate], not only by dossier. Because there, soft skills are important.
>
> (Professor in materials science and engineering in a Swiss HEI)

After the exposure of arguments for the recruitment of local or national candidates for doctoral positions, we examine the question whether in the concrete case of Norwegian and Swiss higher education there are fundamental systemic or institutional mechanisms which may promote the recruitment of candidates either on the local/national or the international doctoral students' market.

X.3. Systemic Recruitment Mechanisms and the Degree of Internationality

When comparing legislation and related practices in terms of doctoral students' recruitment of both countries, we notice that generally speaking, Swiss regulations are shaped by Federalism and display some degree of variation, whereas they are more unified in Norway. Furthermore, recruitment procedures[126] are generally more strictly regulated for doctoral students in Norway than in Switzerland.

A first example which illustrates the differences between Switzerland and Norway, concerning the degree of diversity and strictness, consists in the legal requirements and practices related to the *announcement of vacant doctoral positions*. Norwegian university boards may make academic appointments without prior advertisement of the vacancy only for special reasons and in case of unanimity (Ministry of Education and Research 2005). In practice, vacant doctoral positions are generally announced at least in newspapers and on internet. In contrast, the minimal legal requirement for assistant positions of for instance the University of Lausanne consists of announcements by billposting within the concerned Faculties (Conseil d'Etat du canton de Vaud 2007). Thus, depending on the individual professors' will, job vacancies are or aren't known at a more public level than the (public) HEI's building…

A second such difference concerns the *necessity* for applying doctoral candidates *to previously involve a potential future supervisor in the application process*. The "Standard regulations for the degree of Philosophiae Doctor (PhD)" published by the Norwegian Association of

126 When speaking about recruitment procedures for PhD positions in Norway and Switzerland one has to pay attention to the following difference: the admission to doctoral education in Norway is conditioned by the reception of a paid position as PhD student (or of a funding source other than from HEIs that assures personal financial support), whereas this is not necessarily the case in Swiss higher education. Thus, in many cases doctoral candidates can be admitted to Swiss doctoral education without having any funding. However, as all Swiss doctoral students who get any funding from HEIs (mostly as teaching or research assistant) at a given time also have to fulfil admission conditions, the latter can be considered *de facto* also as conditions to recruitments as doctoral students.

Higher Education Institutions (Universitets- og Høgskolerådet - UHR) recommends an application procedure which includes among others a detailed plan for completion of the thesis and a project proposal which both "shall be prepared in collaboration with the principal academic supervisor" (UHR 2004: 2). In other words, this means that applicants are obliged to contact and involve potential supervisor(s) already during their application process. This recommendation is generally adopted in the individual PhD regulations of Norwegian HEIs. Only a small number of PhD regulations of Swiss HEIs require the formulation of a doctoral research project as condition for admission (Baschung 2008). However, even in those cases this requirement does not necessarily concern the phase before the employment as assistant. In practice, the project formulation is often carried out during the initial phase of the assistantship and, thus, cannot be considered as requirement for the recruitment for a doctoral position.

A third important difference between Norway and Switzerland concerns the *selecting authority* for doctoral students: at least from a legal point of view, Norwegian doctoral students are always selected by a committee of several people, whereas, the selection power largely remains up to the individual professor in Switzerland. The Norwegian Act relating to universities and university colleges (2005) declares that appointments to academic (among which doctoral) positions are to be carried out by the university board, a subordinate body or by one or more appointment committees on the basis of expert assessments. In practice, evaluations of candidates are carried out by a committee situated at institute or Faculty level and composed of several professors or one professor and other academic staff. Only few Swiss HEI and disciplinary sub-units of HEIs know such collective forms of candidates' evaluation and selection. And even in the relatively rare cases where candidates are evaluated by a committee of several members, the ultimate decision to recruit a candidate is, in practice, mostly taken by an individual professor. Interestingly, this difference in individual power of professors in the recruitment of doctoral students also persists independently of the financial source of the doctoral position. First, concerning institutionally funded doctoral positions, this can be illustrated for instance by the case of humanities: Swiss professors in this field (like in most other fields) normally have about the same number of institutionally funded "assistant positions". Thus, those positions are to a wide extent earmarked. In the case of humanities at University of Bergen, the number of institutionally funded PhD positions per professor is not automatically given but determined in a competitive manner. Concretely, it depends on the evaluation of the research projects suggested by the applying candidates for doctoral positions (who have to indicate a potential supervisor). Second, even in the case of externally funded PhD positions (e.g. by research funding agencies or industry), Norwegian professors – again in opposite to their Swiss counterparts – cannot choose themselves the candidate but depend on the ranking of applying candidates and final selection made by the respective committees.

Thus, on the basis of those differences concerning three elements – namely the announcement of vacant doctoral positions, the necessity to previously involve a potential future supervisor in the application process, and the selecting authority – one may make the hypothesis that the first and third elements would rather favour patronage and local recruitments in Switzerland, whereas, the second one could prevent international recruitments in Norway. As Bleiklie and Høstaker (2004) point out, it is difficult to document relations of patronage beyond statements of interviews. However, according to the following numbers, one can at least say that the first and third elements do not seem to impede international recruitments in Switzerland: in 2008, 45% of all doctoral students within Swiss HEIs are from abroad, whereas the part of doctorates awarded to foreigners[127] within Norwegian HEIs only attains 25%. However, as figures 7 and 8 show, both countries display a clear tendency towards generally higher foreign representation.[128]

127 Unfortunately, only number of doctors and not of doctoral students were available with regard to internationality.

128 I would like to thank Stefanie Frölicher from the Swiss Federal Statistical Office (BFS) and Terje Bruen Olsen from the Norwegian Institute for Studies in Innovation, Research and Education (NIFU-STEP) for providing and producing data which did not exist as such in a standardised manner.

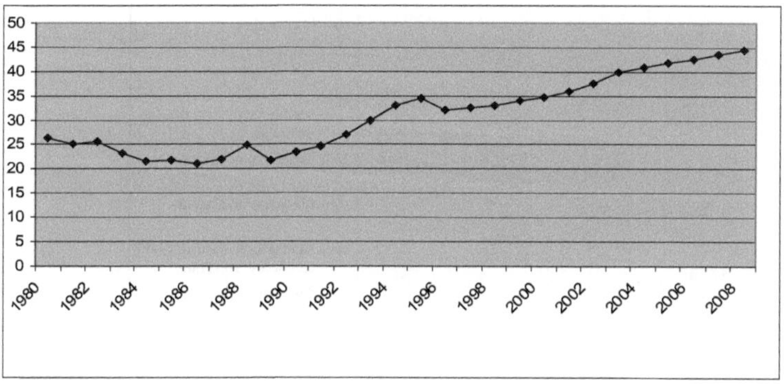

Figure 7: Part of foreign doctoral students in Swiss Higher Education in %
Source: Swiss Federal Statistical Office, 2009; own calculations.

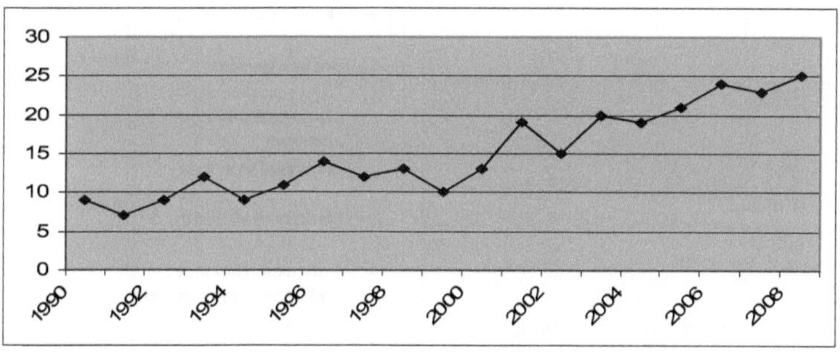

Figure 8: Part of Norwegian doctorates awarded to foreigners in %
Source: NIFU-STEP 2009.

Within the trend of both countries towards higher parts of foreign doctoral students or of doctorates awarded to foreigners, figures 9 and 10 also clearly underline disciplinary differences. The most spectacular growth during the last 10-15 years happened in both countries within mathematics/natural sciences and technical sciences. Especially in Norway and to a lesser extend in Switzerland, this trend is followed by agricultural sciences/veterinary medicine, medicine/health and finally social sciences. Yet, in both countries, the part of foreigners within humanities remains stable.

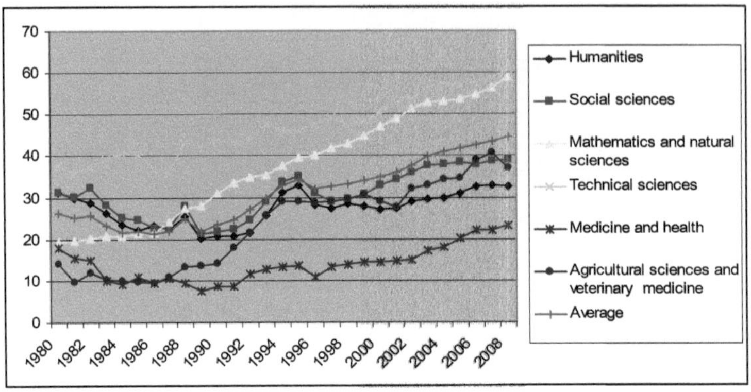

Figure 9: Part of foreign doctoral students in Swiss Higher Education per disciplinary groups in %
Source: Swiss Federal Statistical Office, 2009; own calculations.

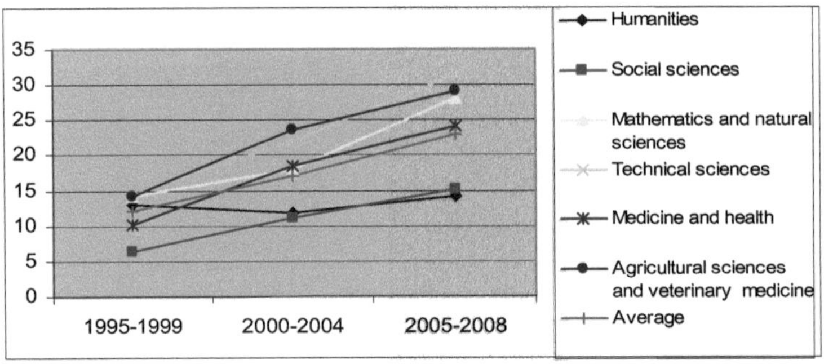

Figure 10: Part of Norwegian doctorates awarded to foreigners in %
Source: NIFU-STEP 2009.

Both countries display a huge increase in the total number of doctoral students/awarded doctorates. In Switzerland, the number of doctoral students almost doubled between 1995 and 2008, from 10,113 to 19,076[129] (out of which 5,707 in mathematics/natural sciences), after a decade of large stability with between 10,000 and 12,000 doctoral

129 It is difficult to say what the exact number of doctoral positions is in Switzerland because they do not exist as such in statistics, but are included under the category "assistants and scientific staff" out of which not all are doctoral students.

students.[130] In Norway, the number of awarded doctorates doubled between 1995 and 2008, from 602 to 1,244 (out of which 284).[131] The number of doctoral students in Norwegian Higher Education in 2008 is 7,776.[132] It is striking that the share of foreign doctoral students/doctors is the highest in the disciplines with the highest total numbers of doctoral students: hence, in both countries, this concerns in particular mathematics and natural sciences. Thus, the growth of foreigners among doctoral students and doctors within mathematics/natural sciences is even more spectacular.

Discipline	**Norway**	**Switzerland**
Humanities	12%	15%
Social sciences (incl. law)	20%	27%
Mathematics and natural sciences	**25%**	**30%**
Technical sciences	17%	12%
Medicine and health	24%	13%
Agricultural science and veterinary medicine	2%	3%

Table 10: Doctoral students of Swiss and Norwegian HEIs per discipline
Sources: Swiss Federal Statistical Office, 2009; Norwegian Social Science Data Service, 2009.

In summary, when comparing doctoral student bodies in Switzerland and Norway, we notice similar developments in terms of overall growth of doctoral students/awarded doctorates and the relative growth of foreigners among them. In addition, in both countries the mathematics/natural sciences and technical sciences display the highest total number of doctoral students/awarded doctorates as well as the highest share of foreigners among them. Nevertheless, two main differences persist between Switzerland and Norway: the absolute number of doctoral students and the relative number of foreign doctoral students are substantially higher in Switzerland than in Norway.

How can one explain differences between countries and disciplines with respect to the doctoral student bodies' degree of internationality? A

130 Source: Federal Office of Statistics. www.bfs.admin.ch, downloaded April 2009.

131 Source: NIFU-STEP. www.nifustep.no, downloaded April 2009.

132 Source: Norwegian Social Science Data Services (NSD). www.nds.uib.no, downloaded April 2009.

number of arguments like varying interest of native graduates, the economic un-/attractiveness of the non-academic job market, graduates' im-/mobility and obstacles related to the national context and scientific disciplines have already been put forward. At least in the Swiss and Norwegian cases, varying legal requirements and practices concerning the announcement of vacant doctoral positions and the selecting authority seem not to have a systematic impact on the degree of internationality. The hypothesis according to which the necessity to previously involve a potential future supervisor in the application process has a negative impact on internationality seems already to be more plausible. However, in any case further explanations are needed in order to explain differences between countries and especially disciplines with respect to the degree of internationality among doctoral students. The next two sections provide such explanations which can be summarised by the availability of different types of resources in the recruitment of international doctoral students.

X.4. Resources for International Recruitments

The study of the eight organised PhD programmes allowed the identification of the following five types of resources which can be considered as (co-)determinative with respect to the quest of doctoral students at international level: financial, organisational, administrative, evaluative and legal resources.

The first type of resource is *financial.* With regard to international recruitments, financial resources play a role regarding at least three issues. The first issue consists in the number of available doctoral positions. In case of small numbers of available positions, professors often renounce to broad advertisement initiatives. A Norwegian professor in molecular biology argued for instance that it would not be worth doing advertisement on a broad international level because he would anyway only have a very limited number of PhD positions at disposal. The case studies showed that the number of available doctoral positions depends on the professors' capacity to generate resources within the own HEI, funding agencies, economy and society. However, according to scientific disciplines' and HEIs those circumstances may vary and thereby influence the number of available doctoral positions. As a second issue, there is no doubt that financial resources also play a role in the concrete ways of advertisement. Announcement in newspapers, journals, internet, etc. have a cost. Therefore, professors sometimes restrict the announcement in media because of financial constraints and thereby, like in the first issue, limit the range of public which can be attained. Finally, even if international students discover the announcement in a way or another, financial resources may still have an impact on the final degree of internationalisation within a HEI. This is due to a certain "risk-minimising logic": before recruiting any doctoral students, professors try to screen candidates as far as possible in order to select the "right" candidates. Among others, this evaluation may consist in interviews with candidates. This activity is perhaps not expensive for local candidates, whereas it generates important costs if it is carried out by flying in candidates from far countries. Our case studies reveal that some recruiters adapt those interview activities to the availability of financial resources what, in case of limited resources, has an impact on the type of invited candidates. For instance, candidates from the same country or Europe are rather invited than those from Asia.

Organisational resources are expressed in the manner announcements and applications for doctoral positions are carried out. We notice forms of announcements and applications which vary between individual and collective organisation. In the individual form of organisation, one position is announced individually and all candidates apply for this only position. Higher organisational resources are expressed by a collective form, where a number of positions within a certain scientific field (but at least officially not coupled to a predefined supervisor) are announced under a common structure bearing a certain label (often without specifying the possibly predefined research subject). In a first step, candidates apply for the structure rather than for one concrete position with one (or several) specific supervisor(s). As a result, there is a pool of candidates for a pool of positions. The underlying idea of the label and the looser definition of positions in terms of research topics consists in getting broader visibility on the international doctoral students' market and thereby more and better candidates.

With the generation of a broader number of applications, another type of resource becomes crucial, namely *administrative resources*. The availability of more or less of such resources determines individual professors' efforts in terms of students' attraction and thereby influences the diffusion of information about open positions at international level. A Swiss professor in materials science indicates for instance:

> I have two to four requests per week from interested people. Thus, if I tell them that they have to apply at our doctoral school, they [doctoral school administration] will break down under the applications. Thus, normally I say that I have nothing, except if I see that somebody is very strong. In this case, I tell them to apply at the doctoral school.
>
> (A Swiss professor in materials science)

Another Swiss professor in finance states:

> I never advertise. I did it a bit in the first year only. Basically, the reason is that if you advertise, you get lots of applications from very marginal students. So it becomes a real job. My friends at London Business School, they get 300-400 applications a year. It becomes a job. Just to sort the applications, if you want to do a good job. I rely more on the word of mouth [...].

Besides administrative resources, *evaluative resources* get an important place in the examination process of applications. Again due to the "risk-minimising logic", a number of selection criteria are used in order to evaluate candidates. Besides basic criteria like a master degree and good grades, additional selection instruments are used in some cases. For instance, letters of recommendation and standardised disciplinary and language tests (e.g. GMAT in finance and TOEFL for English language) sometimes become compulsory parts of the applications. However, recruiters underline that knowledge about the candidates' former HEIs and the authors of the letters of recommendation is necessary in order to properly evaluate the value of those instruments. Some recruiters hint at evaluating applications on the basis of the reputation of applicants' former HEIs and experience with doctoral students coming from the same HEIs as the new applicants. In the case of insufficient knowledge about the candidates' former HEIs, candidates may be eliminated as the following statement of a Swiss professor in finance shows:

> Of course when I get some transcripts from a provincial university in Russia, I don't know what they mean. Also we get them from China and India. The general

> experience for China and India is that we take these students only if they have done a Master in Europe, otherwise it's too risky.
>
> (A Swiss professor in finance)

Finally, according to our interviewees *legal resources* may also turn out to be important in the recruitment of international doctoral students. By the recent introduction of a so called "fast-track", recruiters especially hope to get a better access to the North American doctoral students' market, where students enter the Graduate School (including the Master and doctoral levels) after a four-year Bachelor degree. As good as all PhD regulations of Swiss HEIs already included the possibility to exceptionally accept students with other degrees than a five-year degree (including Bachelor and Master) to certain conditions. The "fast-track" promoters hope to institutionalise this possibility to a broader extent. Some interviewees also emphasise the importance to be flexible in the hiring of doctoral students and not to be legally obliged to respect for instance time-consuming hiring procedures with fixed deadlines.

Those types of resources – especially financial, organisational, administrative and, to a certain extent, also evaluative resources – are to a large extent interdependent. To simplify, collective forms of announcements are often not chosen because there is no minimal number of positions which can be announced at the same moment. As a consequence, positions are announced at a local/national level, with the result that fewer candidates apply, what in turn requires less administrative and evaluative resources. If this relation between the different types of resources is generally confirmed in empirical reality, it does not exclude cases where in spite of rather weakly developed financial resources, the other resources are more strongly available (see the Norwegian finance case study). This may be due, first, to the strong will to recruit doctoral students on the international market and the willingness to make the corresponding efforts or, second, to various perceptions of what a "minimal" number of positions is… However, the availability of those various resources and their interdependence may explain to a certain extent differences between Switzerland and Norway in terms of degree of internationality. Furthermore, it also explains differences of internationality between disciplines. The next section illustrates this argument.

X.5. Recruitment Resource Pools as Promoters of Internationalisation

Since those resources (except the legal one) are quite strongly interdependent, it is not astonishing that they often appear in an accumulated form in practice. We call this accumulated form *"recruitment resource pools"*. Such recruitment resource pools can be found in particular within organisational units called doctoral schools, graduate schools, structured PhD programmes, etc.[133] However, this does of course not mean that each of those organisational units automatically dispose of such a recruitment resource pool. Thus, the term "recruitment resource pool" also provides a possibility to distinguish doctoral schools which are active in the recruitment of doctoral students from those which are not. Since doctoral schools vary for instance in terms of institutional and disciplinary organisation as well as in terms of size, this is also the case for recruitment resource pools. In addition, the degree of availability of each of the different types of resources is, of course, varying according to the recruitment resource pool.

In Switzerland one finds several of those recruitment resource pools. Almost all of them are based in mathematics/natural sciences and technical sciences. They exist for instance in the following organisational units: EPFL Doctoral School, Life Science Zurich Graduate School (LSZGS), the University of Basle's International PhD Program Biozentrum, NCCR Frontiers in Genetics International PhD Program (covering genetics mainly in University of Geneva but also

133 The main criterion to identify those recruitment resource pools consisted in the existence of organisational resources, such as described above. This choice is due to the fact that organisational resources play a particularly crucial role with respect to the number and range of international candidates that can be attained. Its role consists not only in the (theoretical) openness of the doctoral positions with regard to the subject but also in the fact that no preliminary contact between candidates and potential supervisors are necessary. In addition, this choice gets further support from empirical evidence to the extent that identified recruitment resource pools indicate quite high numbers of doctoral students (financial resources) and display the availability of quite highly developed administrative resources, whereas the presence of high numbers of doctoral positions does not necessarily provoke the availability of administrative resources.

other Swiss HEIs). One exception regarding the scientific field is constituted by the Swiss Finance Institute PhD programme. Almost all of those organisational units have been established since the beginning of the 2000s. Thus, they could to a large extent explain the sustained growth of foreigners among doctoral students during the last decade.

From an empirical point of view, we can illustrate the role of recruitment resource pools in particular with regard to financial, organisational and administrative resources. This is done by the following example of natural sciences. And indeed, in 2008, the part of foreign doctoral students within HEIs where recruitment resource pools (RRP) exist is substantially higher than within HEIs without pool structures (see Table 11).

Higher Education Institution	**Total number of doctoral students**	**Percentage of foreign doctoral students**
Federal Institute of Technology Zurich **(with RRP)**	773	**66%**
University of Zurich **(with RRP)**	752	**59%**
Federal Institute of Technology Lausanne **(with RRP)**	123	**67%**
University of Basel **(with RRP)**	601	**61%**
University of Lausanne (without RRP)	453	47%
University of Geneva **(with RRP)**	311	**68%**
University of Bern (without RRP)	254	50%
University of Fribourg (without RRP)	123	50%
University of Neuchâtel (without RRP)	135	49%
Total	3,525	59%

Table 11: Number of PhD students and parts of foreigners in natural sciences per HEI in 2008
Source: Swiss Federal Statistical Office, 2009.

We also notice that those HEIs without RRP are the ones with the lowest number of doctoral students (hence, probably also the lowest number of PhD positions) which confirms the idea of the financial resource as one of the resources supporting internationalisation. Our case studies – covering in particular the RRPs of EPFL, University of Zurich and ETHZ – show that administrative resources are relatively highly developed: administrative staff is employed to handle applications in a first step and to sort them out. This is not necessarily the case in all RRPs. In some cases, this type of administrative work is carried out by scientific staff itself. Efforts for the development of evaluative resources are visible in EPFL and LSZGS. A yearly EPFL report keeps an account among others on the "home universities" of admitted and rejected applicants. Members of the evaluation committee of a PhD programme of LSZGS evaluate candidates not alphabetically but by country. Thus, we make the hypothesis that both measures are ought to further develop evaluative resources. With respect to legal resources, we underline that certain disciplines like finance at University of Zurich recently introduced the possibility of the "fast-track". It is however too early to make an assumption about the effect of this resource.

Finally, with respect to Norwegian Higher Education, almost no recruitment resource pools in a strongly pronounced form have been identified. The PhD programme in Finance at Norwegian School of Economics and Business Administration (NHH) represents an exception. Since a few years, it develops organisational, administrative and evaluative resources in spite of very limited financial resources in terms of doctoral positions. This shows that organisational resources do not exclusively depend on financial resources. Nevertheless, the quasi-absence of highly developed RRPs in Norway may be an indicator for the weak availability of the identified resources and thereby explain, at least to a certain extent, Norway's lower degree of foreigners among doctoral students.

X.6. Summary

The arguments presented in the beginning of this chapter bring not only out that there may be reasons for "local" or "national" recruitments but also that the recruitment of doctoral students on the international student market should not be seen as an objective in itself and that the "best" students do not only exist elsewhere. In other words, the quest of the "best" doctoral students has not necessarily to be limited to the foreign doctoral students market. However, a constantly increasing number of doctoral students of Swiss and Norwegian higher education are recruited abroad. Besides this general trend, the comparison between doctoral student bodies of Norway and Switzerland also confirmed that disparities between countries and disciplines with respect to degree of internationality not only concern the academic labour market as a whole, but also the doctoral student market in particular. The Swiss doctoral student body displays a substantially higher degree of internationality than the Norwegian one whereas mathematics/natural sciences as well as technical sciences stand out against the other disciplines.

Several authors put forward explanations for varying degrees of internationality on the academic labour market: first, competition coming from the non-academic job market (Enders and de Weert 2004) and, second, mobility of doctoral students. Musselin (2004) showed that trans-national mobility among academics is often impeded by formal and informal mechanisms related to the national higher education systems. On the basis of the eight case studies, the present chapter also identified three systemic variables which in the specific case of the Swiss and Norwegian *doctoral* market might have an impact on the degree of internationality of doctoral student bodies: the announcement of vacant doctoral positions, the necessity to previously involve a potential future supervisor in the application process, and the selecting authority. However, crossed with the numbers concerning the share of foreign doctoral students, only the second variable seems to be eligible for providing a more generally valuable explanation of disparities between both countries. Yet, in any case this further variable is not sufficient either to understand disparities between countries and, especially not between disciplines.

Again based on the case studies, this chapter argued that the availability of five different types of resources within HEIs and their disciplines are (co-)decisive concerning the doctoral student bodies' degree of internationality. According to the presence of financial, organisational, administrative, evaluative and legal resources, HEIs and their disciplines are more or less able to attract doctoral students from the international market. The substantially higher availability of those resources – first of all with respect to financial and organisational resources and, to a certain extent, also to administrative and evaluative resources – within Swiss HEIs compared to Norway and within mathematics/natural sciences compared to other scientific disciplines, helps explaining different degrees of internationality between those two countries and disciplines. The example of natural sciences within Swiss HEIs also showed that a particular high development and accumulation of those resources, so called "recruitment resource pools", has a significant effect within one same discipline. Indeed, the doctoral student body within natural sciences of HEIs with recruitment resource pools display a considerably higher degree of internationality than those without or less developed recruitment resource pools. Of course, the availability of such resources is not simply a given thing. At least to a certain extent, those resources can be developed. However, the development of such resources depends among others on the willingness or strategy of national, institutional, disciplinary and individual actors.

XI. Conclusions

During the last two decades, doctoral education in Switzerland and Norway – as in other European and extra-European countries – has undergone profound quantitative and qualitative change. The number of doctoral students doubled in Switzerland and even tripled in Norway. Yet, this quantitative growth could not hide qualitative problems. Different reports have identified issues like completion rates, overall duration and supervision of doctoral students as being problematic. Although the diagnosis varied to a certain extent according to the scientific disciplines and countries, the need for doctoral education's reform has become increasingly evident. Later than in other countries and only gradually, doctoral education's reform has been placed on the national political agendas. This national agenda setting has been accompanied by the elaboration of guidelines and recommendations – aiming at improving doctoral education – at the European level, among others in the framework of the "Bologna reform" and the "Lisbon agenda".

In parallel to doctoral education's agenda setting at European political level, yet, rarely as its consequence, a series of actors outside and especially inside Swiss and Norwegian HEIs have begun to act. Since about a decade, they participated in the creation and running of different kinds of doctoral and research schools. In this context, two basic questions have been dealt with in this study: first, can one observe any changes in the Swiss and Norwegian university governance – or in other words in higher education's polity and politics – on the example of doctoral education's reform, and, if yes, how can those changes be characterised? Second, what does doctoral education's reform in terms of changing practices consists of?

Indeed, concerning doctoral education, a series of dislocations of power could be noticed in Swiss and Norwegian university governance: first, a large number of actors outside HEIs – like national and partly regional governments and bureaucracies, research funding agencies, rectors' conferences and companies – and inside HEIs – like central institutional and Faculty leaders and bureaucracies as well as individual professors and supervisors intervene in varying manners on doctoral education. Thus, decisions about doctoral education are not anymore exclusively taken in the framework of the traditional apprentice-ship model. The second observation consists in the supervisors' loss of power as individuals, but maintenance or even increase of their power as college! Concretely, decisions concerning for instance types and, even to a greater extent, contents of activities of the examined doctoral schools are largely taken by the supervisors' colleges in a collective manner. Thus, this means, in opposite to what has been put forward by Gingras and Gemme (2006), the academic profession's monopole on doctoral education's core is not basically challenged. As a third observation, it can be said that the state, the public research funding agencies and companies did not intervene directly and in an operative manner on doctoral education. Yet, through their manner of intervention, they endow the colleges with considerable power vis-à-vis their rectorates and presidencies. Hence, instead of putting themselves in a strong position, they rebalance the power within HEIs in favour of the colleges of academics! A fourth, important statement must be made concerning the colleges as such. The case studies have shown that the enforced power of the colleges does not correspond to a general comeback to university governance based on "academic self-governance" (Boer et al. 2008). Firstly, because the other actors nevertheless have some power, and, secondly and most importantly, because the composition of the college which holds power may strongly vary. The college may have a "traditional" composition, consisting of all chair-holders of a given discipline within a given HEI. Yet, it may also consist of a part of these chair-holders, of an interdisciplinary or even inter-institutional group of supervisors. Hence, colleges are partly redefined and thereby go beyond existing institutional structures' boundaries. In other words, existing governance structures of HEIs are put into question! This observation made for doctoral education confirms Henkel's (2007) general statement about British HEIs: existing boundaries between HEIs and their environment as well as between scientific disciplines are much less clear-cut than before the 1970s. In this context, Henkel further distinguishes academics who lost their power from academics who increased their power. Thus, the identification of redefined colleges in Swiss and Norwegian doctoral education – containing actors who interact with actors beyond traditional institutional boundaries – seems only to reflect broader observations about dislocation of power in higher education and research. Members of redefined colleges distinguish themselves from other academics who could not or did not want to adapt to this new context. A fifth interesting finding of this analysis consists in the fact that the powerful colleges base part of their power on the use of New Public Management elements like standards and measures of performance and shift to greater competition. This finding objects assumptions existing in scientific literature according to which New Public Management instruments reinforces rectors, presidents or deans at the expense of the academic profession (Schimank 2005). In contrast, empirical findings confirm what has been underlined by Meek (2003), namely that inputs for managerial reforms can also come from the academic profession. A sixth statement concerns the durability of this power dislocation in favour of the colleges. Being largely depending on mostly instable funding of governments, research funding agencies and companies, the colleges' gained power may also be subjected to variation! Thus, the pendulum might move to the HEI governing bodies, once the colleges do not anymore succeed in finding support by these other actors. Last but not least, one must not forget the object of the increased managerial power, namely doctoral students. Whether more or less increased managerial power is exercised through the state, institutional leaders and/or the colleges themselves, final pressure is transmitted on this last actor in the chain!

Besides those seven general findings about dislocation of power in Swiss and Norwegian university governance on the example of doctoral education, another main contribution of this study consists in the findings related to variation in the nature of university governance. If the management of doctoral education is certainly increasingly shaped by elements of the New Public Management narrative, this is by far not the only and neither necessarily always the dominating narrative. The choice of eight case studies according to four variables – namely national political systems, types and size of HEIs as well as scientific disciplines – and the "measurement" of governance through a number of key-elements of three public management narratives allowed to examine patterns of university governance in a more sophisticated way than many studies using a macro approach did. General patterns in terms of relations between combinations of variables and management stories shine out and allow to formulate the following thesis in an ideal-type manner: on the one side, elements of New Public Management have the biggest chance to impose on a broad basis in case of hard and applied sciences situated in small, specialist HEIs within centralised countries. On the other side, it is the Network Governance narrative which is likely to impose in soft pure sciences, situated in larger, generalist HEIs of federal countries. Correspondingly, mixed forms of those two combinations of characteristics lead to situations in between the New Public Management and Network Governance poles. The closer a combination of characteristics is to one of the ideal-type combinations, the closer a case can be situated to one of the two poles.

After this presentation and discussion of governance patterns, attention is turned to changing practices in doctoral education. On the basis of the chosen doctoral and research schools, six types of changes could be identified. They concern doctoral students' recruitment, curricular component, supervision, scientific exchange, follow-up as well as their career. Regarding doctoral students' recruitment, efforts in terms of their attraction and selection could be noticed. Those actions go beyond traditional practices consisting of advertisement within local or national newspapers and direct recruitments of local graduates through individual supervisors. Instead, doctoral positions are advertised on a broad international level in the name of a PhD programme or doctoral school label, applications are evaluated by groups of supervisors and pre-selected applicants are often invited to interviews in situ. New curricular components appear in all case studies, though with huge variations in terms of volume and conditions of evaluation. Thus, in addition to their usual training through research, doctoral students attend courses. Courses can be distinguished between those, which focus on a mono-disciplinary scientific field, those, which concentrate on an interdisciplinary scientific field and those, which can be summarised as transferable skills courses focusing on academic work. Multiple supervision could be identified as third reform element. Instead of being advised by one only supervisor, doctoral students more or less regularly interact with a thesis committee, composed of at least two supervisors from inside and sometimes outside the doctoral students' laboratory or HEI. New practices of interaction focussing on doctoral students' research and training, which go beyond usual exchange between doctoral student and his supervisor(s) or, in the case of laboratory based sciences, the research group, are qualified as forth change in doctoral education. Such practices, which we qualify as “scientific exchange”, include interactions within a group of doctoral students, mostly enlarged by local and external invited scholars and often consist of retreats and conferences specifically organised for doctoral students. A fifth change brought by some doctoral schools consists in regular reporting about doctoral students’ progress in research and training. The underlying idea of this reporting consists of an initial definition of a research and training project, sometimes containing deadlines, and its regular examination. In mostly yearly cadences, doctoral students and/or their supervisor(s) write reports about doctoral students’ progress. Delays have to be justified. In addition, the quality of doctoral students’ supervision may also be a topic dealt with in such reports. Finally, concerning doctoral students’ career, some efforts are visible in terms of doctoral students’ placement after graduation and courses about career planning.

However, not all of those reform elements are implemented in each doctoral or research school. A series of variables can explain differences in their presence. First, the disciplinary variable seems to have a particular impact on recruitment practices, the curricular component’s content, volume and mode of evaluations as well as scientific exchange activities. Even if it was not possible to interrogate underlying disciplinary characteristics in the framework of this study, it seems plausible to explain varying practices – or in-/existing reform elements – regarding those three issues by following the basic argument put forward by Trowler and Becher (2002), that is to say that academic cultures – and related practices – are closely connected to fields of enquiry. Second, the variable “size” certainly has an impact on varying practices – or in-/existing reforms – in terms of recruitment and supervision. For instance, small institutions have difficulties to carry out certain collective recruitment procedures and multiple supervision practices. Third, the institutional variable – in terms of uniform institutional practices – may also have an impact on recruitment of doctoral students. Finally, the national variable, in terms of centralised vs. federal state but also in terms of a favourable non-academic labour market, has an impact on follow-up mechanisms and promotion activities for academic careers. Follow-up mechanisms systematically exist in the centralised Norwegian state, whereas they appear only in some particular cases in federal Switzerland. In addition, the rather favourable non-academic labour market of both countries does not really incite the active creation of new activities for the promotion of graduated doctors' academic careers.

What can be said about the relationship between governance patterns and reform issues and what are the results in terms of changes of doctoral education's overall character? Regarding doctoral education's overall character, four broad tendencies resulting of the observed governance patterns, and therefore varying according to the case study – and probably even more according to unobserved examples of Swiss and Norwegian doctoral education – could be identified. It is argued that tendencies consist of a certain structuring, standardisation and opening of doctoral education, whereas its academic character is maintained. Principally as a consequence of the New Public Management narrative's main elements like explicit standards and measures of performance, a structuring and standardising effect on doctoral education could be noticed. Structuring may take place for instance with respect to schedules of doctoral students' application, training and research production. Standardisation concerns for instance the content and evaluation of the training programme. The Network Governance narrative's emphasis on networks of actors allowed the identification of inter-institutional and/or even interdisciplinary colleges which manage the organisation of common training activities for doctoral students and thereby bring increased opening of doctoral education. The latter may take place regarding doctoral students' choice of training activities, their scientific environment, supervision and career. Finally, as mentioned, central components of doctoral education – like the curricular component and supervision of doctoral students – still are mainly steered by the academic profession. This may be the main reason why existing forms of doctoral education still are strongly dominated by an academic character. No general reform movement towards applied doctoral research has been observed, neither in Switzerland, nor in Norway. In addition, observed changes in doctoral education, particularly in terms of additional training activities, rather seem to focus on the academic character of doctoral education.

Demonstrated changes in terms of management and practices also clearly illustrate the changing role of the doctorate and doctoral students. The doctorate is not anymore considered as an exclusively "private" or personnel matter of doctoral students. According to the actor, doctoral students have been recognised as a central resource for science production, success of particular colleges of academics and HEIs, and even economic competitiveness! This has also an important impact on academic work as a whole. Effects on the work of doctoral students – but also their supervisors – like formalisation, intensification, collectivisation and specialisation can be observed. In addition, professionalisation takes place at the administrative level.

However, it is important to underline that described changes in Swiss and Norwegian doctoral educations' management and practices are not only varying between observed cases but that they do by far not apply to the whole higher education sector of Switzerland and Norway. In other words, there is still much to be done, especially because there is much to win with a "well-tempered reform" of doctoral education. A study carried out by the Swiss Statistical Office (Bundesamt für Statistik 2010) indeed showed that Swiss doctors whose doctoral training went beyond the traditional apprenticeship model, perceive their communication and social competences as being clearly improved. Of course, there is no general identical reform recipe to be applied to all HEIs, scientific disciplines and individual doctoral students. Situations of departure and related needs vary too strongly. However, without pretending that such kinds of reform only have generally positive effects, it is undoubtedly worth for all involved actors to thoroughly reflect about existing management and practices in terms of doctoral students' recruitment, curricular training, supervision, scientific exchange, follow-up and career, and possible improvements. Besides, doctoral students' basic conditions in terms of funding and working load apart the doctoral thesis should not be neglected either because they also partly condition improvements regarding the other mentioned issues. In case of successful improvements, the often opaque number of failed doctoral students could be reduced, the quality of research could be raised and the academic and non-academic labour markets would get better trained doctors!

A second argument for further change in doctoral education is related to the national higher education systems as a whole. We noticed that, besides a very recent Norwegian initiative, alternative doctoral programmes with explicit applied or professional focus do not yet exist, at least not under a specific label. Hence, we argue that from a systemic point of view, the development of an explicit professional doctorate or project based doctorate might be an interesting perspective, in particular for HEIs which, in principle, are (ought to be) more oriented towards applied research, like the Swiss universities of applied sciences and the Norwegian university colleges. Several advantages would be related to the development of such alternative doctoral degrees within those kind of HEIs: first, a larger diversity of doctoral degrees and, hence, of competences in terms of human resources could be developed for the knowledge based economy requiring diversified range of needs; second, doctoral projects of explicitly applied character could generate human resources, explicitly prepared for careers within such HEIs (without being limited to such a kind of career). Thus, instead of recruiting their staff from universities, who often has the ambition of carrying out basic research and who lead those HEIs to an academic drift, more appropriately trained staff could be recruited; third, this could lead to a better balance between different kinds of HEIs and thereby favour differentiation without favouring stratification.

Bibliography

Allen, C.M., Smyth, E.M. and Wahlstrom, M. (2002). "Responding to the Field and to the Academy: Ontario's evolving PhD". *Higher Education Research & Development*, 21(2): 203-214.

Amaral, A., Fulton, O., and Larsen, I.M. (2003). "A Managerial Revolution?". In Amaral, A., Meek, V.L. and Larsen, I.M. (Eds.), *The Higher Education Managerial Revolution?* Dordrecht, Boston, London: Kluwer Academic Publishers, pp.275-294.

Asklin, B. and Stensaker, B. (2002). "Academic Leadership: Prescriptions, Practices and Paradoxes". *Tertiary Education and Management*, 8(2): 113-125.

Auriol, L. (2007). "Labour Market Characteristics and International Mobility of Doctorate Holders: Results for Seven Countries", *OECD Science, Technology and Industry Working Papers*, 2007/2, OECD Publishing. doi:10.1787/310254328811.

Austin, A.E. (2002). "Preparing the Next Generation of Faculty. Graduate School as Socialization to the Academic Career". *The Journal of Higher Education*, 73(1): 94-122.

Bache, I, Flinders, M. (Eds.) (2005). *Multi-level Governance*. New York: Oxford University Press.

Bartelse, J., Beerkens, H.J.J.G. and Maassen, P.A.M. (2000). "Graduate Education in Germany, the Netherlands, Sweden and the United Kingdom". In National Science Foundation, Division of Science Resources Studies (Ed.), *Graduate Education Reform in Europe, Asia, and the Americas and International Mobility of Scientists and Engineers*, Proceedings of an NSF Workshop. Arlington, VA: NSF, pp.101-184.

Baschung, L. (2008). "Inventaires des standards minimaux relatifs au doctorat". Rapport final à l'intention de la Conférence des Recteurs des Universités Suisses, CRUS, OSPS.

Baschung, L. (2010). "Changes in the management of doctoral education. A case study analysis based on three Public Management narratives". *European Journal of Education*, 45(1): 138-152.

Baschung, L., Benninghoff, M., Goastellec, G. and Perellon, J. (2009). "Switzerland: Between Cooperation and Competition". In Paradeise, C., Reale, E., Bleiklie, I. and Ferlie, E. (Eds.), *University Governance. Western European Comparative Perspectives*. Dordrecht: Springer, pp. 153-175.

Becher, T. and Trowler, R. (2001). *Academic Tribes and Territories. Intellectual Inquiry and the Culture of Disciplines*. Second ed. Buckingham: Open University Press.

Bleiklie, I. (1998). "Justifying the Evaluative State: New Public Management ideals in higher education". *European Journal of Education*, 33(3): 299-316.

Bleiklie, I. (2009). "Norway: From Tortoise to Eager Beaver?". In Paradeise, C., Reale, E., Bleiklie, I. and Ferlie, E. (Eds.), *University Governance. Western European Comparative Perspectives*. Dordrecht: Springer, pp.127-152.

Bleiklie, I., and Høstaker, R. (1994). "From Individual Pursuit to Organised Enterprise: Norwegian Higher Education Policy and the Postgraduate Curriculum". *European Journal of Education*, 29(3): 305-22.

Bleiklie, I. and Høstaker, R. (2004). "Modernizing Research Training-Education and Science Policy Between Profession, Discipline and Academic Institution". *Higher Education Policy*, 17: 221-236.

Bleiklie, I., Høstaker, R. and Vabø, A. (2000). "An Academic Profession?". In Bleiklie, I., Høstaker, R. and Vabø, A. (Eds.), *Policy and Practice in Higher Education. Reforming Norwegian Universities*. London and Philadelphia: Jessica Kingsley Publisher, pp. 221-60.

Borrell-Damian, L. (2009). "Collaborative Doctoral Education. University-Industry Partnerships for enhancing Knowledge Exchange". EUA Publications.

Boud, D. and Tennant, M. (2006). "Putting doctoral education to work: challenges to academic practice". *Higher Education Research & Development*, 25(3): 293-306.

Braun, D. (1999). "Changing Governance Models in Higher Education: The Case of the New Managerialism". *Swiss Political Science Review*, 5(3): 1-24.

Braun, D. and Merrien, F.X. (1999). *Towards a new model of governance for universities?* London and Philadelphia: Jessica Kingsley.

Braun, D. and Benninghoff, M. (2003). "Policy learning in Swiss research policy - the case of the National Centres of Competence in Research". *Research Policy*, 32(10): 1849-1863.

Broch, I. and Hyllseth, B. (2004). "Doctoral Studies and Qualifications in Europe and the United States: Status and Prospects. Norway". In Lincoln, D. (Ed.), *Studies on Higher Education*. Bucharest: UNESCO-CEPES, pp. 99-118.

Bühlmann, F. (2005). "'Organisatorische Widerspenstigkeiten': New Public Management im Alltag einer kantonalen Verwaltung der Schweiz". *Swiss Journal of Sociology*, 31 (1): 31-53.

Bundesamt für Statistik (2006). "Das Schweizer Hochschulsystem im internationalen Kontext. Ein Ländervergleich anhand statistischer Daten", Neuchâtel.

Bundesamt für Statistik (2008). "Hochschulabsolventen und Hochschulabsolventinnen auf dem Arbeitsmarkt. Erste Ergebnisse der Längsschnittbefragung 2007", Neuchâtel.

Bundesamt für Statistik (2010). "Die Ausbildung und die berufliche Situation von Promovierten. Ergebnisse aus dem Schweizerischen Hochschulinformationssystem und der Hochschulabsolvent/ innenbefragung 2007". Neuchâtel.

Bundesministerium für Bildung und Forschung (2008). "Bundesbericht zur Förderung des wissenschaftlichen Nachwuchs". Berlin.

Campbell, S.P., Fuller, A.K. and Patrick, D.A.G. (2005). "Looking beyond research in doctoral education". *Front Ecol Environ*, 3(3): 153-160.

Christensen, T. and Lægreid, P. (2007). "Introduction – Theoretical Approach and Research Questions". In Christensen, T., Lægreid, P. (Eds.), *Transcending New Public Management. The Transformation of Public Sector Reforms*. Aldershot: Ashgate Publising, pp. 1-15.

Christensen, T. and Lægreid, P. (2001). "New Public Management: The effects of contractualism and devolution of political control". *Public Management Review*, 3(1): 73-94.

Clark, B.R. (1983). *The Higher Education System. Academic Organizations in Cross-National Perspective.* Berkeley, CA: University of California Press.

Clark, B.R. (1993). "Introduction". In Clark, B.R. (Ed), *The Research Foundations of Graduate Education. Germany, Britain, France, United States, Japan.* Berkeley, Los Angeles, Oxford: University of California Press, pp. XV-XXI.

Clark, B.R. (1995). "The United States. Competitive Graduate Schools". In Clark, B.R. (Ed.), *Places of Inquiry. Research and Advanced Education in Modern Universities.* Berkeley, Los Angeles, London: University of California Press. Berkeley, Los Angeles, London: University of California Press, pp. 116-158.

Clark, T., Sweet, R., Gruber, K.H., Lourtie, P., Santiago, P. and Sohlman, A. (2006). "Thematic Review of Tertiary Education. Norway". In OECD (Ed.), *Thematic Review of Tertiary Education.* Paris: Organisation for Economic Cooperation and Development.

Damrosch, D. (2006). "Vectors of Change". In Golde, M. and Walker, G. (Eds.), *Envisioning the Future of Doctoral Education. Preparing Stewards of the Discipline.* San Francisco: Jossey-Bass, pp. 34-45.

De Boer, H. (2003). "Who's Afraid of Red, Yellow and Blue? The Colourful World of Management Reforms". In Amaral, A., Meek, V.L. and Larsen, I.M. (Eds.), *The Higher Education Managerial Revolution?* Dordrecht, Boston, London: Kluwer Academic Publishers, pp. 89-108.

De Boer, H., Enders, J. and Schimank, U. (2008). "Chapter 3. Comparing Higher Education Governance Systems in Four European Countries". In Soguel, N. and Jaccard, P. (Eds.), *Governance and Performance of Education Systems.* Doordrecht: Springer, pp. 35-54.

Deem, R., Hillyard, S. and Reed, M. (2007). *Knowledge, Higher Education, and the New Managerialism. The Changing Management of UK Universities.* Oxford: University Press.

Delamont, S., Atkinson, P., Parry, O. (1997). "Critical Mass and Doctoral Research: reflections on the Harris Report". *Studies in Higher Education*, 22(3): 319-331.

Dimmen, A. and Kyvik, S. (1998). "Recent changes in the governance of higher education institutions in Norway". *Higher Education Policy*, 11: 217-228.

Dunn, W.N and Miller, D.Y. (2007). "A Critique of the New Public Management and the Neo-Weberian State: Advancing a Critical Theory of Administrative Reform". *Public Organization Review*, 7: 345-358.

Elgar, F.J. and Klein, R.M. (2004). "What You Don't Know: Graduate Deans' Knowledge of Doctoral Completion Rates". *Higher Education Policy*, 17: 325-336.

Enders, J. (2002). "Serving many masters: The PhD on the labour market, the everlasting need of inequality, and the premature dead of humboldt". *Higher Education*, 44: 493-517.

Enders, J. (2004). "Higher Education, Internationalisation, and the Nation-State: Recent Developments and Challenges to Governance Theory". *Higher Education*, 47: 361-82.

Enders, J. (2004a). „Research training and careers in transition: a European perspective on the many faces of the Ph.D". *Studies in Continuing Education*, 26(3): 419-429.

Enders, J. (2005). "Border crossings: Research training, knowledge dissemination and the transformation of academic work". *Higher Education*, 49: 119-133.

Enders, J. (2005a). "Brauchen die Universitäten in Deutschland ein neues Paradigma der Nachwuchsausbildung?". *Beiträge zur Hochschulforschung*, Heft 1.

Enders, J. and de Weert, E. (2004). "Science, Training and Career: Changing Modes of Knowledge Production and Labour Markets". *Higher Education Policy*, 17: 135-152.

Engelage, S., Hadjar, A. (2008). "Promotion und Karriere: Lohnt es sich zu promovieren? Eine Analyse der Schweizerischen Absolventen-studie". *Schweizerische Zeitschrift für Soziologie*, 34(1): 71-93.

Engelage, S., Schubert, F. (2009). "Promotion und Karriere – Wie adäquat sind promovierte Akademikerinnen und Akademiker in der Schweiz beschäftigt?". *Journal for Labour Market Research*, 43(3): 213-233.

EUA (European University Association) (2005). "Doctoral Programmes for the European Knowledge Society. Final Report".

EUA (European University Association) (2007). "Doctoral Programmes in Europe's Universities: Achievements and Challenges. Report prepared for European Universities and Ministers of Higher Education". EUA Publications 2007.

EUA (European University Association), Bundesministerium für Bildung und Forschung, Bundesministerium für Bildung, Wissenschaft und Kultur (2005). "Bologna Seminar on „Doctoral Programmes for the European Knowledge Society". Conclusions and Recommendations". Salzburg, 3-5 February.

Evans, T. (2002). "Part-time Research Students: are they producing knowledge where it counts?". *Higher Education Research & Development*, 21(2): 155- 165.

Schweizer Bundesrat (2007). "Botschaft über die Förderung von Bildung, Forschung und Innovation in den Jahren 2008-2011". Bern.

Felli, R., Goastellec, G., Baschung, L., and Leresche, J.-P. (2006). "Politique fédérale d'encouragement de la relève académique et stratégies institutionnelles des universités". *Les Cahiers de l'Observatoire*. Lausanne: Observatoire Science, Politique et Société, Université de Lausanne.

Ferlie, E., Musselin, C., and Andresani, G.-L. (2009). "The Steering of Higher Education Systems. A Public Management Perspective". In Paradeise, C., Reale, E., Bleiklie, I. and Ferlie, E. (Eds.), *University Governance. Western European Comparative Perspectives*. Dordrecht: Springer, 1-19.

Ferlie, E. (1996). "The creation and evolution of quasi-markets". In Ferlie, E., Ashburner, L., Fitzgerald, L., Pettigrew, A. (Eds.), *The New Public Management in Action*. Oxford University Press, pp. 56-87.

Fluder, R., Hildbrand, T. (1997). "Funktionswandel des Mittelbaus am Beispiel der Universität Zürich". *FS-DT*, Bern: Schweizerischer Wissenschaftsrat.

Gerring, J. (2004). "What Is a Case Study and What Is It Good For?". *American Political Science Review*, 98(2): 341-54.

Giauque, D. (2006). "La nouvelle gestion publique en action: vers une bureaucratie libérale". In Perrot, M.-D., DuPasquier, J.-N., Joye, D., Leresche, J.-P. and Rist, G. (Eds.), *Ordres et désordres de l'esprit gestionnaire. Où vont les métiers de la recherche, du social et de la santé ?* Lausanne: Editions Réalités Sociales, pp. 41-53.

Giauque, D. and Emery, Y. (2008). *Repenser la gestion publique: bilan et perspectives.* Lausanne : Presses Polytechniques et Universitaires romandes.

Gibbons, M., Limoges, C., Nowotny, H., Schwartzman, S., Scott, P. and Trow, M. (1994). *The new production of knowledge.* London, Thousand Oaks and New Delhi: Sage Publications.

Gingras, Y. and Gemme, B. (2006). "L'emprise du champ scientifique sur le champ universitaire et ses effets". *Actes de la recherche en sciences sociales,* 164 : 51-60.

Goedegebuure, L., et al. (1994). "International Perspectives on Trends and Issues in Higher Education Policy". In Goedegebuure L., Kaiser, F., Maassen, P., Meek, L.V., Van Vught, F. and de Weert, E. (Eds.), *Higher Education Policy: An International Comparative Perspective*. Oxford: Pergamon Press, pp. 315-348.

Golde, C.M. (2006). "Preparing Stewards of the Discipline". In Golde, C.M., Walker, G.E. (Eds.), *Envisioning the Future of Doctoral Education. Preparing Stewards of the Discipline.* San Francisco: Jossey-Bass, pp. 3-20.

Gornitzka, Å., and Larsen, I.M. (2004). "Towards professionalisation? Restructuring of administrative work force in universities". *Higher Education*, 47: 455-471.

Gumport, P.J. (1993). "Graduate Education and Research Imperatives. Views form American Campuses". In Clark, B.R. (Ed), *The Research Foundations of Graduate Education. Germany, Britain,*

France, United States, Japan. Berkeley, Los Angeles, Oxford: University of California Press, pp. 261-293.

Gumport, P.J. (1993a). "Graduate Education and Organized Research in the Unites States". In Clark, B.R. (Ed), *The Research Foundations of Graduate Education. Germany, Britain, France, United States, Japan.* Berkeley, Los Angeles, Oxford: University of California Press.

Gumport, P.J. (2005). "Graduate education and research: Interdependence and strain". In Altbach, P.G., Berdahl, R.O., Gumport P.J. (Eds.), *American higher education in the twenty-first century: Social, political and economic challenges*, 2nd Edition, Baltimore: The Johns Hopkins University Press, pp. 425-461.

Gregory, R. (2007). "New Public Management and the Ghost of Max Weber: Exorcized or Still Haunting?". In Christensen, T., Lægreid, P. (Eds.), *Transcending New Public Management. The Transformation of Public Sector Reforms*. Ashgate Publising.

Groneberg, M. (2008). "Doktorierende in der Schweiz. Portrait 2006". Center for Science and Technology Sudies. CEST 2007/8.

Hablützel, P., Haldemann, T., Schedler, K. and Schwaar, K. (1995). *Umbruch in Politik und Verwaltung*. Bern, Stuttgart and Wien: Haupt Verlag.

Harman, G. (2002). "Producing PhD Graduates in Australia for the Knowledge Economy". *Higher Education Research & Development*, 21(2): 179-190.

Harman, K. (2002a). "The research training experiences of doctoral students linked to Australian Cooperative Research Centres". *Higher Education*, 44: 469-492.

Heen, E.F. (2002). "Research priorities and disciplinary cultures: friends or foes? A cross-national study on doctoral research training in economics in France and Norway". *Higher Education Policy*, 15: 77-95.

Hellström, T. (2004). "Between a rock and a hard place: Academic institutional change and the problem of collective action". *Higher Education*, 48: 511-528.

Henkel, M. (2007). "Shifting Boundaries and the Academic Profession". In Kogan, M. and Teichler, U. (Eds.), *Key Challenges to the Academic Profession* (Vol. 65). Paris and Kassel: UNESCO/ INCHER-Kassel.

Herman, C. (2009). "Political transformation and research methodology in doctoral education". *Higher Education*, DOI 10.1007/s10734-009-9261-6.

Hood, C. (1991). "A Public Management for All Seasons?". *Public Administration*, 69: 3-19.

Hood, C. (1995). "The 'new public management' in the 1980s: Variations on a theme. *Accounting, Organisations and Society*, 20(2-3): 93-109.

Hooghe, L., Marks, G. (2003). "Unraveling the Central State, but How? Types of Multi-level Governance". *American Political Science Review*, 97(2): 233-243.

Holley, K. (2009). "The challenge of an interdisciplinary curriculum: a cultural analysis of a doctoral-degree program in neuroscience". *Higher Education*, 58: 241-255.

Huisman, J., de Weert, Egbert and Bartelse, J. (2002). "Academic Careers from a European Perspective. The Declining Desirability of the Faculty Position". *Journal of Higher Education*, 73(1): 141-160.

Jones, L.R., Schedler, K. and Wade, S.W. (1997). *International perspectives on the new public management*. Greenwhich and London: JAI Press.

Jongbloed, B. (2003). "Marketisation in Higher Education, Clark's Triangle and the Essential Ingredients of Markets". *Higher Education Quarterly*, 57(2): 110-135.

Joye-Cagnard, F. (2007). *La construction de la politique de la science en Suisse. Enjeux scientifiques, stratégiques et politiques. 1944-1974.* Thèse de doctorat en histoire contemporaine (dir.: Prof.Dr.Antoine Fleury), Département d'Histoire générale, Université de Genève.

Kehm, B.M. (2004). "Developing Doctoral Degrees and Qualifications in Europe: Good Practice and Issues of Concern - a Comparative Analysis". In Sadlak, J. (Ed.), *Studies on Higher Education.* Bucharest: UNESCO, pp. 279-98.

Kehm, B. (2006). "Doctoral Education in Europe and North America: A comparative Analysis". In Teichler U. (Ed.), *The Formative Years of Scholars*. Wenner-Gren International Series, pp. 67-78.

Kehm, B. M. (2006a). "Doctoral Education in Europe: New Structures and Models". In Krücken, G., Kozmutzky, A. and Torka, M. (Eds.), *Towards a Multiversity? Universities between Global Trends and National Traditions*, Bielefeld: transcript Verlag, pp. 132-53.

Kehm, B.M. (2007). "Quo Vadis Doctoral Education? New European Approaches in the Context of Global Changes". *European Journal of Education*, 42(3): 317-319.

Kickert, W. (1997). *Public Management and Administrative Reform in Western Europe*. Edward Elgar Publications.

Kiley, M. and Austin, A. (2008). "Australian postgraduate research students still prefer to 'stay at home': reasons and implications". *Journal of Higher Education Policy and Management*, 30(4): 351-362.

Knoepfel, P. (1995). "Le NPM: est-ce la panacée?". *Swiss Political Science Review*, 1(4): 130-138.

Knoepfel, P. (1996). "Plädoyer für ein tatsächlich wirkungsorientiertes Public Management". *Swiss Political Science Review*, 2 (1): 151-164.

Kogan, M. (1996). "Comparing Higher Education Systems". *Higher Education*, 32: 395-402.

Kwiram, A.L. (2006). "Time for Reform?". In Golde, M., Walker, G. (Eds.), *Envisioning the Future of Doctoral Education. Preparing Stewards of the Discipline*. San Francisco: Jossey-Bass, pp. 141-166.

Kyvik, S. (2002). "Evaluering av norsk forskerutdanning". Oslo: NIFU.

Kyvik, S., Tvede, O. (1998). "The Doctorate in the Nordic Countries". *Comparative Education*, 34 (1): 9-25.

Kyvik, S., Olsen, T.B. (2007). "Doktorgradsutdanning og karrieremuligheter. En underssøkelse blant to årskull doktorgradskandidater". NIFU-STEP: rapport 35/2007.

Lane, J.-E. (2000). *New Public Management*. London: Routledge.

Lauglo, J., Olsen, T., Aasen, P. Stensaker, B. and Hetland, P. (2004). "På vei mot Innlandsuniversitetet - en vurdering av mulige PhD-program". NIFU-STEP. Arbeitsnotat 15/2004.

Lepori, B., Baschung, L. and Probst, C. (2010). "Patterns of Subject Mix in Higher Education Institutions: A First Empirical Analysis Using the AQUAMETH Database". *Minerva*, 48: 73-99.

Leresche, J.-P. and Benninghoff, M. (2006). "La nouvelle gestion publique et les métiers de la recherche". In Perrot, M.-D., DuPasquier, J.-N., Joye, D., Leresche, J.-P. and Rist, G. (Eds.), *Ordres et désordres de l'esprit gestionnaire. Où vont les métiers de la recherche, du social et de la santé ?* Lausanne: Editions Réalités Sociales, pp. 74-79.

LERU (League of European Research Universities) (2007). "Doctoral studies in Europe: excellence in researcher training".

Lévy, R., Roux, P. and Gobet, P. (1997). "La situation du corps intermédiaire dans les hautes écoles suisses". Berne: Conseil suisse de la science.

Lienhard, A., Ritz, A., Steiner, R. and Ladner, A. (2005). *10 Jahre New Public Management in der Schweiz. Bilanz, Irrtümer und Erfolgsfaktoren*. Bern, Stuttgart and Wien: Haupt Verlag.

Lijphart, A. (1975). "The Comparable-Cases Strategy in Comparative Research". *Comparative Political Studies*, 8(2): 158-77.

Lockhart, J.C. and Stablein, R.E. (2002). "Spanning the Academy-Practice Divide with Doctoral Education in Business". *Higher Education Research & Development*, 21(2): 191-202.

Mainhard, T., van der Rijst, R., van Tartwijk, J. and Wubbels, T. (2009). "A model for the supervisor-doctoral student relationship". *Higher Education*, 58: 359-373.

Mangematin, V. (2000). "PhD job market: professional trajectories and incentives during the PhD". *Research Policy*, 29: 741-756.

Mangematin, V., Mandran, N. and Crozet, A. (2000). "The Careers of Social Science Doctoral Graduates in France: the influence of how the research was carried out". *European Journal of Education*, 35(1): 111-124.

Maurer, E. and Zeltner, E. (1997). "Einführung von Graduiertenkollegs in der Schweiz". Bern: Schweizerischer Wissenschaftsrat.

McLaughlin, K., Osborne, S.P. and Ferlie, E. (2002). *New Public Management. Current trends and future prospects*. London and New York: Routledge.

Meek, V.L. (2003). "Introduction". In Amaral, A., Meek, V.L. and Larsen, I.M. (Eds.), *The Higher Education Managerial Revolution?* Dordrecht, Boston, London: Kluwer Academic Publishers, pp. 1-29.

Mendoza, P. (2007). "Academic Capitalism and Doctoral Student Socialization: A Case Study". *The Journal of Higher Education*, 78(1): 71-96.

Minogue, M., Polidano, C. and Hulme D. (1998). *Beyond the New Public Management. Changing Ideas and Practices in Governance*. Cheltenham and Northampton: Edward Elgar.

Moguérou, P. (2005). "Doctoral and Postdoctoral Education in Science and Engineering: Europe in the international competition". *European Journal of Education*, 40(4): 367-392.

Mora, J.G. (2001). "Governance and Management in the New University". *Tertiary Education and Management*, 7(2): 95-110.

Musselin, C. (2001). *La longue marche des universités françaises*. Paris: Presses Universitaires de France.

Musselin, C. (2004). "Towards a European academic labour market? Some lessons drawn from empirical studies on academic mobility". *Higher Education*, 48: 55-78.

Neave, G., van Vught, F. (1991). *Prometheus bound: The changing relationship between government and higher education in Western Europe*. Oxford: Pergamon Press.

Neumann, R. (2002). "Diversity, Doctoral Education and Policy". *Higher Education Research & Development*, 21(2): 167-178.

Neumann, R. (2007). "Policy and practice in doctoral education". *Studies in Higher Education*, 32(4): 459-473.

OECD (2003). *Tertiary Education in Switzerland*. Reviews of National Policies for Education.

Olsen, T. (2004). *Forskningspolitikk*. NIFU-STEP. Nr.2.

Olsen, T. (2007). "Doktorgrad - og hva så? Om doktorenes yrkeskarriere". NIFU-STEP. Rapport 20/2007.

Paradeise, C., Reale, E., Goastellec, G., and Bleiklie, I. (2009). "Universities Steering between Stories and History". In Paradeise, C., Reale, E., Bleiklie, I. and Ferlie, E. (Eds.), *University Governance. Western European Comparative Perspectives*. Dordrecht: Springer, pp. 227-246.

Paradeise, C., Bleiklie, I., Enders, J., Goastellec, G., Michelsen, S., Reale, E., and Westerheijden, D. (2009a). "Reform policies and change processes in Europe". In Huisman, J. (Ed.), *International Perspectives on the Governance of Higher Education,* London: Routledge.

Pearson, M. (1996). "Professionalising Ph.D. education to enhance the quality of the student experience". *Higher Education*, 32: 303-320.

Perellon, J.-F. (2001). "The Governance of Higher Education in a Federal System: The Case of Switzerland". *Tertiary Education and Management*, 7(2): 211-24.

Perellon, J.-F. (2003). "The Creation of a Vocational Sector in Swiss Higher Education: balancing trends of system differentiation and integration". *European Journal of Education*, 38(4): 357-370.

Perellon, J.-F. (2006). "Higher Education in Switzerland. Update and reflections on current trends and likely futures". *Les Cahiers de l'Observatoire*, No. 14.

Pollitt, C. (2007). "Convergence or divergence: what has been happening in Europe?". In Pollitt, C., Van Thiel, S. and Homburg, V. (Eds.), *New Public Management in Europe: adaptation and alternatives.* Palgrave Macmillan, pp. 10-25.

Pollitt, C., Bouckaert, G. (2004). *Public Management Reform. A Comparative Analysis, 2nd Edition,* Oxford: Oxford University Press.

Prewitt, K. (2006). "*Who* Should Do *What*: Implications for Institutional and National Leaders". In Golde, C.M. and Walker, G.E. (Eds.), *Envisioning the Future of Doctoral Education. Preparing Stewards of the Discipline.* San Francisco: Jossey-Bass, pp. 23-33.

Probst Schilter, C. (2009). *Serving Different Masters – The Communication Doctorate in the Knowledge Society*. PhD dissertation presented at the Faculty of Communication Sciences, Università della Svizzera italiana, Lugano.

Rekilä, E., Larimo, J. and Tauriainen, K. (1999). "Do changing state steering mechanisms have an impact on academic leadership at universities". *Tertiary Education and Management*, 5: 261-277.

Rhodes, R.A.W (1997). *Understanding Governance*, Buckingham, Oxford University Press.

Schimank, U. (2005). "'New Public Management' and the Academic Profession: Reflections on the German Situation". *Minerva*, 43(4): 361-376.

Schreitener, U. (2002). "Schweizerisches Graduiertenkolleg der Sozialwissenschaften im SPP 'Zukunft Schweiz'. Evaluationsbericht zu Händen der Programmkoordination und des Schweizerischen Nationalfonds (SNF)". CHE. Centrum für Hochschulentwicklung.

Sadowski, D., Schneider, P., and Thaller, N. (2008). "Do We Need Incentives for PhD Supervisors?". *European Journal of Education*, 43(3): 315-329.

Salminen-Karlsson, M. and Wallgren, L. (2008). "The interaction of academic and industrial supervisors in graduate education". *Higher Education*, 56(1): 77-93.

Shambaugh, R. N. (2000). "Reframing Doctoral Programs: A Program of Human Inquiry for Doctoral Students and Faculty Advisors". *Innovative Higher Education*, 24(4): 295-308.

Smeby, J.-C. (2000). "Same-gender relationship in graduate education". *Higher Education*, 40: 53-67.

Stark, J., Lowther, M., Sharp, S. and Arnold, G. (1997). "Program-level curriculum planning: An exploration of faculty perspectives on two campuses. *Research in Higher Education*, 38(1): 99-130.

Teichler, U. (1996). "Comparative Higher Education: Potentials and Limits". *Higher Education*, 32: 431-65.

Teichler, U. (2006). "Future Challenges for Doctoral Studies in Germany". In Gorzka, G. and Lanzendorf, U. (Eds.), *Europeanising*

Doctoral Studies. The Russian Federation and Germany on the Way to Bologna. Kassel: Kassel University Press, pp. 25-37.

Tennant, M. (2004). "Doctoring the knowledge worker". *Studies in Continuing Education*, 26(3): 431-441.

Tight, M. (2004). "Research into Higher Education: An a-Theoretical Community of Practice?". *Higher Education Research & Development*, 23(4), 395-411.

Thune, T. (2009). "Doctoral students on the university-industry interface: a review of the literature". *Higher Education*, 58: 637-651.

Trow, M. (1973). *Problems in the transition from elite to mass higher education*. Carnegie, Comission Higher Education, Berkeley, CA.

Usher, R. (2002). "A Diversity Of Doctorates: fitness for the knowledge economy?". *Higher Education Research & Development*, 21(2): 143-153.

Weber, K. (1999). "Switzerland. Discussion of University Reform and its Implementation". In Braun, D. and Merrien, F.X (Eds.), *Towards a New Model of Governance for Universities? A Comparative View*. London and Philadelphia: Jessica Kingsley Publishers, pp. 141-162.

Weidman, J.C. and Stein, E.L. (2003). "Socialization of doctoral students to academic norms". *Research in Higher Education*, 44(6): 641-656.

Welch, A.R. (1997). "The peripatetic professor: the internationalisation of the academic profession". *Higher Education*, 34: 323-345.

Young, C., Curty, P., Hirt, M., and Wirth Bürgel, K. (2009). "Zur Lage des akademischen Mittelbaus. Befragungsstudie and den kantonalen Universitäten und ETH". Schlussbericht zuhanden des Staatssekretariats für Bildung und Forschung. Bern: Staatssekretariat für Bildung und Forschung.

Zinman, J. M. (1994). "Prometheus bound: science in a dynamic steady state". Cambridge: Cambridge University Press.

Governmental and Institutional Sources

Conseil d'Etat du canton de Vaud (2007). *Règlement du 13 juin 2007 sur les assistants à l'Université de Lausanne.*

CRUS (2006). "Planification stratégique 2008-2011 des hautes écoles universitaires suisses". 18. Bern: Conférence universitaire suisse.

CRUS (2006a). "Zwischenbericht 2005/2006 der CRUS zum Stand der Erneuerung der Lehre an den Universitären Hochschulen der Schweiz im Rahmen des Bologna-Prozesses einschliesslich des Reporting 2005 zum Kooperationsprojekt "Bologna-Initialkosten". *Arbeitsberichte zur Umsetzung der Bologna-Deklaration in der Schweiz*, 154. Bern: Rektorenkonferenz der Schweizer Universitäten.

CRUS, ÖRK and HRK (2004). "Zur Zukunft der Promotion in Europa". Gemeinsame Erklärung der Rektorenkonferenz der Schweizer Universitäten (CRUS), der österreichischen Rekorenkonferenz (öRK) und der Hochschulkonferenz (HRK). Bonn, 27.März 2004.

EPFL (2007). "Répartition budgétaire entre les institutions du CEPF". Lausanne.

EPFL (2008). *Ordonnance sur le doctorat délivré par l'Ecole polytechnique fédérale de Lausanne du 26 janvier 1998* (Etat le 1er septembre 2008). 414.133.2.

EPFL (2008a). *Directives sur la formation doctorale à l'Ecole polytechnique fédérale de Lausanne du 21 novembre 2005*, (révisées le 1er septembre 2008).

EPFL (2008b). *Doctoral Program in Materials Sciences and Engineering. Program Regulations for the Candidacy Examination.* Entry into force 1st September 2008.

ETH-Rat (1997). „ETH-Bereich. Strategische Planung 2000-2003". 24.September 1997.

ETH-Rat (2003). "Strategische Planung 2004-2007. Lehre und Forschung im ETH-Bereich". 25.Februar 2003.

ETH Zürich (2000). *Verordnung über das Doktorat an der Eidgenössischen Technischen Hochschule Zürich.* Vom 16.Dezember 2000 (Stand am 1.März 2005). 414.133.1.

ETH Zürich (2008). *Verordnung über das Doktorat an der Eidgenössischen Technischen Hochschule Zürich.* 1.Juli 2008 (Stand am 1.September 2008). 414.133.1.

European Commission (2003). "The Role of Universities in the Europe of Knowledge". Brussels, 5.2.2003. COM(2003) 58 final.

European Commission (2003a). "Research in the European Research Area: One Profession, Multiple Careers". Brussels, 18.7.03. COM(2003) 436 final.

European Council (2000). "Presidency Conclusions". Lisbon European Council, 23 and 24 March 2000.

Faculty of Mathematics and Natural Sciences of University of Oslo (2008). *Supplementary Regulations to the Regulations pertaining to PhD studies at the Faculty of Mathematics and Natural Sciences and the University of Oslo.* Resolved at the Management of the Faculty meeting, 12.February 2008 pursuant to the Regulations pertaining to philosophiae doctor (PhD) at the University of Olso, approved by the Board of the University of Oslo, 21 June 2007.

Humanistisk fakultet Universitet i Bergen (2002). "Handlingsplan for forskarutdanninga ved HF". Revidert 14.3.2006.

Kunnskapsdepartementet (2008). "Statusrapport for Kvalitetsreformen i høgre utdanning". St.meld. nr.7 (2007-2008).

LAU (1999). *Loi fédérale du 8 octobre 1999 sur l'aide aux universités et la coopération dans le domaine des hautes écoles.* 414.20.

LEPF (1991). *Loi fédérale du 4 octobre 1991 sur les écoles polytechniques fédérales.* 414.110.

LSZGS (2009). "Annual Report 2008". Zürich.

Mathematisch-naturwissenschaftliche Fakultät der Universität Zürich (2002). *Promotionsordnung der Mathematisch-naturwissenschaftlichen Fakultät der Universität Zürich.* 415.463.

Mathematisch-naturwissenschaftliche Fakultät der Universität Zürich (2002a). *Studienordnung zur Promotion an der Mathematisch-naturwissenschaftlichen Fakultät.* Revidierte Fassung vom Juli 2005.

Ministers responsible for Higher Education (1999). "The European Higher Education Area". The Bologna Declaration of 19 June 1999. Joint declaration of the European Ministers of Education.

Ministers responsible for Higher Education (2003). "Realising the European Higher Education Area". Communiqué of the Conference of Ministers responsible for Higher Education in Berlin on 19 September 2003.

Ministers responsible for Higher Education (2005). "The European Higher Education Area – Achieving the Goals". Communiqué of the Conference of European Ministers Responsible for Higher education, Bergen, 19-20 May 2005.

Ministers responsible for Higher Education (2007). "Towards the European Higher Education Area: responding to challenges in a globalised world". London Communiqué. 18 May 2007.

Ministers responsible for Higher Education (2009). "The Bologna Process 2020 – The European Higher Education Area in the new decade". Communiqué of the Conference of European Ministers Responsible for Higher Education, Leuven and Louvain-la-Neuve, 28-29 April 2009.

MLS (2004). "MLS Programme Report 2003". Zürich.

MLS (2006). "MLS Programme Report 2005". Zürich.

MLS (2009). "MLS Programme Report 2008". Zürich.

Norwegian Council of Universities (1996). *Standards regulations for the degree of dr.philos. (and equivalent degrees).* Recommendation of the Norwegian Council of Universities as of 09.12.96.

Norwegian Ministry of Education and Research (2005). *Act Relating to Universities and University Colleges.* 1 April 2005.

NHH (2007). "Facts and Figures 2007. A taste of NHH". www.nhh.no. Downloaded: March 2009.

NHH (2007a). *Regulations for the Philosophiae Doctor (PhD) degree at the Norwegian School of Economics and Business Administration (NHH)*. Adopted by the NHH Executive Board on 26 april 2007.

NHH Finance (2008). *Agreement on admission to the organised doctoral programme at the Norwegian School of Economics and Business Administration (NHH)*. April 2008.

Osterwalder, Konrad (2006). "Doktoratsprogramme und die ETH Graduate School". *Print. Die Hauszeitung der ETH Zürich*. Oktober 2006.

Pro*Doc Intermediale Ästhetik. Spiel – Ritual – Performanz (2008). "Wissenschaftlicher Zwischenbericht – Ausbildungsmodul. 1.10.2006-31.5.2008". Basel.

På Høyden (2008). *PhD-fabrikken*. Bergen. 3.6.2008.

SNF (1999). "National Centres of Competence in Research NCCR. Programme Call". 39. Bern: Swiss National Science Foundation.

SNF (2007). "Jahresbericht 2006". Bern.

SNF (2009). "Parlamentarische Initiative. Erleichterte Zulassung und Integration von Ausländerinnen und Ausländern mit Schweizerischem Hochschulabschluss". Stellungnahme des Schweizerischen Nationalfonds SNF. Beschluss des Präsidiums des Forschungsrats vom 1.September 2009.

SNF/CRUS (2007). *Reglement über die Gewährung von Beiträgen für Doktoratsprogramme (ProDoc)*. Bern. 13.November 2007.

Stjernø, S. (2008). "Sett under ett. Ny struktur i høyere utdanning". NOU (Norges offentlige utredninger).

Swiss Finance Institute (2009). "Activity Report 2007-2008". Geneva.

UFD (2003). *Retningslinjer for tilsetting i stilling som stipendiat ved universiteter og høgskoler*. Oslo: Utdannings- og forskningsdepartementet.

UFD (2005). "Commitment to Research. Report No.20 to the Storting". In Oslo: Norwegian Ministry of Education and Research.

UHR (2003). "Forskerskoler i Norge? Om mål og organisering av forskerskoler i norsk forskerutdanning." Oslo.

UHR (2003a). *Standard Regulations for the Degree of Philosphiae Doctor (Phd)*. Norwegian Council for Higher Education, (revised 24 June 2004).

UHR (2007). "Guidelines for the Evaluation of Candidates for Norwegian Doctoral Degrees". Recommended by the Norwegian Association of Higher Education Institutions, 23 March 2007.

UHR, NFR (2006). "Utredning av ordning med nasjonale forskerskoler i Norge". Oslo: Universitets- og høgskolerådet, Norges forskningsråd.

UHR, NFR (2006a). "Ny ordning med nærings-Ph.D. instilling fra arbeidsgruppe". Utdannings- og forskningsdepartementet, Norges forskningsråd.

Université de Lausanne, Faculté des hautes études commerciales (2006). *Directives pour les Doctorats avec mention Finance*. Lausanne.

Université de Genève, Faculté des sciences économiques et sociales (2009). *Règlement d'Etudes du Doctorat ès Sciences Economiques et Sociales*. Genève.

Universität Zürich (2008). *Promotionsordnung über das Doktorat in Wirtschaftswissenschaften an der Wirtschaftswissenschaftlichen Fakultät der Universität Zürich*. 15.12.2008.

Universität Zürich, Wirtschaftswissenschaftliche Fakultät (2009). *Doktoratsordnung*. 27.5.2009.

Università della Svizzera italiana, Facoltà di scienze economiche (2006). *Regolamento degli studi di dottorato.*

University of Bergen (2003). *Regulations for the doctoral degree philosophiae doctor (PhD) at the University of Bergen*. Approved by the University Board of Governors 12 June 2003.

University of Bergen (2003a). *Agreement relating to inclusion in the organised training of researchers.*

Universitetet i Bergen (2009). "Handlingsplan for forskerutdanning. Fra livsverk til karrierestart ved Universitetet i Bergen 2008-2015".

Universitetet i Oslo (2004). *Rammebetingelser for forskerskoler ved UiO*. Vedtatt av Forskningskomiteen 1.november 2004.

University of Oslo (2007). *Regulations for the degree of Philosophiae Doctoral (Ph.D.) at the University of Oslo*. Adopted by the Board of the University of Oslo on 21 June 2007 pursuant on the Act of 1

April 2005, No. 15 relating to universities and university colleges, § 3-3.

Universitet i Oslo (2008). *Forskerskoler I forskerutdanningen.* 6.10.2008.

Universität Zürich Erweiterte Universitätsleitung (2007). *Empfehlungen der Erweiterten Universitätsleitung für die Gestaltung der Doktoratsstufe an der Universität Zürich.* Fassung nach der Sitzung der EUL vom 20.März 2007.

Universität Zürich (1998). *Gesetz über die Universität Zürich.* Vom 15.März 1998 (Fassung vom 1.Juli 2002). 415.11.

Universität Zürich Fachstelle Studienreform (2007). *Muster für die Promotionsordnungen der UZH.* Januar 2007.

List of Acronyms

AI	Aesthetics of Intermediality
BFUG	Bologna Follow-Up Group
BSM	Biomolecular Structure and Mechanism
CRUS	Conférence des Recteurs des Universités Suisses/Rectors' Conference of Swiss Universities
CSO	Centre de Sociologie des Organisations/Center for the Sociology of Organisations
CSS	Conseil Suisse de la Science/Swiss Science Council
CUS	Conférence Universitaire Suisse/Swiss University Council
CUSO	Conférence universitaire de Suisse occidentale
ECTS	European Credit Transfer System
EFTA	European Free Trade Association
EHEA	European Higher Education Area
EPFL	Ecole Polytechnique Fédérale de Lausanne/Federal Institute of Technology Lausanne
ERA	European Research and Innovation Area
ETHZ	Eidgenössiche Technische Hochschule Zürich/Federal Institute of Technology Zurich
EUA	European University Association
GMAT	Graduate Management Admission Test

GRE	Graduate Record Exam
HEI	Higher Education Institution
IFE	Institutt for Energiteknikk/Institute for Energy Technology
LAU	Loi d'aide aux universities/Federal Act on Financial Assistance to Universities
LEPF	Loi fédérale sur les écoles polytechniques fédérales/Law on the Federal Institutes of Technology
LSZGS	Life Science Zurich Graduate School
MCB	Molecular and Computational Biology
MER	Maître d'Enseignement et de Recherche
MLS	Molecular Life Sciences
MSE	Materials Science and Engineering
NCCR	National Centres of Competence in Research
NHH	Norges Handelshøyskole/Norwegian School of Economics and Business Administration
NFR	Norges Forskningsråd/Research Council of Norway
NIFU-STEP	Norwegian Institute for Studies in Innovation, Research and Education
NPM	New Public Management
NTNU	Norwegian University of Science and Technology
OECD	Organisation for Economic Co-operation and Development
PRIME	Policies for Research and Innovation in the Move towards the European Research Area
RRP	Recruitment Resource Pools

SFI	Swiss Finance Institute
SMN	Senter for materialvitenskap og nanoteknologi/Centre for Materials Science and Nanotechnology
SNF	Schweizerischer Nationalfonds zur Förderung der wissenschaftlichen Forschung/Swiss National Science Foundation
SUN	Steering of Universities
SWOT	Strengths, Weaknesses, Opportunities, Threats
TBLR	Tekst, bilde, lyd og rom/Text, Image, Sound and Space
TOEFL	Test Of English as a Foreign Language
UFD	Utdannings- og forskningsdepartementet/Ministry for Education and Research
UiB	Universitetet i Bergen/University of Bergen
UHR	Universitets- og Høgskolerådet/Norwegian Association of Higher Education Institutions
UNIGE	Université de Genève/University of Geneva
UNIL	Université de Lausanne/University of Lausanne
UNIZH	Universität Zürich/University of Zurich
USI	Università della Svizzera italiana/University of Lugano